REVOLUTION ON THE PAMPAS

A Social History of Argentine Wheat, 1860–1910

LATIN AMERICAN MONOGRAPHS, NO. 1

INSTITUTE OF LATIN AMERICAN STUDIES

THE UNIVERSITY OF TEXAS

REVOLUTION ON THE PAMPAS

A Social History of Argentine Wheat, 1860–1910

by JAMES R. SCOBIE

PUBLISHED FOR THE INSTITUTE OF
LATIN AMERICAN STUDIES BY THE
UNIVERSITY OF TEXAS PRESS, AUSTIN

Title page photo. Revolution on the Pampas: Plowing. Photograph reproduced by permission of Dodd, Mead & Company from *The Real Argentine* by J. A. Hammerton. Copyright 1915 by Dodd, Mead & Company.

OTHER BOOKS BY THE AUTHOR

La disolución de un triunvirato: Urquiza, Mitre, Derqui.
Seminario de Estudios de Historia Argentina,
Buenos Aires, 1960.
Correspondencia Mitre-Elizalde (co-editor).
Universidad de Buenos Aires, 1960.
Argentina: A City and a Nation.
Oxford University Press, New York, 1964.
*La lucha por la consolidación
de la nacionalidad argentina, 1852–1862.*
Hachette, Buenos Aires, 1964.
*Three Years in California: William Perkins' Journal of
Life at Sonora, 1849–1852* (co-editor).
University of California Press, Berkeley, 1964.

To PAT

PREFACE

The foundations for contemporary Argentina were built in the second half of the nineteenth century. Today when dining on baby beef at Corrientes Once or La Cabaña in Buenos Aires, or buying a leg of mutton in London, or opening a can of Argentine corned beef in the United States, one is benefiting from the best-known of these foundations—Argentina's emergence as producer of some of the world's finest meats. Less appreciated is the parallel agricultural* revolution, the rise of Argentina from an importer of wheat in the 1870's to the world's third-largest exporter of wheat thirty years later. Behind this economic accomplishment lies the social history of an agricultural heartland, the pampas. The predominance of the city and the province of Buenos Aires, the absentee land-tenure system, the poverty and ignorance of the sparse rural population, the heavy Italianization of the country, all are part of the story of Argentine wheat.

It is the purpose of this study to trace the agricultural and social development of the Argentine wheat zone during the significant years from 1860 to 1910. Someday it may be possible to present a composite picture of Argentine agriculture or even to explore the vast topic of Western man's conquest of the grasslands' frontier. For the moment research warrants concentration on a more modest theme: the meaning and implications of wheat in forming present-day Argentina.

The financial support for this study is gratefully acknowledged: a grant from the Organization of American States and a faculty fellowship from the Social Science Research Council in 1959–1960, and grants from the Institute for International Studies, University of California, Berkeley, and from Indiana University, Bloomington. Investigation can be accomplished only with the patient and understanding cooperation of many persons and institutions. I owe a particular debt of gratitude to the personnel of the General Library of the Univer-

---

* Throughout this study the term "agriculture" is used in the sense of crop farming as distinct from livestock.

sity of California, Berkeley; and in Buenos Aires, to the directors and personnel of the Archivo General de la Nación, Biblioteca de la Facultad de Ciencias Económicas de la Universidad de Buenos Aires, Biblioteca del Banco Central, Biblioteca Nacional, Bolsa de Cereales, Bolsa de Comercio, Bunge y Born, Instituto Nacional de Tecnología Agropecuaria, Facultad de Agronomía de la Universidad de Buenos Aires, Jewish Colonization Association, Junta Nacional de Granos, Museo Mitre, *Review of the River Plate*, Sociedad Rural Argentina, and Tornquist y Cía; to Alberto Dodero for use of his private collection of accounts of Argentina by foreign travelers; to the administration of the colony of Moisesville, Santa Fe; to the director and personnel of the experimental station of Rafaela, Santa Fe; and to numerous citizens of Esperanza, Santa Fe. I am especially indebted to five men who guided me in special aspects of my research: Sergio Bagú, Alfredo Estévez, Horacio Giberti, Alfredo Montoya, and Juan L. Tenembaum.

Grateful acknowledgment is made to the following publishers for permission to reproduce photographs: A. & C. Black, Ltd.; Cassell and Company, Ltd.; G. P. Putnam's Sons; and Dodd, Mead & Company.

J. R. S.

CONTENTS

ILLUSTRATIONS

Title Page: Revolution on the Pampas: Plowing

(Following page 62)

1. A Mud Rancho of Italian Tenant Farmers in the Cereal Zone
2. A Prosperous Italian Colonist Family in the Province of Santa Fe around 1900

(Following page 78)

3. A Typical North Italian Colonist Family in Argentina around 1910
4. The Main Street of Azul in the Province of Buenos Aires around 1910
5. A Typical Rural Town in the Cereal Zone, Melincué in Southern Santa Fe
6. A Typical Oxcart Used in the Argentine Cereal Zone

(Following page 94)

7. Threshing Wheat on the Pampas around 1910
8. Loading Bags of Cereal at a Station of the Southern Railroad around 1910
9. Bagged Wheat Awaiting Shipment at a Station of the Southern Railroad
10. Loading Bags of Wheat by Chute at the Port of Rosario around 1900

(Following page 110)

11. The Riverbank at Buenos Aires around 1880, Prior to Construction of the Docks
12. Grain Elevators of the Central Argentine Railroad at the Port of Buenos Aires

MAPS

TABLES

REVOLUTION ON THE PAMPAS

A Social History of Argentine Wheat, 1860–1910

i. THE PAMPAS: *A Perspective*

The Argentine pampas of the sixteenth century were the first grassland frontiers encountered by European man. The rim of these great plains was skirted by those same conquistadors who toppled mighty Indian empires and explored a hemisphere in search of gold and souls. Yet for three centuries the economic needs and way of life of the Spaniards imposed no demand to conquer and settle the pampas. These grasslands continued to belong to the deer, the flamingos, the ostriches, and later to wild horses and cattle. On the eastern half, where the rainfall was sufficient, the tall, coarse pampas grass blanketed the land. Only the thistle and the *ombú*, that gnarled and spreading native tree, rose above this immense sea of grass to break the skyline. The very flatness hindered drainage. The runoff from the torrential downpours fed a few wandering streams and more frequently collected in huge swamps or saline depressions. To the west the pampas grass grew sparser and finally gave way to thorny brush and cactus.

Certain nomadic Indian tribes considered this land their home and, after the Spaniards introduced the horse, the Indian ranged far and wide over its expanse. The gaucho, that offspring of the conquistador and the Indian woman, was equally at home here, although he usually came to hunt wild horses and cattle. The Spaniard and then the Argentine parceled out these unsettled lands as vast estates, but the incentive of ownership brought relatively few of the Hispanic population from the towns to live in such remote and lonely surroundings. Those who did come led an existence little different from that of their gaucho laborers: a diet composed wholly of meat and the strong brew of *yerba mate*, or Paraguayan tea; a simple garb suited to wind, rain, dust, and work on horseback; a thatched hut with a cot made of hides, some ox skulls for chairs, and a few pegs from which to hang heavy silver spurs or ornate bridles. By the nineteenth century a few of the very wealthy might aspire to a more Europeanized way of life. They constructed long adobe sheds around a central patio and whitewashed them. They sank wells, planted willows and fruit trees, raised vegetables and chickens, and for protection against wild herds and marauding Indians dug wide ditches surrounding their oases of civilization. Some eccentrics experimented with such rarities as wire fences, imported stallions, rams and bulls, and ornamental trees and flowers. But life was simple and luxuries were few even for those who might literally own half a province.

By 1910 this scene had vanished. The gaucho had passed into legend, to be replaced by the peon, a capable and often skilled laborer but one who lacked the savage freedom of his forebears. The wild herds were gone. The vast emptiness of the horizon had been broken. Civilization had descended on the pampas.

Wherever the railroad tracks penetrated these grasslands, villages appeared at intervals of from ten to twenty miles. Often they were no more than two rows of unadorned houses facing a broad dirt road. A brick station house, looking uncomfortably British in these bare surroundings, provided the focus for both the street and the settlement. The villages that had enjoyed longer establishment and some prosperity boasted a church and a municipal building to form a square which the station house still dominated.

The development of the land, like that of the villages, was linked to the railroads. A bushel of wheat, a bale of wool, a prime steer had value only when the one or two hundred miles to Buenos Aires, Rosario, or Bahía Blanca could be bridged easily. The foundation of the new Argentina rested on these products. Here the blades of a gang plow sliced the tough sod and cut the roots of the coarse pampean grass. Wheat, flax, or corn would soon flourish in the virgin soil. There a thousand acres of alfalfa grew through the stubble of a recently cut wheat field to provide pasturage for a herd of prize Shorthorns. Across the changing face of the pampas sprouted novel features—windmills, barbed-wire fences, and dirt roads.

The dependence on rangy wild animals, useful only for hides, tallow, and salted meat, diminished as soon as refrigeration made it possible for meat to survive the ocean voyage and to be sold in the markets of Liverpool, London, or Southampton. The British consumer's demand for high-quality prime beef guided the cattleman. Fences closed blooded Shorthorn, Hereford, and Black Angus stock into alfalfa pastures, while through selective breeding, legs and necks were shortened and weight was increased. The rise of dirt farming and sheep ranching accompanied this shift in the cattle economy. Wheat for British flour mills, corn for England and the Continent, wool for Belgian and French carpet factories, all provided stimuli for further exploitation and settlement of the pampas.

Thus was the domain of the gaucho and the Indian radically altered. The Indians were exterminated in an organized military campaign. The gaucho lost his economic and cultural identity when he was no longer needed to ride down the wild herds of horses and cattle. European immigrants, those hardy souls who survived the attraction of the coastal cities, now penetrated the pampas. Population was still sparse and distances were large. A man and his family might scratch the surface of five hundred acres in order to raise a wheat crop. Ten thousand acres might carry only two thousand head of cattle, handled easily enough by a dozen peons. But the farmers, sharecroppers, hired men, and peons, the Italians, Swiss, Germans, and the Irish brought new life, industry, commerce, and values to the pampas.

These changes produced wealth and a civilized life for some of the population. The bare frontier outpost now became a Mediterranean villa, a French château, or a gabled English country house, surrounded by eucalyptus groves and cropped lawns. Rose gardens, tennis courts, and guest houses were necessary adjuncts of this life. Those whose forebears had been able to acquire and keep enormous land grants or who now secured estates enjoyed a gilded existence. Lands whose only worth had been in their herds of wild cattle, lands which could be reached only by horseback or oxcart, lands occupied largely by hostile Indians, underwent a total transformation. British capital had built railroads. Pastoral techniques had been improved and the resources of the pampas were being utilized more thoroughly. Immigrants, newly arrived from European poverty, were available not only for railroad and urban construction but also as sharecroppers, tenant farmers, or peons to raise corn, wheat, flax, and alfalfa, to put up fences, and to tend cattle and sheep. Under such conditions land provided an annual return of from 12 to 15 per cent to the owner and land values often rose 1,000 per cent in a decade.

Those who already had land, power, or money monopolized the

newly developed wealth of the pampas. The man who tilled the soil or cared for the herds eked out a meager existence. If he had left Europe because of poverty and despair, at least he did not starve in Argentina, but few incentives were offered him and, for the most part, title to the land was beyond his grasp. As a peon he lived in a shed near the corrals or in a lean-to in some distant pasture. As a tenant farmer or colonist he might build himself a mud hut. His diet consisted of the cheapest and most readily available food—meat for the herdsman and corn for the farmer. There was little opportunity for education, sociability, or self-improvement. Instability and transiency characterized every aspect of his life. Argentine landowners wanted and needed his labor and seemed determined to make sure that he did not rise out of the laboring class. As a result the small independent landowner or farmer never gained a foothold on the pampas. In this agricultural and pastoral economy the immigrants who prospered were generally those who remained in the cities and busied themselves with commerce and industry.

By 1910 the wealth of the pampas had created a nation of extremes. To step from cosmopolitan Buenos Aires into the colonial atmosphere of Salta was to move backward a hundred years. To leave the château and park of an *estancia* and visit the one-room hovel of an Italian tenant farmer was to explore the opposites of pampean life. But it was in Buenos Aires, now a city of 1,300,000 inhabitants, where the complexity of the new Argentina was most dramatically evident.

Here a new nation was being forged. By the turn of the century, three-quarters of the city's adult population was of European birth, and new arrivals were pouring into the port at the rate of from 10,000 to 20,000 a month. Many, it is true, were transient laborers who crossed the Atlantic each season from Italy or Spain for three or four months' work during the wheat and corn harvest. Others became sharecroppers and tenant farmers. But the great majority never went beyond Buenos Aires and the other coastal cities. The increasing flow of agricultural and pastoral products required many hands—in the stockyards and packing plants, in the flour mills, at the railroad terminals, and on the docks. Profits underwrote more expansion, more buildings, more consumption, and still more immigration. Construction became the city's great industry. *Porteños,* the proud inhabitants of Argentina's major port, called their capital the Paris of the Americas, and Buenos Aires, self-consciously, tried to live up to the claim.

The narrow colonial streets and the one- or two-story houses built around internal patios could not be made to disappear overnight, but *porteños* hoped at least to hide them behind the façade of modernity. Public edifices—the ornate and costly Capitol, the impressive Colón Theater, the columned Supreme Court—vied with the construction of private palaces, commercial and bank buildings, or ultramodern hotels such as the Plaza. A mile-long avenue was pushed west from the presidential palace on the Plaza de Mayo to the new Capitol, and two broad diagonals were opened northwest and southwest from the same plaza. Ambitious projects were studied for the city's first subway system, destined to supplement its extensive streetcar network. The very magnitude of the urban working-class created new jobs and opportunities. The poorest might huddle together in downtown *conventillos*—entire city blocks burrowed by long corridors and honeycombed into tiny rooms—but increasing numbers of the population spread westward from the waterfront. Hundreds of small stores —butcher shops, bakeries, groceries, drugstores, tailor shops, and others—were needed to supply these new districts. Imports naturally increased in response to the tastes and desires that the immigrants brought with them from Europe. Local industries that catered to these demands—macaroni factories, breweries, textile plants, shoe manufacturers—flourished.

As a result of economic growth the spectrum of classes in the cities greatly expanded, and the differences between the various social strata emerged in sharp relief. Previously there had been those who lived decently and those who lived poorly. The mestizo, the day laborer, and the servant had comprised the lower class. Among the well-to-do there had been some gradations in wealth, prestige, or lineage, but on the whole the food, the clothes, the homes, and the amusements of the large landowner, the lawyer, the dry-goods merchant, the shipping clerk, or the university professor had been surprisingly similar. Now that the coast and Buenos Aires were wealthy, free rein was given to conspicuous consumption.

A small elite of established Argentine families with large landholdings jealously guarded its position as the leader of *porteño* society and controlled the principal aspects of the nation's financial and political life. A haughty, self-contained group, it had a select membership that also belonged to the three distinguished clubs of Buenos Aires: the Jockey Club, the Círculo de Armas, and the Club del Progreso. At their offices, over an after-dinner brandy, or on the floor of the congress or the stock exchange, they ran Argentina. It was a genteel society, a gentlemen's club, which regarded the control of the country's destinies as its patrimony and sought to develop Argentina into the richest and most progressive nation in Latin America.

Below this elite extended a kaleidoscopic succession of economic and social groups. Here, very significantly, the opportunities for profit and advancement were not restricted to those who already had power and money. Unlike the pampas, where the principal asset—land—was monopolized by a few, the cities, especially Buenos Aires, provided incentives and opportunities for the immigrant. In an enormous variety of occupations the newly arrived were rewarded in some proportion to their efforts and abilities. It was the immigrant, therefore, who largely created modern Buenos Aires and who found an appropriate niche at every level—as a successful contractor or importer, a railroad manager, a street peddler, a bank clerk, a governess, or a stevedore. And for the moment at least, the immigrant was unconcerned with the political scene. Being a foreigner, he did not expect to vote. His efforts were focused on material advancement and he was content to let the elite rule.

This was the Argentina that emerged as a result of the late nineteenth-century revolution on the pampas. It was a nation dedicated to economic growth and prosperity, but it was also an unbalanced country where the cleavage between urban sophistication and rural primitivism, between the modernity of Buenos Aires and the backwardness of the interior provinces, between the immigrant and the established Argentine, promised conflict rather than harmony.

In the ensuing pages, one aspect of this metamorphosis of modern Argentina will be studied in detail. The story of Argentine wheat is the story of agricultural and social revolution on the pampas. It is also the history of what happened to the immigrant and to the land.

ii. THE LAND: *The Geography of the Wheat Zone*

By 1910 the heart of Argentina's wheat zone lay within a broad belt of the pampas, two hundred miles wide, stretching from Santa Fe in the north to Bahía Blanca in the south (Maps 1 and 2). From approximately 15,000,000 acres sown to wheat, Argentina annually harvested 4,000,000 tons (140,000,000 bushels) and exported more than 2,000,000 tons. To comprehend the upheaval that such a change represents in a period of just half a century, let us pause for a moment to examine the pampas of the 1850's.

The Chilean historian Benjamín Vicuña Mackenna, visiting Argentina in 1855, bemoaned the fact that this fertile plain was used only to raise horses, cattle, and sheep, and he accurately underscored one of the basic causes: "The sad truth is that so long as the pastoral economy provides a return of 30 per cent on capital with virtually no effort on the part of the owner, the demanding and less remunerative occupation of farming has little chance for success . . ."[1] Easy profits, however, were not the sole determinants of the pastoral economy of the pampas at mid-century.

The Indian still pressed in on the settled areas of coastal Argentina. Despite the southern campaign of 1833 to push the frontier to the mouth of the Negro River, despite elaborate treaties and alliances with many of the pampean tribes, despite forts scattered just beyond the Salado River in the province of Buenos Aires, raiding parties continually roamed over the whole area of the pampas. The map of the 1850's presents a startling contrast with that of present-day Argentina. The southern frontier followed the trail from Mendoza

[1] Benjamín Vicuña Mackenna, *La Argentina en el año 1855*, p. 133. This passage and subsequent passages from the Spanish have been translated by the author.

through San Luis and Río Cuarto to Casilda (known as Candelaria before 1870). Here the line of forts traced the frontier southward to the vicinity of Junín, Nueve de Julio, Azul, and Tandil. To the north an equally vulnerable trail marked the frontier, here often subjected to the forays of Chaco Indians. From the city of Santa Fe it ran due west to within fifty miles of the city of Córdoba before it turned north toward the Dulce River and Santiago del Estero.

Beyond this frontier the risk to life and possessions was enormous, and even within it security was only relative. Until the late 1870's, travelers from Buenos Aires or Rosario to Mendoza and Chile had to depend on fast horses, luck, and long-range repeating rifles to save them from marauding Indians. A young North American who crossed to Chile in 1848 was impressed by the deserted region around Candelaria (Casilda) in Santa Fe: "Everything was poor and they were living in the midst of great danger—20 days ago they were attacked by several hundred Indians who have gone south and west on to Cordova."[2] Throughout 1855, Indians repeatedly attacked settlements along Buenos Aires' southern frontier, and one particularly severe defeat to porteño forces caused the Buenos Aires Minister of War to concede: "Up until now we have known that one Christian was a match for two Indians, but now there may be those who will consider even two Christians insufficient to deal with one Indian."[3] An Englishman who settled near Bell Ville (known as Fraile Muerto before 1870) in the province of Córdoba in 1865 stood off a band of fifty Indians only to see them "draw up on the rising ground about a mile from our house, when half their party rode towards our horses, and in a few minutes they had driven them up to their own troop of unmounted horses, and the whole body were off like the wind, in a northerly direction."[4]

It was a relentless war between the Indian and the Christian and one in which the Indian had the upper hand until the national government's ruthless campaign of extermination in 1879. Even the gaucho paled as a horseman beside the Indian. Sweeping across the pampas in bands of from fifty to a thousand, these mounted warriors would descend on settlements and forts alike, drive away the horses for mounts and for food and the cattle for sale across the Chilean

[2] Samuel G. Arnold, Viaje por América del Sur, 1847–1848, p. 189; original English text supplied courtesy of the Rhode Island Historical Society.
[3] Bartolomé Mitre to Pastor Obligado, June 12, 1855; in private archives of Señora Justa D. de Zemborain, Buenos Aires.
[4] Richard A. Seymour, Pioneering in the Pampas, p. 54.

frontier, kill the men, and carry off the women to their camps in remote southern Argentina. Before word of the attack reached the nearest town, even before the sun rose, the band would have left the smoldering ruins a hundred miles behind it and be ready to strike at some other hapless outpost. The pastoral economy and the consequent sparse rural population aided this Indian mode of warfare. Cultivation of the land, requiring greater investment, population, and security, appeared an impracticable dream while the pampas were still the Indians' domain.

The transportation facilities of the 1850's also encouraged coastal Argentina to remain pastoral. Argentina's first locomotive, a survivor of the Crimean War, commenced its run on six miles of track from Buenos Aires to San José de Flores in 1857. But for another decade at least, the oxcart was the principal carrier of freight. An eighteen-year-old Yankee who traveled from Rosario to Mendoza in the company of a caravan of these carts described them as "most cumberous affairs, and in appearance not unlike a *rancho*, or native hut, set upon wheels. The body consisted of a framework of sticks, covered upon the sides and back with small reeds, and roofed with cattle hides, which rendered them secure against the heaviest rain. The carts, which probably exceeded twelve feet in length, were only four feet wide, being mounted upon two wheels of extraordinary diameter . . ."[5] These vehicles, each carrying two tons of merchandise and pulled by six bullocks, traveled in groups of from fifteen to fifty for mutual protection and assistance. The trip from Rosario to Córdoba took a month and that from Buenos Aires to Salta three or four months. One can appreciate the expense as well as the slowness of this type of transportation from the fact that even in the 1830's it cost thirteen times as much to move a ton of goods from Salta to Buenos Aires as from Buenos Aires to Liverpool.[6] After the advent of the railroads in the late 1860's, merchandise was moved by rail for one-twelfth of the charge demanded by oxcarts.[7]

The overland transport charges in Argentina, exorbitant in comparison with those by water or rail, did not interfere with a pastoral economy but they did discourage cultivation of the land. Crops were

[5] Nathaniel H. Bishop, *A Thousand Miles' Walk across South America*, pp. 103–104.

[6] Calculated from ton-league costs quoted by Miron Burgin, *Economic Aspects of Argentine Federalism*, p. 117.

[7] Calculated from statistics given by Thomas J. Hutchinson, *Buenos Ayres and Argentine Gleanings*, pp. 37, 60.

grown on land immediately surrounding the towns, the *tierras de pan llevar* which Spanish tradition had reserved for cereals, fruits, and vegetables. Vicuña Mackenna noted that even with 120,000 inhabitants to be fed, untamed prairies and cattle reached into the very suburbs of Buenos Aires.[8] Yet the small agricultural enclosures around each town sufficed except in periods of drought or crop failure. Then it was frequently cheaper to bring flour from the United States or from Chile through the Strait of Magellan than from Tucumán or Córdoba.

Such local self-sufficiency, imposed largely by transport costs, did not affect the mobile pastoral industry. The sixteenth-century practice of hunting down wild horses and cattle for their hides gradually gave way to the more rational system of rodeos and branding. Gauchos gathered horses, and more particularly cattle, into enormous herds and restricted them to certain locations favored with good pasturage, drainage, and water. Thus were the colonial *estancias* built, without fences or boundaries—vast extensions of land and cattle and few men. Cattle and horses moved about on their own muscle power, and it took only a handful of gauchos to bring them to towns along the Paraná and Uruguay Rivers for slaughter, after which they were processed into salted meat, hides, and fats for export. After 1850, when intensive sheep grazing became dominant in the protected inner ring of the pampas around Buenos Aires, the new products—fleece and skins—were compact and light enough to be carried by oxcart from twenty to eighty miles to the estuary of the Río de la Plata. Bulky items such as corn, flax, cotton, or perishable vegetable and fruit products stood little chance of becoming export items so long as the oxcart rolled along, ponderous and unchallenged.

The psychology and habits of the Argentines of the littoral at mid-century were also powerful deterrents to farming. For three centuries the pampas had been exploited but not conquered. Regardless of the reasons, the doughty Argentines had developed an independent way of life. Almost since the discovery of the area of the Río de la Plata, trade and the pastoral industries had been the only economic attractions of the area and neither required settlement of the land. To buy Europe's fine textiles, furniture, and other manufactured goods from commercial houses in Seville, London, Brussels, or Paris and transship them to Córdoba, Tucumán, or Salta did not involve pro-

---

[8] Vicuña Mackenna, *La Argentina en el año 1855*, p. 133.

duction or industry in Buenos Aires, Rosario, or Santa Fe. Similarly, the exploitation of the pampas required a minimum of settlement and laborers. The rodeo replaced the cattle hunt because it was more practical and profitable to bring semitamed cattle or horses to market on hoof than to roam over endless miles of pampas in pursuit of totally wild creatures. The *saladero*, or meat-salting plant, introduced efficient utilization of the whole animal. The development of sheep grazing intensified the use of pasture and increased the value of land in Buenos Aires. But these activities did not involve colonization; they merely represented systematic use of nature's reproductive process. That man's participation in this process was not essential had been amply demonstrated by the spread of wild horses across the pampas after the Spanish abandoned their first settlement at Buenos Aires.

Indeed, for many years there had been little need to improve on nature. From their settlements around the margins of the pampas, the town merchant and the gaucho were able not only to create and tap a current of trade between Europe and the interior provinces but also to exploit an immense and well-stocked natural range. On the pampas, cattle, sheep, and horses doubled their numbers every three years, enough to support a modest population with modest tastes.[9] The animals were admirably suited to their markets. The scrawny, tough long-horned cattle produced fibrous lean meat excellent for salting, a good commercial tallow, and thick, durable leather. Since mares were never ridden in Argentina, those not used for breeding contributed their hides and grease for export. Sheep, as one British observer noted, were "very inferior; the quality and quantity of their wool, which is of all colours, being very coarse; they are also ill-shaped, long-legged, lank-bodied, and very difficult to fatten; in a word, they are a degenerate race, the consequence of total neglect."[10] But what more was demanded by European carpet factories?

The result was that the inhabitant of the coast—whether gaucho, lawyer, *estanciero*, or merchant—became accustomed to a source of easily exploited natural wealth which demanded little attention. Nineteenth-century European travelers often interpreted this easy adjustment as laziness, shiftlessness, improvidence, stupidity, or

[9] *Ibid.*, pp. 120–121; Wilfrid Latham, *The States of the River Plate*, pp. 182–183.

[10] William MacCann, *Two Thousand Miles' Ride Through the Argentine Provinces*, I, 275.

worse. They saw the muddy, rutted streets, the rotting carcasses of horses and oxen, the filthy drinking water, the dirty markets, the stagnation of small towns, and bemoaned Argentina's lack of progress, industriousness, or ambition. They never ceased to marvel that the owner of thousands of head of cattle and acres of land should live in "a hut of stakes, cornstalks and mud [with] two or three holes knocked through its sides to serve as windows and ventilators."[11]

The environment had nurtured different values. A gaucho subsisted on meat and *yerba mate,* not because he disliked fruit and vegetables but because their acquisition meant a sustained labor and residence quite foreign to his nomadic habits. He often remained in his saddle twenty hours at a time and displayed astounding courage and strength in his everyday occupations. But heaven help the man who asked him to lift a spade! For that kind of work—sinking wells or digging defensive ditches against Indians and stampeding herds—Irish laborers had to be attracted by fabulous daily wages (high enough so that a worker could earn enough in three weeks to buy a flock of fifteen hundred sheep and set himself up as a sheepman).[12] Throughout the coastal area bread was a scarce item. Butter, eggs, milk, and vegetables were far more expensive in the coastal towns than in the cities of Europe. Rents were exorbitant, but it was the cost of labor rather than of construction materials that made them high. If a field of wheat, an orchard, a plot of vegetables were cultivated, if some cows were stripped of their few pints of milk, if some bricks were laid, it was usually by the hands of immigrants and not of the natives of coastal Argentina. By inclination and habit the vast majority of the population had little interest in tilling the soil and scorned manual labor.

The wheat belt of 1910, then, was anything but an agricultural zone in the 1850's. What was to become one of the world's breadbaskets was still the domain of hard-riding gauchos and hostile Indians, settled only on its fringes by a people who had little use for farming. Yet the chief ingredient of the startling transformation was already present—the land. What was this land? How was it formed? What sort of climate did it enjoy? What plants and animals did it support? The answers to these questions emphasize the importance of geography to the future of the wheat zone.

[11] Bishop, *A Thousand Miles' Walk across South America,* p. 82.
[12] Calculated from data in MacCann, *Two Thousand Miles' Ride Through the Argentine Provinces,* I, 99.

In our consideration of the Argentine wheat belt we will focus our attention on the humid pampas, although in a limited fashion we shall consider an even larger scene of wheat cultivation which includes the southern and central portions of the province of Entre Ríos in the Argentine Mesopotamia. Entre Ríos has distinct geographical and political boundaries, but the region of the humid pampas is not so easily delimited. In the absence of natural boundaries the soil, temperature, rainfall, and vegetation must serve as approximate guides. With these as indicators, the humid pampas may be said to extend westward from the Atlantic Ocean and the Paraná River to the sixty-fourth meridian (Map 1). The northern corners almost touch the cities of Santa Fe and Córdoba. The southern boundary is the Colorado River and again the Atlantic Ocean.[13]

The erosion of wind and water on ancient geological formations built these vast plains. The bedrock of the pampas, crystalline and granitic, is the shattered and fragmented edge of one of the earth's oldest land masses, Brasilia, which underlies much of Uruguay and Brazil. But in most of the Argentine littoral, this jagged bedrock is buried under hundreds of feet of sediment, fine clay, sand, and wind-blown dust, or loess. Recent artesian perforations have encountered bedrock at a depth of more than 1,000 feet near the city of Buenos Aires and at more than 2,000 feet at Guanaco, in the western part of the province of Buenos Aires, and at Bell Ville in Córdoba, while beneath the Salado River the bedrock is estimated to be at a depth of 16,000 feet. Only here and there do the granite remains jut to the surface: the island of Martín García in the estuary north of the city of Buenos Aires; the hills of Tandil rising to 1,500 feet above sea level and those of Ventana with several peaks of 4,000 feet in the southern part of the province of Buenos Aires; the hills of Córdoba with some elevations of 5,000 feet; and the low hills of the arid western extension of the pampas beyond the sixty-fourth meridian.[14]

The Argentine coastal plains, therefore, are made up almost totally, and in great depth, of loose deposits of sand and clay. Except in the hills of southern Buenos Aires, rocks and gravel are practically unknown. Indeed, it was noted in the Indian campaign of 1879 that many of the soldiers and officers had never before seen a pebble and

[13] Federico A. Daus, *Geografía de la República Argentina*, I, 132.
[14] Francisco de Aparicio and Horacio A. Difrieri (eds.), *La Argentina. Suma de geografía*, hereinafter cited as *Suma de geografía*, I, 406–407; Preston James, *Latin America*, pp. 328–329; Daus, *Geografía de la República Argentina*, I, 44, 55–63.

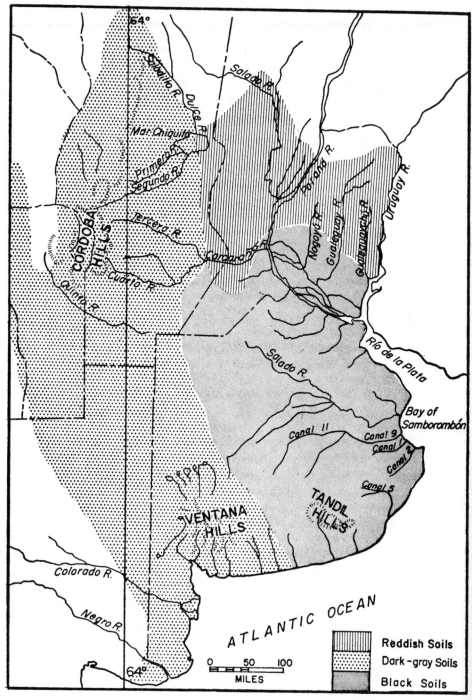

Map 1. Drainage System and Soil Types of the Pampas

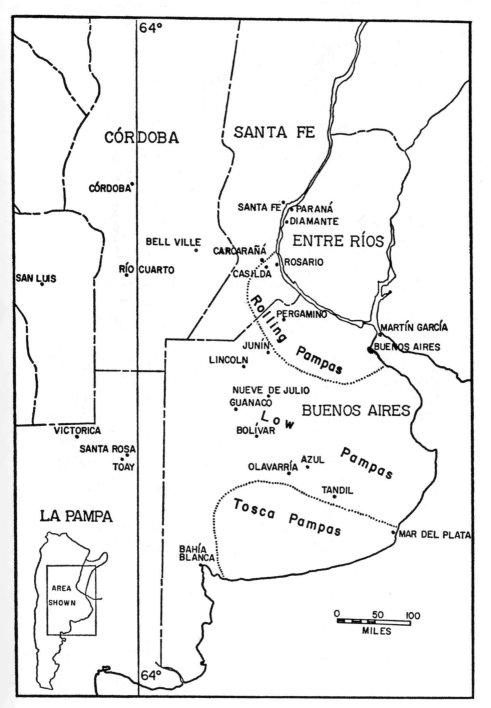

Map 2. Towns of the Pampas Region

filled their pockets with the strange souvenirs which they found along the Colorado River. Over the aeons, volcanic ash from the hilly region of the pampas, fine wind-blown rock particles from the Andes and Patagonia, and sedimentary deposits have contributed to the building process. The top layer of soil is, of course, of most recent formation. Ranging in depth from a few feet to several yards, it is the result of a continued mixing of loess and alluvium, both sand and clay, with the humus of an enormous grassland. Recent investigations have defined three types of soil in coastal Argentina (Map 1). The dark-gray soil of western Buenos Aires, eastern La Pampa, and southeastern Córdoba, formed in a semiarid environment, tends to be alkaline, relatively sandy, rich in calcium but poor in organic materials. The black earth of most of Buenos Aires, southern Santa Fe, and Entre Ríos is only slightly alkaline, with occasional deficiencies in calcium and phosphorus, but it contains a considerable amount of clay and is very rich in organic materials. To the north, in central Santa Fe and Entre Ríos, the soil becomes reddish in color, apparently owing to its evolution in a warmer climate; it contains less organic material and more clay than the black earth but is basically just as fertile.[15]

The pampas have almost universally been characterized as a vast sea or a level plain, but as Vicuña Mackenna noted in 1855: "They are rather a series of long slopes or vast swells, often almost imperceptible, yet sometimes abrupt when they form ravines or washes."[16] The relief of the pampas divides this section of the country into three distinct regions. The *rolling pampas* form a 100-mile-wide band from Buenos Aires to Rosario; from the 30- to 50-foot bluffs along the Paraná River, they slope very slightly upward toward the upper Salado River. In a recent geological era, after the pampas had already been formed, this region rose above the surrounding country. Since the movement was not always simultaneous, the result is a rolling countryside with very gradual contours. The effect has been heightened by flat-bottomed valleys cut by many small streams which flow into the Paraná River. The highest elevation of this region is only 300 feet above sea level, and rarely is there a rise or fall of more than 5 feet per mile. In the southern portion of the province of Buenos Aires, a somewhat similar terrain with a maximum elevation of 700

[15] Aparicio and Difrieri, *Suma de geografía,* IV, 62–70, 73–96.
[16] Vicuña Mackenna, *La Argentina en el año 1855,* p. 145.

feet above sea level surrounds the Tandil and Ventana hills. This is the region of the *tosca pampas*, with hard limestone layers just beneath the surface of the soil. Between these two regions and extending west and north lie the *low pampas*. From the slough of the Salado River, which rain frequently converts into a series of vast lakes and swamps, the land rises slowly toward the west. But even here the swells are frequently imperceptible and are interspersed with broad depressions; the 650-foot (200-meter) contour line is encountered for the first time in the vicinity of the sixty-fourth meridian or the western limit of the humid pampas.[17]

The formation and relief of this land contribute to the peculiar drainage-system of the pampas. In such a broad plain, the relative absence of major rivers is notable. The *rolling pampas* and the *tosca pampas* are drained by numerous small stream beds and gullies which empty, respectively, into the Paraná River and the Atlantic. For the large area of the *low pampas*, however, surface drainage is very poor. In the north, of the several streams that rise from the Córdoba hills, only the Tercero River and the Cuarto River (subsequently the Saladillo), by joining forces to become the Carcarañá, manage to reach the Paraná. The rest flow north into the large salt lake of Mar Chiquita or, as the Quinto River, merely disappear into the sandy soil of southeast Córdoba. The slight rise in elevation around the rim of the *low pampas* marked by the Tandil and Ventana hills in the south, the *rolling pampas* in the north, and the granite uplift near the sixty-fourth meridian, prevents easy runoff. The only way for the water to get out is toward the Bay of Samborombón and to reach this it has to cross hundreds of miles of alternating swells and depressions, aided only by the very slight slope eastward. The result is that the streams often form series of small salt lakes. Or, where the water table is close to the surface and where the absorbency of the soil is reduced by a high clay content, the rains create huge shallow lakes. Similarly, the Salado River, the only major watercourse of the *low pampas*, is a source of floods rather than drainage; even man-made canals to the south have done little to avert periodic inundations.[18]

[17] Aparicio and Difrieri, *Suma de geografía*, I, 423–428; Daus, *Geografía de la República Argentina*, I, 132–138; James, *Latin America*, pp. 329–330; Pierre Denis, *The Argentine Republic*, pp. 167–173. Daus's classification is preferred to those of James and Denis.

[18] Daus, *Geografía de la República Argentina*, I, 242–247, 261–265.

Entre Ríos presents slightly different relief-features and is relatively well drained in its central section. Rather than a terrain of gradual swells, the countryside here is characterized by many small knolls, never more than 300 feet above sea level and usually no more than 30 feet above the surrounding land. The slight southward slope of the land is followed by the Nogoyá, Gualeguaychú, and Gualeguay Rivers as well as by the major Paraná and Uruguay Rivers. Innumerable small streams and washes in turn drain into these rivers. Below Diamante, the lower Paraná, no longer held in check by a rocky channel, spreads its bed over a broad delta—a maze of branches and loops from 30 to 50 miles wide. A large portion of southwestern Entre Ríos is consequently exposed to seasonal floods.

The climate of the coastal region is also an important factor of the environment in which Argentina's agricultural and social revolution took place. Rainfall, temperature, and winds all play their role in determining the success and extension of wheat growing.

Both banks of the Paraná River enjoy an average annual rainfall of from thirty-six to thirty-nine inches. Precipitation declines slightly to the west, although all of Santa Fe and the *low pampas* in Buenos Aires are still within the thirty-two-inch limit. Over this eastern portion of the pampas and in Entre Ríos, rainfall is fairly evenly divided throughout the year with the scantiest precipitation in the winter months of June and July, a secondary minimum in January and February, and heavy rains in the spring (September) and fall (March). Most important to the agriculturist, however, is the dependability of rainfall, and here the record is not so favorable. At Buenos Aires, which presents the most stable conditions, there were several sharp departures from the average within the period 1860 to 1910. Three years—1861, 1867, and 1893—brought serious droughts, with less than twenty-four inches of rainfall, whereas 1895 and 1900 saw disastrous downpours, culminating in March 1900 with twenty-one inches in a single month.[19]

The *tosca pampas* and western Buenos Aires, southeastern Córdoba, and northeastern La Pampa receive an annual precipitation ranging from twenty-four to thirty inches. The twenty-inch average —the minimum for nonirrigated crops—follows a curve from Bahía Blanca through San Luis to Santiago del Estero. Although in this

[19] Walter G. Davis, "Clima de la República Argentina," in *Censo agropecuario nacional de la República Argentina en 1908*, III, 647–648.

area there is no clear-cut rainy season, in contrast to the coast, rains tend to occur during the months from October to March.[20] The predictability of rains is also less sure here than on the coast. The *tosca pampas* and the western extension of the *low pampas* are exposed to periodic drought and the slough of the Salado to serious floods. Raising crops along the western limits of the humid pampas near the twenty-inch rainfall curve is a distinct gamble, for only a slight decline from the average will burn seedlings or dry up the maturing plants.

A further factor for the agriculturist to consider is the timing of the rains and their dependability within certain months. Maize, for example, requires a period of summer rain to mature. Such rain most frequently occurs in northern Buenos Aires and southern Santa Fe, while southern Buenos Aires, Córdoba, and La Pampa tend to have dry summer months. Wheat, on the other hand, needs spring rains and a dry summer, a general characteristic of the humid pampas but more pronounced as one moves west or south from Buenos Aires.

The humid pampas lie in a temperate zone. Summer temperatures (January) on the *rolling pampas* average 75°F. but will cover a range of from twenty to thirty degrees during a twenty-four-hour period. The winter average (July) is 42°. Humidity is high along the Paraná River and the Atlantic coast, especially in winter, when the average reaches a disagreeable 85 to 90 per cent. To the west and north, average summer temperatures are two or three degrees higher than on the *rolling pampas*, while the range on the *tosca pampas* is several degrees lower. Humidity drops sharply beyond the coastal fringe. Winter temperatures decrease southward to Bahía Blanca's July average of 36°. On the *rolling pampas* frosts are mild and occur only during the winter months of June through August; rarely do temperatures dip below 22°. To the south and west, with dry atmosphere, clear skies, and no wind, the danger of killing frosts increases markedly. The growing season drops from 290 days at Buenos Aires and 260 days at Pergamino to 240 at Bahía Blanca and 210 at Victorica in La Pampa.[21] More dangerous for the farmer is the fact that to the west and south of the humid pampas, frosts are more likely to be irregular and occur occasionally as late as November. Snow is

[20] Aparicio and Difrieri, *Suma de geografía,* II, 70–78; Denis, *The Argentine Republic,* p. 162.
[21] Aparicio and Difrieri, *Suma de geografía,* II, 30–34.

an extreme rarity in most of the humid pampas, although one brief snowfall per year can be expected in southern Buenos Aires and La Pampa.

Wind has been a major determinant of life on the pampas and its erosive action still vitally affects agriculture. From the estuary of the Río de la Plata southward to Bahía Blanca, along the southwest coast of Entre Ríos, and in dry western Buenos Aires and eastern La Pampa, lie countless sand dunes, sometimes one hundred feet high and extending over many square miles. Many of these are covered by vegetation and have become dead dunes. Anything that upsets nature's balance, however, such as drought, cultivation, or over-stocking of the range, exposes the sand particles to the force of the wind and causes the dunes to move. Charles Darwin, on his visit to the pampas during the 1830's, observed that the trampling of horses and cattle around rain-filled depressions often resulted in the forma-tion of dunes. Man's penetration into the pampas and his use of plow and harrow on the dry western lands made the problem acute. In the twentieth century, certain areas of La Pampa, Buenos Aires, and Córdoba threatened to become another Dust Bowl.[22]

For the agriculturist, the immediate effect of the winds on his crops is more meaningful than any potential erosion the land might suffer. The most severe pampean storms generally occur in the spring and early summer, when crops are in a critical stage of development. They may bring much-needed water, but they may also bring hot dry winds that sear the land, torrential downpours and floods, clouds of suffocating dust and sand, or whipping rounds of wind and hail. The hot, humid north wind, so irritating to human nerves, often ends with the famous pampero, followed by cool, dry breezes from the southwest. Wilfrid Latham, a British sheepbreeder, has left a classic description of a pampero of the 1860's:

The day has been close and oppressive; towards afternoon a dark leaden colour marks the line of sky on the horizon, and gradually rising against the wind, assumes dyes of deep purple and brown. . . . Suddenly the wind veers and comes with a rush, which nearly sweeps you from the saddle; before it is possible to dismount, the blinding dust pours over you, striking sharp against the skin. Denser and denser it drives. . . . In a few moments, total darkness envelopes everything—not the thin darkness of night, but an impenetrable, 'palpable' darkness, no object being discernible an inch

[22] *Ibid.*, IV, 121–138; Denis, *The Argentine Republic*, pp. 173–175.

from the eyeball. We had such a storm last year, and numbers, terrified, believed the day of judgment at hand: old men and children were swept away and lost or bruised; in the city, the crash of glass, the cracking of walls, bursting of doors, and in more than one instance the crumbling of walls of houses, and the cries of the affrighted, added terror to the scene. . . . In the 'campo', 'ranchos' and sheds were unroofed, and flocks and herds driven leagues before the storm.[23]

At times the pampero blows with such force as to drive the waters of the estuary onto the Uruguayan shore, leaving hundreds of yards of riverbed momentarily exposed on the Argentine side. Such a storm is known as a "dirty pampero" (*pampero sucio*). It has many of the characteristics of a tornado and will flatten crops, drive cattle and sheep before it, and leave a trail of destruction in its wake. More common is the "clean pampero" (*pampero limpio*), a milder storm whose effects are limited largely to heavy rains, spectacular lightning and thunder, and a general cleansing of the atmosphere. The south-easter, like the pampero, tends to follow periods of intense humidity and brings with it violent rains and high gusts of wind. Its effect on the estuary of the Río de la Plata is the reverse of that of the pampero, for it drives the water before it into the low-lying regions of Buenos Aires and Entre Ríos. Although more common to the northwest provinces, hail frequently accompanies summer thunderstorms over the pampas, especially in Córdoba and La Pampa. Damage to crops is usually localized, but until hail insurance became commonplace in the early twentieth century, hailstorms could mean serious losses for the individual farmer.

Grasses were the principal vegetation of the pampas. Spanish settlers applied the term "coarse grasses" to distinguish the several families of tough perennials, ranging from the tall clumps of pampas grass with their silky white plumes to the thick matting of *puna* grass. "Soft grasses" were the clovers, thistles, Indian barley, foxtail, or mustard accidentally imported by the Spanish; these sprang up wherever livestock grazed or trampled down the coarse grasses. The process was helped by vast fires, both deliberate and accidental, which often swept the pampas at summer's end when the coarse grasses were tinder-dry.

By the 1850's the soft grasses had emerged victorious in the area from Buenos Aires to the Salado River and north over most of the

[23] Latham, *The States of the River Plate*, pp. 28–29.

rolling pampas. Thistles characterized this zone. During the winter
they formed an impenetrable barrier from ten to twelve feet high
along the roads north from Buenos Aires. At winter's end the stalks
withered and died, and with the spring rains the soft grasses, clover
as well as thistles, burst forth with renewed vigor. For several months
the pasturage was excellent. By mid-century these soft grasses had
turned the region around Buenos Aires into a vast sheepwalk. Cattle
might nourish themselves on the coarse grasses and produce the excellent tough lean meat needed by the *saladeros.* Sheep, however,
could survive only where soft grasses grew. As a result, sheep took
over as soon as the herds of horses and cattle had eaten away or
killed out coarse grass and refined the pasturage. Soil and climate
decreed that this refining process could not move west indefinitely,
although the limit had not been reached by the 1850's. An arc from
Mar del Plata through Tandil, Olavarría, Bolívar, and Lincoln to
Rosario would eventually mark an approximate frontier for the soft
grasses.[24]

Vegetation on the pampas underwent few other changes as the
result of the activities of the Spaniards. Thomas Hinchliff, a British
traveler of the 1860's, noted that north of the city of Buenos Aires
"the sloping land between the Quintas [suburban residences] and
the river was principally covered with alfalfa, or lucerne, which
grows there with remarkable vigour, and seems capable of producing
good crops in seasons where the ordinary grasses of the country dry
up from want of rain."[25] But for the moment there was no need or
thought of using that plant's deep roots to provide rich and permanent forage on the pampas.

Scrub vegetation lined the borders of the humid pampas: dwarf
mimosas on the Colorado River; certain types of thorny brush on the
Tandil Hills; the mimosas of the Córdoba Hills and northern Santa
Fe. Along the Paraná River and the estuary of the Río de la Plata
trees invaded this grassland: the laurel; the bamboos; the *ombú* with
its corklike wood and bark; the spiny clump of the tala rising to a
height of thirty feet; the *ceibo* or *ceibal*, Argentina's national tree with
its scarlet flowers. The only tree that was widely planted in the pampas environment was the peach, and curiously enough not for its
fruit. It owed its popularity to the fact that a peach tree matured in
three years and consequently provided an excellent source of fire-

[24] Daus, *Geografía de la República Argentina,* I, 337.
[25] Thomas Hinchliff, *South American Sketches,* p. 58.

wood. Although the imported eucalyptus, poplar, willow, *paraiso*, and *robinia* subsequently did extremely well in the eastern portion of the pampas, beautification of *estancia* headquarters and cities was a concern of the late nineteenth century, not of the 1850's.

The addition of horses, cattle, sheep, and dogs was the only significant change in the animal kingdom during the three centuries following the arrival of the Spanish. Before effective occupation of the humid pampas began in the second half of the nineteenth century, these grasslands had the aspect of a huge game-preserve and indeed hunting was the major sport for travelers in the Argentine pampas. The Paraná River and the Paraná Delta, the streams of Entre Ríos, the marshes and lagoons of the Salado slough, the rain-filled depressions of the pampas supported an extensive wildlife: flocks of strikingly beautiful pink flamingos and endless varieties of ducks; herons and swans; and valuable furbearers such as the nutria, weasel, and jaguar. Across the grasslands roamed numerous herds of the small pampean deer, several types of foxes, and, in the north, the puma. This was the home of the armadillo, the partridge, and the rhea, that smaller and less elegantly plumed cousin of the African ostrich. Perhaps most characteristic of the wildlife was the *vizcacha*, similar in habits if not in size to the North American prairie dog. In appearance, *vizcachas* resemble large-headed, rather square-nosed hares. They tend to group together in villages, each family living in an extensive underground tunnel which is frequently shared with a pair of burrowing owls. As occupation of the pampas progressed, their burrows became a distinct hazard to the galloping horseman, and their taste for maize made them a nuisance to farmers.

The opening of the pampas brought drastic changes in the patterns of wildlife. First to vanish were the deer. The vast numbers of birds and wild animals decreased or moved to remote areas as their breeding grounds, food supply, and lairs dwindled or disappeared before the advance of horses, cattle, packs of wild dogs, and man himself. Human perspectives also shifted. Just as the *vizcacha* changed from a curiosity to a pest, so did one of the pampas' more casual visitors, the locust, become a plague. The flights of these brown insects had mattered little when the land belonged to wild horses and Indians. But when man began to till this soil, the locust turned into a calamity.

Such then was the ecological picture of the pampas in the 1850's. A grassland lay waiting to be conquered: its potential was enormous and unsuspected; its limitations were vast and untested. The simple geographical outline of the preceding pages was largely unknown. Where could rainfall be counted on to support a crop? Where did the danger of frost cancel out man's tillage of the soil? What crops were suited to what soils? The answers to these and many more questions would be found only by costly and painful experience.

Settlement had nibbled at the edge of the pampas. But by and large the Argentines at mid-century had no need or desire to undertake the sedentary settling of the land. They were able to tap the animal wealth without undue exertion. Any conquest would have to look elsewhere for its army. There might have existed visionary leaders and statesmen who could understand that this land had to be cultivated and settled if Argentina was to grow, that "to govern is to populate," according to the dictum of one of the country's great thinkers. But the masses of people, in terms of numbers and aptitudes needed to carry out such a dream, were themselves a dream of the future.

Argentina's agricultural and social revolution, therefore, had to wait for the immigrant. The land was there. It remained to be seen what the newcomers would do with it.

iii. THE PEOPLE: *The Immigrant and the Farmer*

During the second half of the nineteenth century, the opportunities of an expanding agricultural economy attracted thousands of Europeans to Argentina. The map of 1869, date of the first national census, shows thirteen clusters of settlement, representing the thirteen provincial capitals. By 1914, when the third census was taken, the center of population had moved toward the pampas and was concentrated in the coastal cities (Map 3).

At mid-century, Argentina's population numbered 1,300,000, barely one-third of which was settled in the future wheat provinces. Almost all of the 100,000 foreigners, however, resided in the coastal cities and in the province of Buenos Aires.[1] A census of the city of Buenos Aires in 1856 showed a foreign population of 38,000 out of 91,000 inhabitants. This foreign element handled the retail trade and provided skilled artisan labor. Most of the city's food supply was raised on surrounding plots tended by immigrants. Outside the city, Irish, Scotch, and Basque herdsmen controlled sheep raising. The Italians completely dominated the river trade, while in towns along the Paraná and Uruguay Rivers, Basques, Italians, and Frenchmen constituted as much as 20 per cent of the population. The foreigner, nevertheless, rarely ventured outside the littoral except for an occasional wandering Italian or French merchant or artisan, and, save for the shepherd in Buenos Aires, he never left the towns or cities.

Statistics from the subsequent national censuses demonstrate the extent and concentration of immigration in the coastal area. Out of a total of 1,800,000 inhabitants recorded by the 1869 census, 200,000

[1] Victor Martin de Moussy, *Description géographique et statistique de la Confédération Argentine*, II, 234.

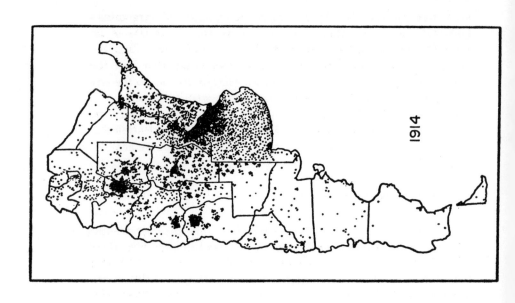

1914

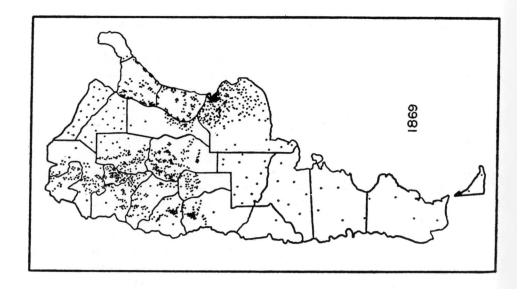

1869

were foreign-born; by 1895, almost one-quarter of Argentina's 4,000,000 were immigrants; by 1914, more than 2,300,000 of an 8,000,000 population had been born abroad. By this latter date, the coastal region contained two-thirds of the total population; here the ratio of immigrants to native Argentines was two to one. In the city of Buenos Aires three out of every four adults were foreigners.

What this influx and concentration of immigrants meant to the political formation of Argentina will be considered, at least tentatively, in the final chapter of this study. For the moment we are concerned with a specific aspect of immigration: the arrival of farmers in a new land.

As with contemporary outpourings into the United States, Canada, and Australia, the source of immigrants was Europe and the reasons were many and diverse. Unfortunately, available statistics are not very enlightening (Table 1 for immigration and emigration, 1871–1910). They record the endless flow as ciphers, without faces, personalities, or origins. In the half-century covered by this study, 1,880,000 of the immigrants to Argentina, or 55 per cent, came from Italy. Spaniards added another 880,000, or 26 per cent. The French accounted for 5 per cent, while the rest were Russians (primarily Jewish), Austrians, Syrians, English, Germans, and Swiss in that order.[2] Since Argentina's great demand, especially in the latter decades, was for agricultural labor, it is not surprising that some 37 per cent declared themselves to be agriculturists. But this is of little help in determining whether the new arrivals were city-bred or farm boys, whether they had cut the bonds with their homeland or were mere birds of passage who planned to return to Europe, whether they had been driven from their homes by despair or drawn by the hope and vision of a new life overseas. Only official Italian statistics shed some light: from 1876 to 1900 they show an emigration to Argentina of 444,000 from the prosperous but overpopulated northern agricultural districts as contrasted with 263,000 from the depressed south of Italy, a period when southern Italy sent 523,000 of her sons to the United States, while the north sent only 73,000. The next period—1901 to 1913—saw southern Italy balance the north in emigration to Argentina with 328,000 to 316,000, but the comparison with the United States is still instructive, for the south now sent 1,700,000 to the

[2] Calculated from statistics in Juan A. Alsina, *La inmigración en el primer siglo de la independencia*, p. 22.

United States as contrasted with the north's 347,000.[3] Such statistics reinforce our impression of the northern Italian's importance in Argentine development and carry also the implication that the preparation and aspiration of many of these immigrants were agricultural—whether or not they achieved their hopes for such a life in Argentina.

In the absence of clear-cut statistical indications we must turn to the reception of the immigrant himself. The Argentina of the 1850's was still virtually unknown in Europe. To Irish sheepherders, English merchants, and Italian river captains who had prospered, this was a promised land. But this select element, which did little to alter the traditional economy, was not what Argentine statesmen were seeking. Their country needed a major injection of European laborers if it was to be anything other than a land of scrawny cattle and sheep. The habits of three centuries were deeply embedded: an urban population that subsisted on commerce, politics, and on enormous herds exploited with a minimum of labor. Only a revolution could transform this deserted land with its scattered provincial capitals and river ports into a civilized, prosperous, and growing country. The dreamers and statesmen had at hand a ready illustration of what could be done—the immigration to the thirteen North American colonies, which in a century had built a powerful agricultural and industrial nation. If more lessons were needed, there were the contemporary experiences of Canada and Australia. Little wonder that to the generation which overthrew the country's *de facto* ruler, Juan Manuel de Rosas, Argentina's urgent need was immigration.

One might expect, therefore, to find a mammoth propaganda effort launched in Europe to preach Argentina's attractions, to see the immigrant welcomed with open arms, courted and pampered, or at least presented with the tools to secure the hoped-for revolution. The realities of the Argentine scene, however, were far different from the illusions of statesmen and publicists. Governments might make ambitious plans, but they lacked the funds and the power to execute them. Sporadic civil war raged between the provinces and Buenos Aires from 1852 to 1862, and from 1865 to 1870 the nation was involved in the disastrous Paraguayan War. As political stability gradually increased in the 1870's the prevalent spirit of *laissez faire* dominated government policy. National authorities rode out two economic booms—1882–1889 and 1904–1912—and their ensuing depressions,

---

[3] SVIMEZ, Associazione per lo sviluppo dell'industria nel Mezzogiorno, *Statistiche sul mezzogiorno d'Italia 1861–1953*, p. 117.

with a minimum of official interference and at no time took active measures to direct the economic development of the country. Politics continued to be the absorbing and profitable passion of native Argentines, while commerce, business, and construction were developed by immigrants. Land values increased a hundredfold, but this very increase conspired, in the absence of government action, to keep ownership out of the hands of the immigrants. With the subjugation of the Indian and the expansion of the frontier, huge tracts offered at public auction could be secured only by those with capital, credit, or influence. When the further rise of land values brought subdivision, speculators and investors outbid the agriculturists. At the same time, rural life in Argentina was not so difficult as it was transitory. The North American frontiersman might readily have changed places with the Argentine farm laborer insofar as working conditions were concerned. But in Argentina the pressures were against a farm environment. The tenant farmer was relentlessly pushed from plot to plot because the *estanciero* wanted the land for raising cattle or sheep. Pastoral interests accepted agriculture as the initial step in planting alfalfa pastures but leased land to farmers only long enough to break up the sod and prepare the land for pasturage. The landowner also preferred the short lease that permitted periodic increases in rents. In surroundings that favored the large unit, the small-farm owner found himself at the mercy of equally restrictive forces—petty officials, discriminatory railroad rates, and powerful market interests. The land remained something to be exploited in order to secure the maximum return in the shortest time, without regard for the consequences. As a result the immigrant rarely sank roots in the land, and the city rather than the farm increasingly became the purveyor of rapid and easy advancement for the newly arrived.

Official or semiofficial colonization was the first effort essayed by the Argentine authorities to attract masses of rural laborers from Europe. The number of immigrants was small and their initial agricultural and economic impact was even less. But the experiments were significant as an illustration of the problems and attitudes of the Argentine rural environment.

Bernardino Rivadavia, a precursor of the liberal-minded Argentine statesmen of mid-century, had already attempted in 1825 to contract European farm families for the area of the Río de la Plata. But the fruit of his efforts—three small colonies of Scots, English, and Germans—had a fleeting existence and soon dissolved as a result of civil strife and the unsympathetic pastoral tradition. Immigration continued throughout the Rosas regime, but it consisted mostly of ambitious young men drawn by opportunities in commerce and sheep grazing. Few were attracted to agricultural pursuits except those who tended small garden plots around the coastal cities. Certainly the Rosas government lent no official encouragement to immigration and demonstrated no interest in agricultural settlements.

Immediately after the fall of Rosas in 1852, several entrepreneurs approached the national and provincial governments with ambitious projects for agricultural colonies. The basic terms of these projects were outlined in a contract in 1853 between the governor of Corrientes and Auguste Brougnes, a French doctor of some experience in Argentina. The colonizer was to introduce a specified number of families and settle them on selected public lands. The government agreed to grant land (most often a unit of twenty *squares,* or eighty acres) to each family, with ownership rights after cultivation for a certain number of years. Agricultural implements, seed, housing, animals, and initial food stocks were also to be provided by the government with the expectation of repayment after two or three years. Such contracts usually exempted the settlers from taxation for a few years. The colonizer was to be repaid for his efforts in attracting colonists and transporting them to Argentina either by a grant of public land adjoining the colony or by shares from the harvests of the colonists. In that same year, 1853, the new Argentine constitution added liberal encouragement to immigration by guaranteeing religious freedom and granting foreign residents most of the privileges of citizenship without incurring such obligations as military service.

On paper the terms appeared advantageous to all. The colonists, who presumably would be recruited from the poorer classes in the European countryside, were to be aided through their initial stages and would emerge at the end of four or five years of hard work as independent landowners. The government, which held endless tracts of virgin public lands, would be able to settle an industrious class in the rural zones, build a thriving agricultural economy, and increase the value of its public domain. The colonizer, as a good capitalist, would profit in the degree to which the colony prospered.

During the 1850's and 1860's several entrepreneurs concluded colonization contracts with the Corrientes, Entre Ríos, and especially the Santa Fe governments. The execution of these contracts showed that the agricultural conquest of the littoral and the pampas and its conquest on paper were quite different matters. The colonizers usually turned over recruitment in Europe to some established emigration firm, such as Beck and Herzog of Basel. Frequently those persuaded to enlist had no agricultural experience and were recruited from the desperately poor of the German and Swiss cities. Far worse than this was the fact that the provincial governments invariably lacked the funds or the initiative to carry out their part of the bargain. When Brougnes delivered 160 colonists to Corrientes in January 1855, it was discovered that the provincial government had taken no measures to receive them, to provide housing or food, or even to survey and measure the land for their colony. When in early 1856 Aaron Castellanos brought 840 colonists to settle Esperanza, Santa Fe, he met the same official neglect of reality: "There had been no thought taken of measures of the first importance for the colonists; no houses built, no wells dug, no corrales ready for the cattle which were to be delivered by the government. No arrangements made for public order, no system of overseering [sic] to teach the colonists what they ought to do; no church and no hospitals."[4] It was not surprising, therefore, that the Brougnes colony promptly dissolved, and that the Esperanza colony was saved only by a loan from the national authorities.

Perhaps even more significant was the fact that official colonization, from the start, was relegated to marginal zones, either of dubious pastoral value or exposed to Indian raids. The richest of the pastoral provinces, Buenos Aires, gave no encouragement to the efforts of early colonizers. Only by accident did it fall heir to one colony in the 1850's: eleven families, who could not be included in the Esperanza venture, emigrated directly to Buenos Aires in 1856 with the aid of Beck and Herzog. Foreseeing the increased value agriculture might bring to their lands in northern Buenos Aires, several progressive cattlemen arranged for tiny family-grants of nine acres each from the municipality of Baradero. On the other hand, the central portion of the province of Santa Fe, where most of the early colonization ventures were located, was considered largely marginal to the pastoral economy and, ironically, it was also a poor zone for wheat. Many years later the Argentine Ministry of Agriculture was to list much of this area as submarginal for wheat cultivation. But this was of no matter during early colonization. The crucial factor was that

[4] William Perkins, *The Colonies of Santa Fe. Their origin, progress and present condition with general observations on emigration to the Argentine Republic,* p. 19.

cattle and sheep had not prospered here, and consequently the land had not acquired the value of Buenos Aires' rich pastoral holdings. Hence it was open for any venture—even agriculture. The presence of Indian tribes from the Chaco further reduced the pastoral value of these lands. Yet the Santa Fe authorities broke their original contract and relocated the Esperanza colony as an outpost twenty miles from the city of Santa Fe. Many were the advocates of immigration on just those terms: a ring of agricultural settlements that would protect Argentina's primary interest and basic source of wealth—the pastoral industries.

With such obstacles official colonization was doomed and, except for a few frontier establishments, ended in the 1860's. But government colonization, especially that of Santa Fe, had shown a way to utilize marginal lands. Colonization projects were now underwritten by private initiative. With the aid of Charles Beck-Bernard (of Beck and Herzog), General Justo José de Urquiza had established the colony of San José on his enormous holding near the Uruguay River in 1857. The following year Richard Foster, an English landowner, founded the colony of San Gerónimo Norte, just west of the city of Santa Fe. During the 1860's fifteen more colonies were established, most of them private ventures and all of them located in the province of Santa Fe.

Despite its apparent failure, official colonization had introduced two important changes to the Argentine scene, changes which were dramatized as the initiative passed to private hands: European agriculturists were actually settled on the land, and wheat cultivation expanded. Although their numbers were small, European families had been drawn to Argentina and had sunk their roots in the land. No one could deny that they had suffered enormous hardships. The experience at Esperanza was typical. During the initial four years, drought, locusts, and the colonists' ignorance of agriculture erased the slightest hope for a harvest, and the colony showed a total loss. The constant menace of Indian attack which forced the colonists to go armed to their fields, the arduous labor needed to transport the harvest twenty or thirty miles to a town or river, and the frequent hostility of the native Argentine population were not calculated to make life easy for these newcomers. But they did survive. These colonies did not dissolve, as each preceding experiment had done. At the end of four or five years, they began to show their vitality, to expand, and even to attract additional settlers. Esperanza, which started with 840 men, women, and children in 1856, had 1,856 inhabitants by 1869. San Gerónimo Norte grew from 100 souls to 958; several miles to the south the important colony of San Carlos, established in 1858 by Charles Beck-Bernard and the Santa Fe government, expanded from a few hundred settlers to 1,992. At the same time it is valuable to remember that these agricultural settlers represented a relatively small percentage of the total immigration to Argentina. Net immigration—that is, those who remained in Argentina—totaled 10,000 in 1870; 28,000 in 1871; 58,000 in 1872; and 47,000 in 1873. A government report in 1872 listed thirty-two colonies, official and private, in Santa Fe and three in Entre Ríos with a total population of only 17,000.[5]

The second important change introduced by the official colonies and carried forward by privately financed ones was the expansion of wheat cultivation. There were a few wheat areas such as the *chacras*, or small farms, of Chivilcoy, almost one hundred miles west of Buenos Aires, where the former tenants had been given the opportunity to become proprietors of their lands by Buenos Aires legislation in 1857. But the bulk of wheat consumed in the coastal cities— and bread was a wholly urban commodity—was grown on the farms and garden plots surrounding these cities. From the start, however, Esperanza, San Carlos, and the other Santa Fe colonies dedicated themselves primarily to wheat and thus added extensive virgin land to the production of that cereal. Wheat possessed three valuable advantages: it could be grown by the most inexperienced agriculturist; it could be stored; and in days when all freight still moved by lumbering oxcart its compactness meant relatively low transport costs. The steady rise in urban population, more and more oriented to the European taste for bread, increased demand and maintained high prices. Argentina in the early 1870's was still a net importer of wheat, and consequently the colonies reaped handsome profits when crops were good (Table 2). The importance of the colonies was indicated by the fact that, in 1872, they produced almost one-quarter of the national wheat crop, or some 20,000 tons.[6]

By 1870 agricultural colonization was firmly established in Argentina. Although governments, national and provincial, had proved less than the ideal executors of such projects, they had given the nec-

[5] Guillermo Wilcken, *Las colonias. Informe sobre el estado actual de las colonias agrícolas de la República Argentina*, Appendix, Table I.
[6] *Ibid.*, Table II.

essary impulse. Landowners and private colonization companies now turned to the colony system to exploit marginal pastoral lands, especially in central Santa Fe. The procedure was simple. In effect, it meant that an entrepreneur extended sufficient credit to a contracted colonist to transplant him from Europe or Buenos Aires to eighty acres of virgin soil on the frontier and to start him as an agriculturist. With a fertile soil, worth next to nothing, the individual colonist stood a fair chance to repay such an advance and to emerge as proprietor of those eighty acres. The immigrant was hardly coddled, but if he possessed courage and determination the colonization contract was a substantial improvement over agricultural prospects in crowded Europe.

Had it not been for the railroad, private colonization would doubtless have been limited to the slow expansion characteristic of the 1860's. The first railroads radiated from Buenos Aires to serve the surrounding pastoral region. As previously mentioned, the first stretch of track in Argentina—the Western Railroad—was completed in 1857 with six miles extending due west from the city. In 1864 another company, the Northern Railroad, finished a twenty-mile length of track northward, while in 1867 still another group of entrepreneurs completed the Southern Railroad's line to Chascomús, seventy miles south of the *porteño* city. But the event that signaled a new horizon for agriculture was the inauguration in 1870 of the Central Argentine Railroad from Rosario to Córdoba (Map 4). As part of the concession to the English company that had constructed the line, a strip three miles wide on each side of the track had been granted to a subsidiary, the Central Argentine Land Company, for colonization. In 1869 intensive recruiting got under way in Switzerland and soon expanded to Italy, and by March 1870 the first colony, Bernstadt, was established thirteen miles west of Rosario. The company offered lots ranging in size from eighty to one hundred sixty acres for direct sale to colonists. Or, for those without capital, the land was offered for rent at a small fixed charge per year with an option for future purchase once the colonist had accumulated funds. Advances in animals, equipment, food, and housing could also be secured from the company, to be repaid from the proceeds of future harvests. Within a year, three more colonies were started along the Santa Fe portion of the Central's track—a total of 3,000 inhabitants who promised agricultural prosperity for their communities and commercial

THE IMMIGRANT AND THE FARMER

benefits to the railroad.[7] Changes in administrative policy in London and a resultant concern with immediate profits interrupted colonization, and the Land Company did not resume active promotion of its settlements until the 1880's. But agriculture had been given new encouragement. A large area of Santa Fe, formerly isolated by distance from cities and rivers, was made accessible by the railroad, and since neither cattle raising nor sheep raising had taken root in that zone, colonists were able to turn the cheap lands to wheat production. Private companies copied the terms of the Central Argentine Land Company and offered lots to agriculturists on the installment plan with payments spread from three to ten years.[8] Individual landowners increasingly saw the advantage of agricultural colonies as a means of raising the value of their vast holdings. Typical was the notice in *La Nación* for January 29, 1876:

Messrs. Videla and Latorre, residents of the province of Santa Fe, are thinking of establishing a colony on their property. The total area of the colony will be two square leagues divided into 160 concessions each measuring four *squares* on the front by five deep [the standard unit of eighty acres]. The most advantageous conditions will be made available to settlers, such as lumber for construction, oxen, tools, etc. In addition, no charge will be made for surveying and for the registration of deeds.

Agriculture—and in its early stages the word meant wheat cultivation—thus came to Argentina indirectly. Under official and later under private auspices it penetrated first into the marginal areas of central Santa Fe. Then with the transportation facilities of the Central Argentine Railroad and the administrative leadership afforded by the Central Argentine Land Company, wheat colonies blossomed in southern Santa Fe. Subdivisions of Santa Fe lands for sale to colonists returned from three to four times their value to the large landowner.[9] Since much of this land was deserted or provided only inferior pasturage, landowners were delighted with the profit and were willing to surrender ownership of some of their lands to agriculturists. The 1860's and 1870's, therefore, marked a golden era for the colonist. Conditions of life were rugged and facilities few,

[7] *Ibid.*, pp. 147–183.

[8] Jonas Larguía, *Informe del inspector de colonias de la provincia de Santa Fe, 1876*, p. 37.

[9] Estanislao S. Zeballos, *Descripción amena de la República Argentina*, II, *La región del trigo* (1883), p. 245.

but for the industrious European peasant, ownership of land was a definite possibility in Argentina.

Wheat production increased proportionately to the expansion of the colonies. Argentina, which had imported wheat ever since the colonial period, now promised not only to meet the rising internal demand but also to provide a surplus for export. Small shipments of wheat left Argentina for Paraguay in 1871, for Belgium in 1872 and 1873, for England in 1874; in 1878 the total export of wheat exceeded the import. President Nicolás Avellaneda, in his annual message to Congress in 1879, hailed the shipment of 4,500 tons of wheat to Europe on April 12 and praised the progress of colonization and agriculture in Santa Fe. His visit to those colonies later that same year emphasized official appreciation of this new phase of Argentine economic progress. Despite the inaccuracy of early statistics, figures from contemporary numbers of the *Boletín del departamento nacional de agricultura* show a trend toward increasingly larger areas sown to wheat in Santa Fe, and almost entirely accounted for by the colonies: from 89,000 acres in 1873 and 1874 to 144,000 in 1875; 174,000 in 1876; 247,000 in 1877; 295,000 in 1878; 312,000 in 1879; and 338,000 in 1880.

The economic revolution which Argentine statesmen had been attempting to encourage by means of immigration and agriculture attained some of its goals after 1880. It converted Argentina into a world breadbasket as well as into a major supplier of beef for European markets. It provided Buenos Aires with the wealth and population that made the city the envy of the rest of South America. Yet this revolution destroyed the colonization system and the small independent farmer. The pampas had been conquered economically, but socially they remained outside the nation, an area exploited but not possessed.

The changes which now took place were intimately linked with the predominantly pastoral interests of Argentina's coastal region. Agriculture had started in an area where the production of cattle and sheep was of secondary importance. The agricultural colonies of Santa Fe had played a major role in making Argentina self-sufficient in wheat production. But they were too few and absorbed too small a proportion of the increasing numbers of immigrants to alter Argentina's economy or social structure in any drastic fashion.

The revolution on the pampas came about not because of the

colonies but because of the needs of the pastoral industry—the very interests which had initially rejected the whole concept of immigrants on the land. Three factors molded those needs. The Conquest of the Desert, completed by General Julio Roca in 1880, brought tranquility to the pampas and eliminated the Indian as a frontier menace. Extensive railroad building in the following decades, especially of the Western and the Southern, made it possible to move wool, hides, animals, and cereals to the coast rapidly and cheaply. Finally, the whole emphasis of the pastoral economy began to shift, especially in the 1890's, from primary dependence on wool, hides, and salted meat, to an increasing interest in the production of animals that could supply choice meat as well.

The elimination of the Indian brought tremendous advantages to the pastoral industries. As has been noted, cattle acted as a refining agent on the tough pampean grass, breaking it down to permit the spread of softer grasses suitable for sheep forage. Since the production of hides and salted meat called for no special attention or feed, cattle had always been pushed toward the frontier, the very area where the animals were most exposed to Indian raids. From mid-century on, a thriving commerce had existed through the southern passes with Chile—the sale by pampean Indians of cattle driven off from the ranches around Tandil and Azul. Now not only had the raids ended, but also Buenos Aires' southern boundary had been extended to the mouth of the Negro River. From one year to the next, the area available for pastoral exploitation had doubled in size. These new lands, as huge holdings, passed directly into the hands of powerful pastoral interests or speculators. Roca's expedition had been financed in part by the sale of government bonds, each worth four hundred silver pesos and exchangeable for a square league chosen as the frontier advanced. In 1882 public auction offered remaining frontier lands in lots as large as 100,000 acres.

The railroads altered the rural scene even more drastically than had the expulsion of the Indians. Wherever the rails reached, the fruits of the land acquired added value, and utilization of vast new areas became possible. Wheat was no longer limited to the customary radius of twenty or thirty miles from a river or a city; cattle could be moved to pasturage or market by rail instead of on the hoof; and not only could wool be shipped but the sheep themselves could be easily brought to Buenos Aires for slaughter. The pastoral and agricultural exploitation of new lands was, therefore, a direct result of

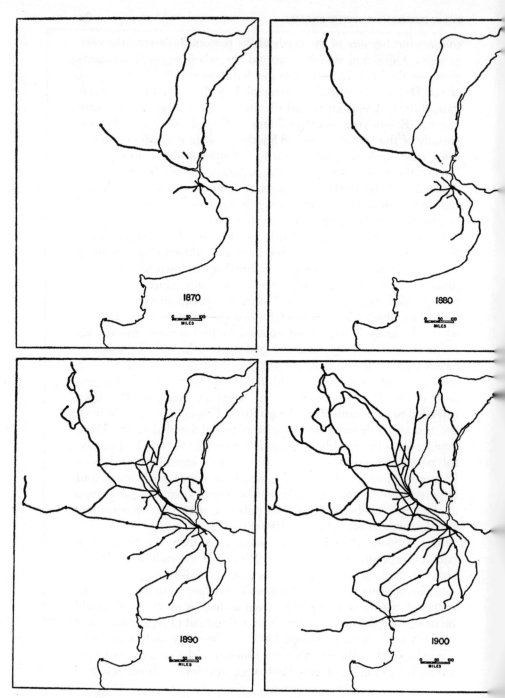

Map 4. Expansion of the Argentine Railroad System, 1870–1900

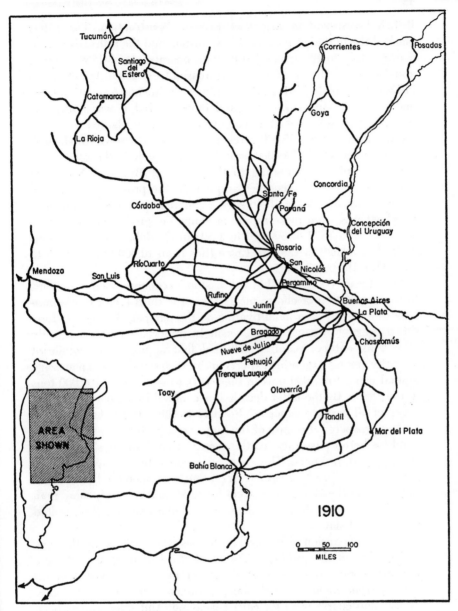

Map 5. Argentine Railroad System in 1910

British investment in Argentine railroad construction. The 1880's marked the period of most rapid expansion, and the railroads played a major role in the general economic boom of 1882–1889 (Map 4 and Table 3). The miles of track increased from 460 in 1870 to 1,570 in 1880, to 7,800 in 1891. Initially railways in Buenos Aires stimulated and aided that province's pastoral interests, but it was noticeable that the increasing wheat acreage was invariably planted alongside the rail lines. From 125,000 acres in 1873, the area sown to wheat in Buenos Aires rose to 790,000 acres in 1891, largely in the zone of the Western Railroad extending to the towns of Bragado, Nueve de Julio, Pehuajó, and Trenque Lauquen. In the provinces where the pastoral industry did not hold such a dominant position, the advance of wheat was even more rapid: in Santa Fe, production rose from 20,000 tons in 1872 to 500,000 in 1891; in Córdoba, from 8,000 tons in 1875 to 80,000 in 1891; in Entre Ríos from 10,000 tons in 1878 to more than 100,000 in 1891.

An internal change within the pastoral economy itself—the shift to the production of choice meats—was the third factor that stimulated the spread of crop cultivation on the pampas. As noted before, sheep grazing became an increasingly important pastoral activity after mid-century. Wool, which had first appeared in significant quantity among Argentine exports in the 1830's, rose from an average annual export of 7,000 tons in the 1840's to well above 100,000 tons in the 1880's. By the latter decade it accounted for 55 per cent of the value of all pastoral exports.[10] Relative to the cattle industry, sheep raising prospered. Because of the higher return from sheep and their need for better pasturage, cattle were displaced and pushed toward the exposed frontiers. The demand created by European carpet factories for coarse, unwashed Argentine wool increased even more rapidly than the European market for hides and certainly more than the static or even declining demand of Cuba and Brazil for salted meat to feed slaves.

Yet real expansion of pastoral industries was curtailed by the type and quality of the products. The wool clip had been the only important nineteenth-century modification in a pastoral system inherited from colonial times. Sheep products were limited to skins, grease, and coarse wool for carpet weaving. And since, as has been mentioned, mares were never ridden by the gaucho, those not used

[10] Alois E. Fliess, *La producción agrícola y ganadera de la República Argentina en el año 1891*, p. 320.

for breeding yielded hides and tallow. Cattle were utilized for their hides, fat, and stringy lean meat. For a land sparse in population and not too extravagant in aspirations this had been enough. But the spirit of progress and the liberal ideas evident after the 1850's stimulated the desire to modernize and improve Argentina's pastoral wealth.

Meat was the obvious key. In the coastal areas it constituted the cheapest item in the diet, and frequently it was merely thrown away: during the 1860's the carcasses of 60 per cent of the slaughtered cattle were never utilized for meat.[11] Yet for Europe's rapidly expanding urban population meat was a luxury far beyond the reach of the poor. But how bridge the Atlantic and bring about the meeting of supply and demand? Several entrepreneurs bankrupted themselves trying to develop a European taste for salted meat. Food habits and custom proved too strong, and the strips of dried grayish meat relished by Brazilian slaves were rejected even by the slum-dwellers of Paris and London. More successful were efforts to reduce the juices of the meat to paste form. Liebig's Meat Extract, manufactured in Entre Ríos and in Uruguay, was widely used in the hospitals and poorhouses of Europe in the 1860's and soon became a popular household item on the Continent. Inventive minds, meanwhile, tried to dehydrate meat, pack it in vacuum tins, inject it with preservatives, but without commercial success. The method of getting unspoiled meat to Europe, however, was only one side of the problem. Several far-sighted landowners who organized the Sociedad Rural Argentina in 1866 understood what it would take three decades for the majority of cattlemen to comprehend: that the stringy beef produced by native stock would never appeal to European palates regardless of its preparation. Through their organization and through their journal, the *Anales,* they commenced a pioneering campaign to teach cattlegrowers the rudiments of selective breeding: that pedigreed bulls were not mere curiosities, and that fences and alfalfa were the essential ingredients of a new era. But until a European market was assured, the *saladero* and hide market reigned supreme, and few could see the value of blooded stock, wire fences, or refined forage.

The problem of securing this much-needed market was solved in the 1880's by two methods: frozen meat and on-the-hoof shipments. The French led in the initial attempts to transport frozen meat across

[11] Horacio C. E. Giberti, *Historia económica de la ganadería argentina,* p. 161.

the Atlantic; in 1876 an experimental shipload of chilled carcasses arrived in Buenos Aires from Rouen. Although at a banquet the leaders of *porteño* commerce and society were barely able to choke down cuts which had aged for three months under less than perfect refrigeration, they were enthusiastic about the idea of refrigeration. Subsequently, frozen meat (−22° F.) won out over chilled (32°) as more suited to the long voyage and the rudimentary level of technology. In the meantime British interests, already at work on the transport of mutton from Australia, took over from the French and established packing plants in Buenos Aires and outlets in England. Through their Australian experience and owing to serious technological limitations, meat packers soon discovered that it was easier to handle mutton than larger carcasses. The effect on the sheep industry was immediate. Since packing plants paid 50 per cent more than tallow factories for sheep carcasses, there were powerful incentives to produce an animal which could be used for meat as well as for wool.[12] As a result, the Lincoln was introduced to modify or replace the previously dominant Merino breeds, and sheepgrowers suddenly became interested in selective breeding and superior pasturage.

Cattlegrowers, little affected during the 1880's by the packing plants, received their incentive from on-the-hoof shipments. There had always been an extensive live-cattle trade across the frontiers to Chile, Bolivia, Paraguay, Brazil, and Uruguay, whose consumers were even less demanding than the Argentine market. In the 1870's several exporters attempted to send live cattle to Europe, but although shipping problems were easily solved, the quality of the animals turned the ventures into commercial failures. Only in the late 1880's did success finally crown the repeated efforts to ship and sell live cattle. Then, within five years, the low price and vastly improved quality of Argentine beef enabled it to displace United States and Canadian cuts as the choice of British consumers. The incentive for change was the same as that given by the packing plants to sheepgrowers. Shippers for the overseas market needed tame fat animals of breeds preferred in Europe, and for these they were willing to pay far higher prices than the *saladeros* paid for scrawny native stock. As a result the British consumer imposed the Shorthorn, producer of the famous marbleized roast beef, on Argentina. With the Shorthorn bulls came the demand for fences to tame cattle, to pre-

12 *Ibid.*, p. 171.

vent the mixing or degeneration of stock, and to avoid losses. Since pampas grass put little fat on cattle, special pastures of rich forage near the ports had to be developed to fatten the animals in preparation for the long ocean voyage.

The pastoral interests, which had not concerned themselves with the immigrant and certainly had not invited him onto the land, now found in the late 1880's that their economy was changing radically. With the conquest of the Indians they acquired vast new holdings. The railroads made the products of the hinterlands available to world markets and extended the horizons of both pastoral and agricultural expansion. The markets for frozen mutton and live cattle in Europe, especially in England, demanded extensive changes in pasturage, breeding, and care. In such a framework the immigrant could find a niche.

Agricultural immigrants, however, were doomed to enter pastoral areas as servants of already-existing economic interests. In these zones the principal obstacle to the independence of the immigrant was the high cost of land. Pastoral lands in the province of Buenos Aires had traditionally been the most expensive in the whole littoral. In 1888, acre for acre, holdings in Buenos Aires were worth four times the price of similar holdings in Santa Fe (Table 4). As a result the immigrant did not encounter in Buenos Aires the peculiar situation found in Santa Fe, where owners had been willing to sell a part of their holdings in order to increase, by proximity to cultivated areas, the value of the remainder. The *porteño* landowner, on the contrary, had no desire to subdivide his property, at least not at the prices which the penniless new arrival could hope to amortize. Accustomed to the large expanses required by a pastoral economy, the *estanciero* had also become used to rapid increases in the value of his lands. The expulsion of the Indians and the construction of railroads had not deceived such expectations; and the new bonanza created by European consumption of the pedigreed beef inflated them still further. Typical of this attitude was the cool reception shown by *porteño* cattle kings to a provincial law on Centros Agrícolas passed in 1887 at the height of the boom. Privileges and loans were held out to landowners who established agricultural colonies around railroad stations. There was a flurry of interest among speculators, but hardly any landowners participated; only at the more remote stations of the Western Railroad were a few colonies actually founded.

In the pastoral zone, therefore, the immigrant was limited to being a tenant farmer. He was welcomed or tolerated as a tool to aid in the execution of necessary changes in the economic system. There were new areas to exploit, and tenant agriculture provided income for the owners. For the *estanciero,* it was essential to break up the soil, destroy the pampas grass, and replace it with forage for refined animals. Most of all, the cattle needed alfalfa pasturage, but the landowner could not afford to plant it himself. Some did, and declared the cost of labor and equipment prohibitive. Tenant farming provided the solution, as stated by one cattleman in the *Anales de la Sociedad Rural Argentina:*

The land is first divided into fenced grazing pastures of four to five thousand acres and then subdivided into surveyed numbered lots of five hundred acres each without any intervening barbed wire. These lots are rented on a three-year contract at one and a half paper pesos the acre [for comparison, wheat sold at one to two pesos the bushel] to Italian farmers who bring their own equipment and supplies and agree at the end of the period to leave the land sown with alfalfa, the seed being supplied by the owner.[13]

The wheat production of the 1890's reflected the changing role of agriculture on the pampas (see Table 5 for areas sown and Table 6 for production by provinces). That decade marked the apogee of the Santa Fe colonies and at the same time established tenant farming in the Argentine littoral.

The number of colonies had increased rapidly. In Santa Fe they had risen from 32 in 1872, to 80 in 1884, to 190 in 1887, to 365 in 1895. By 1895 Entre Ríos had added 201 new colonies to the 3 it possessed two decades earlier, while in Córdoba 80 colonies were in operation by the 1890's. Tenant farmers and colonists jointly contributed to Argentina's two largest wheat crops to date: 1893 with a production of 1,600,000 tons and an export of 1,000,000 tons, and 1894 with 2,200,-000 and 1,600,000 tons, respectively (Table 2 shows growth of exports).

The depression of the early 1890's actually aided the colonization movement by halting briefly the rise in land values. For a few years Argentina's peculiar structure of paper money also tended to further agricultural expansion. In 1885 the national currency, which four years earlier had been established on the gold standard, could no longer be backed by gold because of the outflow of that metal. From

---

[13] Benigno del Carril, "Praderas de alfalfa en la República Argentina," *Anales de la Sociedad Rural,* Vol. XXVI (1892), No. 11, p. 274.

then until the end of the century, when the paper peso was stabilized at 44 centavos of the Argentine gold peso, the value of the paper peso fluctuated constantly and was determined by the daily market quotation in gold. The tendency in the 1880's was inflationary, and the government encouraged it with deliberate, and at times illegal, printing of more paper money. For the moment, inflation suited the wheatgrower as well as the most important economic interests in the nation: the stockraisers and exporters. Such paper money enabled the producer to pay his local expenses in continually depreciating script and to receive gold or its equivalent for his exports to Europe. With the depression, the peso continued to lose value for several more years. An article in the British *Corn Trade News* pointed out what this meant to the wheatgrower:

Wheat, whether sold locally or for export, naturally fetched a price based on its gold value in European markets, which price meant a good deal in depreciated paper currency, in which the wheat-grower paid all his outlay, except for agricultural instruments, and a few other articles which were paid for at gold rates. His wages and expenditures being consequently so much less when converted to gold, his profits were therefore considerably higher than in former years. Again, the high gold premium enabled persons having gold to buy wheat lands cheaply, for their value in depreciated dollars remained much the same. A great impetus was thus given to wheat cultivation, and a demand created for labour and capital to still further increase its area.[14]

These benefits lasted for only a few years. Then the appreciation of the peso, the rising costs of labor, land, and implements, and the falling wheat prices wiped out the artificial stimulus.

The mid-nineties marked a definite shift from colonization and small owner-farmers to the much larger units of extensive tenant farming. As we have seen, the colonization principle never penetrated to pastoral Buenos Aires, and the pastoral interests accepted the agriculturist as a servant only in order to open up new lands and plant new pastures. Now, however, depression and crisis struck at Santa Fe itself, the heartland of the colonies. The world price of wheat, on the decline for the last decade, took a particularly sharp fall in 1894, partly in reaction to the emergence of Argentina as a major exporter. The price of land, even when quoted in paper currency, started to rise, as did the agriculturist's single largest expense—

14 Reprinted in *Review of the River Plate*, March 24, 1894, p. 26.

the cost of harvest labor. Caught between rising costs and falling prices, the only apparent answer was to produce more for less, but Santa Fe was precisely the area least able to meet such a challenge. The colonists' lands had been exploited with the absolute minimum of agricultural technique or knowledge. The soil, if not quite exhausted, at any rate could not compete with the virgin land offered by the pastoral zone. Finally, nature added the *coup de grâce*. Locusts and frosts during the growing season and heavy rains at harvest time descended on Santa Fe and Entre Ríos in 1895, 1896, and 1897. The harvest in 1895 dropped to 700,000 tons in Santa Fe from the previous year's 1,200,000, and in Entre Ríos from 330,000 to 170,000. The following year, with a very slight reduction in area planted, the returns dropped still further, to 500,000 tons in Santa Fe and to 100,000 in Entre Ríos. And in 1897, with a substantial 20 per cent reduction in planting as a result of the two previous failures, the harvest amounted to only 300,000 tons for Santa Fe and 30,000 for Entre Ríos.

Under such conditions, the colonization system could not expand or survive. The method by which the colonist gained title to his lands was basically that of working off a mortgage. Very few who had not acquired ownership by the mid-nineties were able to do so subsequently. During the last eight years of the century, the price of wheat fell 40 per cent. The paper peso, which had declined in value to 30 centavos gold in the early 1890's, now appreciated and in 1899 was stabilized at 44 centavos gold, thus wiping out the momentary advantage of production costs in paper and profits in gold. At the same time, the mortgage or colonization contract, fixed while paper money was depreciating, became an unduly heavy charge. The British commercial journal, the *Review of the River Plate*, summarized the results:

Statistics on the subject are not available, but there is no questioning the fact that in the bad years succeeding 1894 much of the land which had been the property of small holders passed into the hands of mortgagees, or creditors who had some kind of lien on the produce, and was cultivated in the first place for their account, and only secondarily for the benefit of the occupier. The agriculturist, in fact, was in the same position as many companies with a heavy debenture debt, the interest on which is little more than covered by the profits. The area under cultivation, it is true increased, but the conditions under which that cultivation was carried on had altered for the worse. The cultivator could hardly make more than a living: this

his creditor was compelled to guarantee him: hence he worked without the stimulus of hope, and on the whole worked badly.[15]

The first statistics on ownership were secured in 1899–1900. At that time Santa Fe with 11,500 wheat farms and Buenos Aires with 8,000 each recorded only 39 per cent of them as owned by the cultivator.[16] The rest were tilled by sharecroppers or tenant farmers.

Not only was tenant farming on the rise, but the center of wheat production was moving south (Tables 5 and 6). The area sown to wheat in Buenos Aires expanded rapidly during the 1890's. From 790,000 acres in 1891, the area rose to 1,000,000 acres by 1895 and to 2,000,000 by 1900; and in 1901, the harvest for the first time exceeded that of Santa Fe. Wheat sprouted in hundreds of fields along the extension of the Southern Railroad to Bahía Blanca. Hastily improvised facilities in that southernmost port began to handle the outflow of grain: 2,000 tons in 1891, 60,000 in 1895, 270,000 in 1900. The Northwestern Railroad of Bahía Blanca and the Western of Buenos Aires planned a connection at Toay (in the territory of La Pampa), and optimists confidently proclaimed Bahía Blanca the future grain emporium of South America.[17]

The next decade saw the culmination of the trends started in the 1880's and 1890's. Wheat, for a time, became Argentina's major export, with Argentina the world's third-largest exporter. The cereal which had contributed 0.3 per cent of the value of Argentine exports in 1878 now in the first decade of the twentieth century made up 25 per cent of the exports (Table 7 shows the percentage of wheat in total exports). The area of wheat cultivation had risen from 2,500,000 to 8,000,000 acres in the 1890's, to 12,000,000 by 1905 and to 15,000,000, or one-third of all the cultivated land, by 1910 (Table 5). Production fluctuated between 3,000,000 and 4,000,000 tons annually and in exceptional years such as 1908 rose to 5,000,000 (Table 6). More than half of each harvest entered the export trade.

Most significant was the redistribution of the wheat area (Tables 5 and 6). Although Santa Fe built back its acreage after the disasters of the mid-1890's, by 1910 it was planting no more wheat than in 1895. Wheat had moved to virgin lands, while other cereals and dairy

[15] *Ibid.*, April 7, 1900, pp. 5–6.
[16] Argentina, Dirección de estadística y economía rural del Ministerio de Agricultura, *Datos estadísticos. Cosecha 1899/1900* (Buenos Aires, 1900), pp. vii–viii.
[17] *Review of the River Plate*, May 16, 1896, p. 5.

farming occupied an increasingly larger percentage of the acreage
in the colonies. The wheat-growing zone of Entre Ríos never did
recover and remained in the vicinity of 750,000 acres. Buenos Aires,
on the other hand, passed the 2,500,000-acre mark in 1902 and by
1910 stabilized at 6,000,000, or more than double Santa Fe's acreage.
Córdoba, a western frontier for Santa Fe, increased its acreage from
750,000 in 1895 to 5,000,000 by 1910. The territory of La Pampa,
Buenos Aires' western frontier, surpassed Entre Ríos' 750,000 acres in
1910 and five years later reached the 2,500,000 mark.

The relative stability of Argentina's export production reflected
the fact that by the end of the first decade of the twentieth century
the harvest risk was spread over a far larger area than that occupied
by the colonies of Santa Fe, northern Buenos Aires, and central Entre
Ríos. The wheat area now encompassed a rectangle 600 miles from
north to south and 400 miles from east to west, and the principal cultivation was concentrated in a broad arc of the pampas stretching
from Santa Fe to Bahía Blanca. The possibility that total disaster
from locusts, hail, frost, drought, excessive rain, or any of the other
myriad dangers faced by the wheatgrower could descend on the
whole area was extremely slight.

With this southward expansion, tenant farming became the rule
throughout the coastal area. As mentioned earlier, in 1899–1900, 39
per cent of the farmers in Buenos Aires and Santa Fe owned their
land; in the next six years ownership declined to 26 per cent in Buenos
Aires and to 37 per cent in Santa Fe. By 1910 these percentages still
held firm, although during the decade the number of wheat farms
had increased from 11,500 to 18,000 in Santa Fe and from 8,000 to
27,000 in Buenos Aires.[18]

Steadily increasing land values and the continued evolution of the
pastoral industry did more to entrench the tenant-farming system
and to drive wheat southward than did any amount of overcropped
land and backward techniques in Santa Fe. Argentine capital, no-
toriously reluctant to enter into railroad, port, construction, or industrial ventures, remained concentrated in conservative, secure, and
very profitable investments in lands. Real estate provided an annual
return of from 10 to 15 per cent in addition to fabulous appreciation
of capital, sometimes amounting to several thousand per cent in a few
decades. Who could blame an Argentine for leaving to foreign capi-

[18] Argentina, Dirección de estadística y economía rural del Ministerio de
Agricultura, Estadística agrícola, 1909–1910 (Buenos Aires, 1910), pp. 80–83.

tal a number of often risky enterprises that paid no more interest and promised little appreciation? It was this very concentration of capital which by the 1880's had inflated land values throughout the littoral and had made land prices in pastoral Buenos Aires four times higher than those of agricultural Santa Fe. In the early twentieth century the increase in land values (Table 4) tended to break up some of the largest estates, which covered hundreds of square miles in the richest coastal zones. Such subdivisions put the land into the hands of investors or speculators, not into those of the tenants who worked it. The former colonizing companies died a natural death sometime in the 1890's. The land was simply too valuable to sell on terms that the small farmer could be expected to amortize. Even the word "colonist" lost its original meaning and became synonymous with a category of tenant farmer.[19]

Land values reached their peak in the period 1903–1907. There was no lack of observers to read the danger signals. Estanislao Zeballos, writing in the *Revista de Derecho, Historia y Letras* in 1903 pointed to the unhealthy rise of urban and rural land prices and warned that such increases—out of proportion to productive capacities—had been the cause of serious depressions in the United States in 1873 and 1893.[20] The *Anales de la Sociedad Rural* warned in 1906 that land prices had reached a critical point and that any natural disaster to crops would bring a crash.[21] Warnings of such a collapse sprinkled the newspapers in early 1907, and a Ministry of Agriculture study documented the decline in total sales as compared with those of 1903. Some readjustment of land values followed, but there was no wholesale collapse; the boom had merely come to an end.

The nation, however, was left with an unfortunate legacy. From 1881 to 1911 land values had increased an average 218 per cent throughout the cereal provinces.[22] These values created a serious problem, that of excessive charges for the land in rents or in crop shares in an effort to justify the sudden rises in price. As early as 1902, the result was forecast:

[19] For the purpose of this study, the term "colonist" is limited to denoting only the earlier Santa Fe prototype, although in Argentine literature on the subject, *colono* is often used to mean a variation of "tenant farmer."

[20] Estanislao S. Zeballas, "Problemas conexos con la inmigración," XV, 544–552.

[21] *Anales de la Sociedad Rural*, January-February 1906, pp. 10–11.

[22] Emilio Lahitte, *La cuestión agraria. Informe*, p. 16.

. . . a veritable intoxication in land values has resulted. The landowner has believed that if in less than ten years a league worth 10,000 pesos can reach the exaggerated price of 100,000, there is no reason for the rents not to continue to increase yearly in that same proportion. In this belief, he does not rent his land in long-term contracts because with each new contract he expects to raise the rent. The result is that as the yield declines with the exhaustion of the soil's nutrients, the rent climbs sharply, rising within six years from 12 per cent of the crop to 18, 20, 22 and even 25 per cent.[23]

In effect, the percentage of the harvest turned over to the landowners by the sharecroppers—using their own equipment—rose from an average of 10 to 12 per cent in the early 1890's to a rate of 20 to 30 per cent twenty years later.[24] Herbert Gibson, an Englishman of long experience in the Argentine pastoral and agricultural industries, concluded in ponderous phrases:

The prospects of the immensely greater profits that were to be derived from the cultivation of the soil in exchange for the more primitive pastoral industry of an earlier age, created in all directions a fictitious and unstable activity. Immigration flowed in to assist an agricultural venture that was to prove an unprofitable one; and when the proof became more apparent, a good deal of emigration began to flow out again. Land which was estimated under the new aegis to yield an enhanced return was revalued on the new basis, and again subdivided to be sold at still greater values to the agriculturist who was to buy it with the proceeds of thrift from an occupation which had not yet yielded the return to justify the estimate of its earlier valorization.[25]

The pastoral industries had already made clear their need for tenant agriculture in the 1880's and 1890's. Two drastic events in 1900 accentuated this orientation. After an outbreak of hoof-and-mouth disease in Argentina, England closed its ports to further shipments of live animals. Overnight the packing plant became the major purchaser and outlet for Argentine cattle. Statistics show the extent of the change. Salted beef, which accounted for 48 per cent of all meat exports in 1887, dropped to 22 per cent a decade later and to 4 per cent by 1907. Live-cattle exports rose from 28 per cent in 1887

[23] A. Dumas, *La crisis agrícola*, p. 9.
[24] Roberto Campolieti, *La chacra argentina*, pp. 118–119; Raúl A. Lastra, *El cultivo del trigo y del maíz*, pp. 12–13.
[25] Herbert Gibson, *The Land We Live On*, p. 11.

to 43 per cent in 1897 only to fall back to 8 per cent in 1907. Meanwhile, within a decade frozen beef increased from a mere 0.2 per cent in 1897 to 51 per cent of all meat exports.[26] Also in 1900 crippling blows struck the important sheep-raising industry. A serious depression in the wool market in France and Belgium coincided with extensive floods in southern Buenos Aires and the death of fourteen million head of sheep. Under such conditions, tenant farming answered many of the landowner's problems. For the sheep farmer faced with decimated flocks and a depressed wool market, tenant agriculture provided a profitable alternative use for his land. The cattleman needed alfalfa pasturage more than ever now that the packing plants placed such a premium on improved, fattened stock. For the man with idle acres, tenant farming promised an income while the value of his land continued to rise.

To the immigrant drawn to Argentina by the hope of an agricultural future, the realities of the scene were often disheartening. Foreigners poured into Argentina, especially in connection with the economic booms of 1882–1889 and 1904–1912. Since much of the prosperity of these booms was linked to the pastoral and agricultural industries, a rural labor-force was needed. Thus many of these immigrants worked the land for several years. But with the exception of the Santa Fe colonists few really settled on the land. Penniless new arrivals might be able to amortize or secure with their labor the machinery and equipment to farm eighty or five hundred acres, but the economics of increased land values and a society of pastoral and class traditions denied them ownership of that land.

The result was pampas without settlers—a frontier filled with migrants. One class which increased markedly after 1890 was totally migratory, the *golondrinas*, literally the "swallows." These were European laborers, mainly Spanish and Italian, who made the long Atlantic crossing in October or November of each year to earn high wages as harvest workers. In two weeks they covered the round-trip cost of their cramped, dirty steerage passage; whatever else they earned in the three or four months' work in the wheat-corn harvest was carried home to Europe with them. Almost as migratory in a social sense were the workhorses of Argentina's agricultural greatness: the sharecroppers and tenant farmers. These were the agri-

[26] Ricardo Pillado, "El comercio de carnes en la República Argentina," in *Censo agropecuario nacional de la República Argentina en 1908*, III, 366.

cultural laborers and little capitalists who cultivated Argentina's boom crops, who planted the alfalfa pastures, who conquered the pampas economically, but who in reality left those plains as empty as in the 1850's. Behind them they left no houses, no schools, no churches, no roads, no villages. The railroads might cut across the expanse, the station master and the storekeeper might create a semblance of a town, but the landowner could turn the land back to cattle, to sheep, or to the wilderness as easily as he had called it into wheat production.

The immigrant grew wheat and planted alfalfa for purebred stock. But for every newcomer who tilled the soil, ten others made their living at urban pursuits stimulated by the income from rural products. Indeed, the wise and the lucky—those who had put aside some funds from agricultural labors—soon returned to the city, where social and economic advance was infinitely easier than in the countryside. The needs of a swelling urban population had to be met. Wheat, wool, mutton, and beef had to be processed; railroads had to be built; public works, houses, streets had to be constructed. Here lay the real opportunities for immigrants, not in rural tasks where they were tolerated only as transients.

Argentina's economic greatness, nonetheless, was created by those who toiled the land. Exports, almost entirely of agricultural and pastoral products, increased from 30,000 gold pesos in 1870 to 390,000 in 1910. And in that latter decade, one-quarter of that new-found wealth was the work of the wheatgrower. Who was he? What sort of a life did he lead? How did he become a part of the new Argentina? The answers are to be found in the substance of the wheatgrower's daily life.

iv. THE WHEATGROWER'S LIFE

The wheatgrower, as we have seen, was first a colonist and then, as the nineteenth century drew to a close, increasingly a tenant farmer. The distinction between the small independent-farmer class and the tenant-farmer class was important for Argentina's agricultural and social future. But in terms of origin and way of life, the colonist, the tenant farmer and, at times, even the migrant laborer were one.

They shared certain basic characteristics. Although there were sprinklings of people from all the regions of Europe, Italians from the northern agricultural districts of Lombardy and Piedmont predominated. Their overpopulated homelands provided little opportunity for advancement. They were poor, but as a general rule they were not in a state of starvation or abject misery. It was partly a push and partly a pull that started them across the Atlantic: the impossibility of advance at home, the hope that they could accumulate some small capital in America and return to Italy, Spain, or France to enjoy it. There were city boys in their midst, but the majority had some link to the land in Europe, either as farmers or rural laborers. They knew farming; but they knew it on tiny plots, on soil that had been tilled for hundreds of years. Sharecropping and high tenant rents were part of their life. They were conservative and illiterate. Neither new techniques nor scientific farming made any impression on them. Extremely materialistic in hoarding away their gains, they cared, at the same time, little about material comforts. Ambitious in the sense of wanting to accumulate a small store of capital, they nonetheless had few desires beyond that of being left alone. They were hard workers but lacked the foresight and vision to organize and diversify their rural labors. When no pressing job presented itself, they found complete idleness their only relaxation. They were a fatalistic and humble people, respectful and fearful of authority—of those who were powerful, or wealthy, or educated.

The Swiss started the rural colonization of Argentina. Most of the Swiss who came to Argentina before 1870 became farmers, and the majority of colonists as of that date were Swiss; 5,900 out of a total of 10,000 Swiss immigrants had settled in agricultural colonies. Comparison with other nationalities is instructive. Before 1870 the Italians with 120,000 immigrants provided 4,200 for the countryside; the French had 1,900 farmers out of 44,000 immigrants; the Germans 1,500 out of 6,000; the English 500 out of 15,000; the Spanish could claim only 200 out of 49,000.[1]

Leadership in agricultural labor, however, soon passed to Italy. Tortugas, the fourth colony established by the Central Argentine Land Company in 1871, can be taken as the forecast of the value and predominance of the north Italian farmer in the wheat-growing regions of Santa Fe, and later of Córdoba, Buenos Aires, and La Pampa. Unlike the first three colonies of the Central Argentine Land Company, which were settled by Swiss and French families, Tortugas was primarily Piedmontese and Lombard.

Unfortunately there are no comparative statistics to indicate with accuracy how many Italians were farmers when they left their homeland and how many became agriculturists upon arrival in Argentina. Telling port authorities—either in Italy or Argentina—that one was a farmer and actually being one were quite different matters, and the statement was certainly no assurance that the individual would fulfill his expectations in a new land. Prior to 1900, the flow of Italians to Argentina was heavily in favor of northern Italy, 55 per cent coming from Lombardy, Piedmont, Venetia, Liguria, and Emilia. After 1900, the balance was readjusted by immigrants from depressed southern Italy, but as previously noted, comparable to emigration to other countries, such as the United States, a much greater proportion—33 per cent—still came to Argentina from the north.[2] We can surmise, because of their rural origins in northern Italy, that a majority of the able-bodied male emigrants had an agricultural background. Yet relatively few continued as farmers in Argentina. Perhaps the figure given above for pre-1870 Italian immigration—4 per cent as agricultural colonists—is too low for the following decades. But one can

[1] *Anales de la Sociedad Rural,* 1872, pp. 60–61.
[2] SVIMEZ, *Statistiche sul mezzogiorno d'Italia 1861–1953,* p. 117.

conclude, in view of the tempting alternatives in the burgeoning coastal cities, that those who actually went out to the land must have had a very strong desire to continue as farmers. Such a conclusion has importance when we examine how wheat was grown. We find poor agriculturists, but not because they were city-bred. Rather it was their illiteracy and conservatism and the radically different ecological conditions which contributed to the poor methods of growing.

The majority of these immigrants, in fact all of those with whom we are concerned here, traveled steerage or third-class. This meant an uncomfortable and crowded two to four weeks below decks, with no baths, inadequate toilets, poor food, monotony, and seasickness. But it was cheap. Argentina is twice as far as the United States from European ports, yet in the 1890's the *golondrina* could pay for his round-trip passage with two weeks' labor in Argentina.

Buenos Aires was the port into which this mass of humanity poured. In the days when contracted settlers were brought from Europe, river steamer and jolting cart immediately carried the colonists off to some remote section of the pampas. This type of immigration, however, was short-lived, and ship captains thereafter merely dumped their human cargo—immigrants who had already paid their passage—on the shore. Since the details of government immigration policy will be explored in a later chapter, suffice it to say here that until 1900 the methods of handling this influx of Europeans were extremely rudimentary. Although there were immigrant commissions and even an immigrants' hotel, by and large the newcomers merely piled in on top of their countrymen in the city's slums. The era of the *conventillos* dates from the 1880's and 1890's. Hunger, dirt, and poverty were nothing new to these immigrants, and in the crowded slums they found conviviality, people who spoke their dialect or tongue, even old acquaintances and friends. In boom times at least, there was no lack of occupations in the rapidly growing city. Immigrants, regardless of origins, appeared as bricklayers, porters, stevedores, masons, housemaids, cooks, grocers, cartmen, peddlers, and beggars. Little wonder that of these arrivals only the migrant rural laborer and those with contracts or determination pressed on through Buenos Aires to the frightening, treeless waste of the pampas.

Those who wanted to get on the land were offered several economic alternatives. The first, chronologically if not in ultimate importance to wheat growing, was the chance to become a colonist. We have already had a glimpse of the development of official, railroad, and private colonization. A company, occasionally provincial or municipal but most often private, offered land to the agriculturist; at first it was a unit of eighty acres, but as wheat growing became more and more extensive the units increased in size to two hundred fifty and eventually to five hundred acres. The ultimate aim of the company was to sell its subdivisions to the colonist; that of the colonist was ownership. The most common procedure, at least after the initial colonizing ventures, was the outright sale of property in cash installments. Under this arrangement the colonist provided his own equipment and seed, assumed all risks, and if successful, gradually paid off his mortgage. Occasionally companies made advances of machinery, seeds, and food to colonists and accepted payments in percentages of the crop, but these terms represented undesirable risks to the company. Actual title to the land was never transferred to the colonist until he had completed all his payments and had canceled all his debts with the company.

Some of the early colonies achieved a sort of linguistic or ethnic unity, and companies usually tried to fill subdivisions consecutively in order to maintain contiguous settlement. The size of a colony ranged from twenty to two hundred families, and in some cases, such as in the province of Santa Fe, colonies became the basis for cities like Esperanza or Casilda. The company frequently provided stores and rented out threshers. A school and church were also added, but the colonists paid for building costs and maintenance. The structure of the colony might have been oriented toward the community. However, since the vast majority of the settlements were commercial ventures, little encouragement was given to any project which did not promise to bring an immediate financial return. Even the practice of model or experimental farms to teach new techniques was largely ignored. Unless the director took a personal interest in his settlers or there were strong ethnic or religious bonds uniting the community, a colony tended to be little more than individual farms scattered over several square miles of pampas.

The tenant farmer did not have even this vague sense of community, fixed location, or possible hope of landownership. His life, nevertheless, was not very different from that of the colonist. Landowners were eager for his labor, especially after 1890. If he truly had nothing except a strong back and the labor of his wife and children to offer, he might start as a *medianero*—a sharecropper who received implements and seed from the landowner and turned over half his harvest in payment. He was at the bottom of the tenant-farmer class. His contract with the landowner limited cultivation of a particular plot to a year or two; then he moved to a new location. His advantage, however, was that he had little to lose. He had no capital and no equipment. If the harvest was bad, he had no rent or mortgage to pay. The landlord shouldered the major portion of the risk and the *medianero* merely provided the labor. If crops were good for several successive years, the *medianero* was able to raise himself into the *arrendatario*, or tenant, category—or if truly wise he would return to the city with his small hoard of capital. For that reason and because of the unwelcome investment and risk incurred by the landowner, the number of *medianeros* tended to decline as wheat growing expanded.

The *arrendatario* was a rural capitalist. His most typical feature was that he had a personal investment in equipment, oxen, and horses in addition to his strong back. Sometimes he might be a man of considerable means who rented large extensions from a landowner and then sublet sections to other *arrendatarios* or *medianeros*. Frequently he was a person of more modest position, yet possessing sufficient funds to purchase a small lot of land. The hope of increasing his capital by extensive agriculture made him a tenant of five hundred acres rather than the owner of fifty.[3] More often, however, he was a former *medianero* or even a migrant laborer who had saved enough money to buy a plow, a harrow, a team of horses, and some bags of seed. For the landowner this type of tenant farming was the most desirable since the whole risk and investment were assumed by the tenant. The owner contributed only the use of his land, which probably had been paying no income before and stood to be improved by cultivation. If a fixed charge could be levied per acre, so much the better, for then the owner collected whether or not there was a harvest. A more usual procedure was to hand over a percentage of the crop, ranging from 10 to 30 per cent according to the value of the land, the distance from transportation facilities, or the particular stage of wheat-growing history. Through a contract, usually oral, an area of from two hundred to five hundred acres was turned over to the tenant for a term of from three to six years. He had to build his own home and, if he chose, shelters for implements, animals, or grain. If there was no stream or waterhole nearby, he had to dig a well for his own

[3] Emilio Lahitte, *Crédito agrícola. La cooperación rural*, p. 35.

use and that of his animals. Yet he received no allowance for improvements when he left, since, for the stock raiser, a house and a shed were obstructions rather than improvements. The tenant was hardly master of his rented land. The contract sometimes allowed him a small portion for pasturage, but only enough for necessary work animals. The rest he was obliged to cultivate, usually with the crop which the landowner designated. If his landlord was a cattleman it was almost certain that he would have to leave the land sown to alfalfa after his last harvest. As tenant farming spread, so did obligations become more onerous, such as having to use the owner's threshing machines, buy bags from him, sell the crop to him, or secure provisions from a specified store.

As can be seen, there was a certain similarity in the contracts which both the colonist and the tenant farmer concluded with the company and the landowner. A rent was being paid on the land, which in one case had the added advantage of paying off a mortgage. But so long as the colonist did not secure clear title to the land, his situation was little different from that of the tenant farmer. Bad harvests could ruin the one just as surely as the other. The colonist possessed a certain equity in his machinery and whatever part of the purchase price he had cleared; the tenant farmer had only his equipment and animals. But in either case the reserve was not very great. With guidance and, most important, with ownership of the land, the colonist might be led toward intensive mixed farming. The tenant farmer, however, was propelled by the hope of immediate profits toward extensive one-crop cultivation which, if nature was kind, seemed to afford the best return in the short run. Unfortunately, as long as the colonist did not actually own his land, the same hopes encouraged him also to follow the one-crop gamble.

A final economic alternative open to the agricultural immigrant was that chosen by thousands of Italians and Spaniards: to become rural migrant laborers or *golondrinas*. The *golondrina's* objectives were different from those of the ownership-minded colonist or the small rural capitalist, the tenant farmer. He had come to earn wages. He either was single or had left his family behind in his homeland. His employer gave him food. He slept where he could, in sheds or in the fields—something not impossible during Argentine summers. His only expense, therefore, was the transatlantic voyage. Four to five months' labor in the wheat-corn harvest could bring him from forty to fifty pounds sterling—five to ten times what he could earn in his homeland—and this represented a net profit to take back to Italy or Spain in May.[4] By the 1900's one hundred thousand such laborers a year entered Argentina, twice the average of the previous decade. In 1911 an Italian census recorded ninety thousand emigrants in Argentina temporarily absent from their families.[5]

These *golondrinas* were a necessary part of Argentina's expanding cereal economy. Employed by colonists, tenant farmers, and *estancieros,* they provided the manpower which Argentina lacked to harvest the record wheat crops. Their social impact on the countryside, however, cannot be compared to that of the colonist or tenant farmer. They were true swallows, men whose cultural significance was hardly greater than that of the machinery used to reap and thresh the grain. When they remained in Argentina, as many did, married, or sent for their families, they ceased to be *golondrinas.*

The colonist and the tenant farmer were, therefore, the principals in the social formation of the wheat-growing zone. In addition to economic motivations, they shared certain similarities in environment, psychology, and way of life.

Isolation was the predominating characteristic of the Argentine rural scene. This was only natural in a pastoral society where few humans were needed in the countryside. But it remained true even after cereal culture had invaded the pampas. Roads had not been necessary before the day of wheat; products moved on the hoof or, as with goods to and from the interior provinces, by oxcart. For this, mere trails across the pampas sufficed. Railroad construction in the 1870's and 1880's leaped over the intermediate stage of road building. British companies, building the railroads as investments, were guaranteed a minimum return on their capital by the Argentine government, and agricultural development insured their profits. Isolation was apparently broken down. Farm and seaport were linked by the railways, but the links were not among the farms themselves nor with rural communities or villages. The railroads were mere feelers which probed into the zones of cereal, cattle, and sheep to gather in freight for the ports. They fulfilled the immediate transport needs of the countryside and at the same time inhibited the construction of roads.

[4] Charles Darbyshire, *My Life in the Argentine Republic,* pp. 102–103, referring to experiences in wheat colonies in 1893–1894.

[5] *Annuario statistico italiano,* 1916, p. 46.

The railroads did not want competition, and so for decades the only roads permitted in Argentina were the mud ruts radiating from the railroad stations.

The agriculturist was submerged in this isolation. The transportation system took his products to market but did nothing to break down the remoteness between him and his fellow men. Roads remained as they had for three centuries—dusty shallow troughs or long canals, according to the season. Only the high-wheeled oxcart could negotiate these tracks. The buggy, the phaeton, the sulky, and the carriage had no place on the pampas. The gaucho and the Indian had molded themselves to their horses and had overcome the distances. The agricultural immigrant, however, never did become a horseman; restricted to the plodding oxen or to foot, he soon resigned himself to the limited horizon of his farm or colony.

The country store—the *pulpería* in Buenos Aires or the general store in Santa Fe—was rural Argentina's only social institution. Its economic aspects will be studied in a later chapter, for it served as provider of merchandise, purchaser of products, banker, and sole dispenser of credit. In the isolation of a lonely countryside, its role as a place of conviviality and a source of information and news was perhaps as vital as its economic functions. In many ways, it took the place of the church, the school, the club, and the plaza, which were conspicuously absent on the pampas.

The origins of the country store were colonial. It had emerged within the pastoral economy. The *pulpería* of Buenos Aires or of the northwestern provinces was, in the original meaning of the term, a bar, a store, and a social club for gauchos. With the development of agriculture, a railway station or a colony became its preferred locations, and its commercial and merchandising interests increased. Rather than glasses of raw cane alcohol, it now dispensed cheap red wine to Italian farmers, and rather than salt and the dried leaves of *yerba mate,* it sold meat, beans, and biscuits. Here, on a Sunday or in the idle season between harvest and planting, the agriculturist could blunt his loneliness, secure the latest wheat prices and harvest rumors, and exchange news with neighbors he never visited. Yet many a farmer was not within reach of a country store; and even when he was, it hardly fulfilled his social needs.

Churches, schools, and clubs did not penetrate into rural Argentina for the simple reason that settlement was dispersed and often temporary. The colonies of Russian Jews in Entre Ríos and Santa Fe and,

1. A Mud Rancho of Italian Tenant Farmers in the Cereal Zone. From *Indian Corn in Argentina: Production and Export* by Frank W. Bicknell.

2. A Prosperous Italian Colonist Family in the Province of Santa Fe around 1900. From *Wheat Production and Farm Life in Argentina* by Frank W. Bicknell.

to a lesser degree, some of the older Swiss colonies of Santa Fe possessed strong religious and cultural unity. But these were rare exceptions. Agriculturists in Argentina, colonists and tenant farmers alike, did not as a rule live in villages and go out each day to cultivate the surrounding fields. Because of extensive agriculture where a great deal of land was superficially tilled, farm homes were spread out at considerable distances from each other. When eighty acres was the basic unit of wheat cultivation, it nevertheless required much walking or riding to reach a neighbor; with five hundred acres, the distance was nearly tripled, and the possibility of social institutions reaching the farm decreased in proportion. Weddings, funerals, and special church holidays might warrant the long trip to town or city. But the priest, clergyman, or rabbi could not minister to widely scattered families that lacked the resources or interest to form a congregation.

Education likewise faced insurmountable problems. The children were needed to work. And even if they could have been spared, where could schools have been built to reach this dispersed population? As soon as one left Buenos Aires and the coastal cities, educational facilities declined sharply in quality and number. In large areas of the wheat zone, they were nonexistent.

The Germans, the Swiss, and the Italians had their singing clubs, their shooting clubs, and their mutual-aid societies. But these were urban institutions. They throve in the towns of the wheat zone, many of which had been former colonies, such as Esperanza, San Carlos, Roldán, and Carcarañá, but not in the countryside. The average agriculturist lived from five to fifteen miles from the nearest railroad station. He probably was forty or fifty miles from the closest town. Distances and lack of transportation spoke for themselves. Isolation wore a different face now. Rather than a horizon broken only by thistles or the lone *ombú,* one could see the huts of several farmers and perhaps the estate of some cattleman. But occupation of the pampas had not linked its inhabitants together.

If the farmer's hut seemed remote from the rural town, it must be realized that the town itself was just as remote, in a cultural and social sense, from the metropolis of Buenos Aires, the bustling ports of Rosario and Bahía Blanca, or the colonial-style city of Córdoba. By 1914, besides the ports and centers adjacent to Greater Buenos Aires, the wheat zone boasted only three cities in the 20,000–30,000 category: Chivilcoy, Junín, and Pergamino, all in the province of Buenos Aires.

The largest nuclei of population in the province of Santa Fe, excluding Rosario and the city of Santa Fe, were Casilda, Cañada de Gómez, and Rafaela, numbering just under 10,000 each. The average rural town had a population between 2,000–6,000; an unpaved main street, a bare plaza, a few stores, several squares of mud-brick houses, the more pretentious of which were plastered or whitewashed on the outside; occasionally a church, a school, some storage sheds, and a railroad station. If it was the seat of a political subdivision, or *partido*, there was probably some sort of town hall on the plaza. The inhabitants were people of modest means and culture. The priest, the police chief, or *comisario*, the justice of the peace, and the schoolteacher represented the aristocracy and authority of the town. Here was no doctor; the apothecary attended any serious ills. No cattleman, no lawyers, no politicians, no bankers resided in it. In short, the average town had little to recommend it. After a visit to Rafaela in 1891, an understanding and usually sympathetic observer of the Argentine scene wrote: "All I can say, however, is that, if ever a man wishes to know what it is to have an inclination to commit suicide, let him spend a week in a camp town in the Argentine."[6] In essence, the town was a small nucleus destined to handle the barest needs of the countryside and to expedite the transportation of products to the coast. Its economic role was perfectly caricatured by the local bakery: located in the heart of the wheat zone, the baker invariably received flour from the mills of Rosario or Buenos Aires.

It is hardly surprising that the immigrant paused before he accepted a rural calling. The desolate countryside and the poverty of the towns contrasted sharply with the opportunities in Argentina's cities. Even without considering the obstacles and difficulties which the wheatgrower faced, these drawbacks were enough to send the ambitious scampering back to Buenos Aires or the coastal ports.

To see how the wheatgrower actually lived, we must strike an average, as we have already done with the transportation system and the town. There were always the scenes of neat brick homes, sheds, milch cows, poultry, garden plots, small orchards of plum and peach trees, and varied crops of some Swiss colony which the propagandist loved to hold up to European immigrants. Unfortunately such pictures were the exception. It is also well to remember that the realities which served as the foundation of such lures had been developed on

[6] Charles E. Akers, *Argentine, Patagonian and Chilian Sketches*, p. 66.

lands of little value, by people who nevertheless had had the opportunity to sink their roots in that land, and who in all likelihood had
put in thirty years of hard labor to achieve such an idyllic agricultural
life.

If isolation ruled the Argentine countryside, transiency dominated
the life of the wheatgrower, molding his psyche and his way of life.
He was already predisposed to look upon his occupation as an in-
terval in which to amass a reserve that could be enjoyed in his homeland. The difficulty, at least after 1895, of securing ownership of the
land and the parallel demand for tenant farmers stimulated this sense
of impermanence. The idea of "home," therefore, had little meaning
for the farmer. His culture placed no value on physical conveniences
and his poverty had inured him to discomfort.

"Home" for the colonist or tenant farmer evoked few of the over-
tones that the word had in its Anglo-Saxon origins. Home was merely
a cheap, temporary shelter from the elements. Rare was the farmer
who, before he secured final title to his land and sometimes not even
then, spent more than a few days on the construction of his house.

The most common structure in the cereal zone was the mud-and-
straw rancho. A rectangle was measured out on the ground and the
soil was tamped down. At the four corners, posts were sunk and the
dirt was tightly packed around them. Saplings were tied or wired to
these posts to form a framework. A roof of straw thatch was added
next. Nearby a pit had been dug where dirt, water, and manure had
been thoroughly mixed. Bundles of straw were now plastered with
this mixture and woven into the framework to form walls. Around
the lower edges of these walls, dirt was piled and packed down. The
completed rancho contained probably from one hundred to one hundred fifty square feet of living space, a doorway closed by a sheepskin
or piece of canvas, and perhaps one or two openings or "windows" in
the walls. Occasionally the interior might be divided into two rooms.
If cooking was done inside, there was a hole near the ridgepole under
the eaves for the smoke. Usually, however, a lean-to, attached to one
side of the rancho, sheltered a small adobe baking oven as well as the
open fire for cooking.

Naturally there were variations in the style and pretentiousness of
this type of building. To enlarge his house a man merely extended
its length or added units around a patio. More substantial dwellings
were built with crude sun-dried bricks formed from clay and grass.
Curiously enough, the sod house never gained widespread accept-

ance on the pampas, although it was well known in Patagonia and the northwest. When the national authorities began to distribute zinc sheeting for use in the antilocust campaigns (discussed at some length in Chapter viii), this material frequently replaced straw thatch as roofing. But the basic plan of the rancho remained unchanged and served to shelter the great majority of Argentina's wheatgrowers.[7]

The interior of the agriculturist's home further reflected his transient life and his lack of concern with physical comforts. Early travelers in Argentina used to be astonished at the furnishings of the gaucho's abode, limited to a few ox skulls on the dirt floor. The farmer's furniture, not so picturesque, was hardly more plentiful. It is true that, as in the pastoral society, much of the day-to-day life went on outdoors or under the kitchen lean-to, and during the summer the family ate, relaxed, and slept outside. A few handmade chairs or benches served as seats, and usually the house boasted a table. Bedding was a pile of sheepskins and ponchos rolled in a corner and sometimes, as a luxury, a bed for the farmer and his wife. Despite the cold and humidity of the winter season, a fireplace or heating was unknown. Fuel, often packed sun-dried dung, was dear enough just for cooking. Lighting was almost as rare. Daylight governed rural hours; candles and kerosene were expensive, and few had the knowledge or desire to read. Clothing likewise was limited to essentials. Cheap cotton fabrics predominated despite winter temperatures which frequently dipped below freezing. Many an adult as well as the children went barefoot the whole year. Sunday clothes were reserved for the special occasion of a visit to town. Everyday trousers and shirts, skirts and blouses, were worn until they were in shreds, then mended and remended.

It can easily be believed that the wheatgrower and his family were oblivious to the habits or even the possibility of cleanliness and hygiene. Sanitary facilities were unknown. Surrounded by the broad expanse of the pampas, it would have been hard to explain to an Italian peasant the reason for an outhouse. Modesty or sanitation was hardly his concern. To his mind, bathing was equally unnecessary. Neither his culture nor his surroundings made personal cleanliness essential. In contrast with tropical northeastern Brazil, where disease

---

[7] Aparicio and Difrieri, *Suma de geografía*, VII, 521–541, *passim*.

had promptly wiped out unwashed German settlers, dirtiness in temperate coastal Argentina imposed no serious penalties.

Their cultural background, transient existence, and ignorance robbed these farmers of the most elementary conveniences. No one who had seen an entire Italian family, from the toddlers up, at work plowing, sowing, reaping, or threshing, would ever have called them lazy. All writers on the wheat zone praised the sober and industrious Piedmontese and Lombards as the best laborers rural Argentina had ever had. An eighteen-hour day of back-breaking labor was routine during the planting and harvest seasons. But almost as a reaction to this, they lapsed into total lethargy during the other seven months of the year. It is true that often there was little else to do, especially when a tenant farmer's contract dictated a single crop, prevented him from keeping hogs or cattle, and forced him to move on after a few years. Certainly the lack of ownership discouraged any effort to plant trees to shelter his rancho from the burning summer sun or to provide fruit for his diet. But around the wheatgrower's house, vegetable plots, chickens, even a few humble pumpkins or squash, were equally rare. Drought, locusts, and tenancy would hardly have been sufficient deterrents had desire, imagination, or knowledge driven the farmer to improve this aspect of his daily life and diet. It was simpler, however, to exist on the standard diet of grease-flavored beans and corn. Even that universal staple of pastoral Argentina—beef—appeared at the wheatgrower's table only in the harvest season, to give strength for the hot, dusty threshing operations. And then it was bought, already slaughtered, from the butcher's cart or shop. Modest in his food, the farmer was equally temperate in his drink. Red wine was the sign of a special social event, a feast day, a visit to town, the arrival of an honored guest. As with beef, hard liquor or cane alcohol made its appearance at harvest time for stimulation rather than for sociability.

Surprisingly enough, some features of the transient life, especially those related to comfort, tended to continue even after a colonist secured title to his land, and thus there is reason to believe that cultural preference had a distinct role in his acceptance of ranchos and lack of furniture. But it was a preference which the Italian, the Spaniard, and the Frenchman did not bring solely from his homeland. Transiency was combined in Argentina with an overwhelming drive toward extensive cultivation. Consequently comforts, which had little value anyway, were sacrificed to the economic goal of putting still greater areas under a single crop. Many who had enough capital to purchase modest plots of land preferred to gamble with the vast expanses which they could rent as tenants. And among owners there were quite a few who continued to live in mud-and-straw ranchos, surrounded by nothing but fields of wheat.

The psychology of extensive farming is quite different from its economics and was so ingrained in the minds of the wheatgrowers that it deserves examination. Studies by the Ministry of Agriculture and the Sociedad Rural indicated that the only way for the small farmer to succeed in Argentina was to diversify. The ideal farm consisted of 160 acres. It was recommended that the agriculturist put 150 of these acres to five distinct uses: pasturage, beans, clover, wheat, and a mixture of clover and wheat, and rotate these among different lots. He should also raise a few pigs, 100 sheep, and 30 milch cows. Such a farm could be handled without any outside labor. In bad years losses would be kept at a minimum and in good years there would be no wage expense to eat into profits.[8] Diversification would spread work over the twelve months of the year, would guard against total loss of a harvest, and would permit more intensive and scientific use of the soil.

The Argentine agriculturists could not grasp the importance of such practices, and it must be added that the pastoral and landed interests saw little value in intensive agriculture. Argentina had land in abundance, and much of it was virgin soil which needed to be refined by plowing. Inevitably, in their effort to wring fortune from nature, farmers took on too much land. If profits could be made from 80 to 100 acres, the wheatgrower, with his limited logic, concluded that they could be tripled or quadrupled on 250 or 500 acres. He combined his meager investments in equipment and machinery with his Mediterranean brawn and attempted to render vastly larger areas productive with the sweat of his brow. But the investment of effort and capital which might have been sufficient to carry the risks of an 80-acre farm obviously could not be expected to meet the losses of crop failure on 500 acres. These evils of extensive farming were compounded by the refusal to diversify crops. Rather than warding off a possible total loss by spreading the risk over several crops and by investing in livestock, the farmer, with a tremendous surge of work,

[8] Roberto Campolieti, "La crisis del trigo," *Anales de la Sociedad Rural*, 1903, pp. 1005–1008, 1215–1219.

planted the entire area to a single crop. Then he sat back and allowed nature to decide his fate. Only too frequently the gamble went against him. If the myriad dangers of nature—a too-mild winter, untimely frosts, drought, locusts, or rain during the short harvest season —did not overtake him and he reaped a bumper crop, the market would catch him in its impersonal grasp and reward him with lowered wheat prices, higher railroad freights, or increased equipment costs. To his limited mental and psychological horizon, there was nothing left to do but to start the same cycle over again the next year and hope that somehow a profit would miraculously emerge.

At the same time, extensive one-crop agriculture suited the pastoral and landed interests. Even the least enlightened landowner realized that the Argentine rural scene was changing and that immigrant labor was essential to that change. European peasants were accepted —as were thoroughbred bulls, improved pasture, and fences—but with the expectation that these immigrants would continue as laborers, planting alfalfa for the stockman or providing rent for the landowner. Since the labor force was still small in comparison with available land, extensive one-crop farming permitted cultivation of the greatest possible area. Contracts sought to encourage this. The landowner frequently told the tenant what crop to plant. He also told him where to buy his supplies, where to thresh his wheat, and where to sell it. Since raising cattle, hogs, or sheep reduced the area under cultivation and distracted the tenant from his primary function, it was forbidden. Fruit trees, permanent housing, and garden plots were discouraged because they placed obstacles on future grazing lands. The landed interests thus conspired with the agriculturist's natural inclinations to further a system of extensive agriculture in Argentina.

Success in the wheat zone was a relative matter. Despite hardships, the first arrivals in each new wheat zone, be it Santa Fe, Córdoba, Buenos Aires, or La Pampa, often made profits and sometimes became owners of their farms. The region of the colonies in Santa Fe became the one area of the pampas with small diversified farms. The *golondrinas* carried back to their homelands a substantial hoard in wages. The tenant farmer probably endured no worse conditions than he would have borne in Italy, Spain, or France and often substantially improved his financial position. A very few, such as Giuseppe Guazzone, who became the largest single producer of wheat in the world, made their fortunes by starting at the bottom as farmers. The expanding wheat area and extensive agriculture, however, worked against small-farm ownership, improved roads, rural social institutions, or better housing. The cultivated acreage increased, but the cultivators did not sink their roots in the pampas. On the contrary, the story of success was most frequently told by those who left the soil after a few lucky harvests and invested their savings in a shop or piece of land in some town or city.

Argentina's greatness as a wheat producer was not made by the few fortunate ones. As Bernard W. Snow, a United States statistician and commercial expert who visited Argentina shortly after the turn of the century, concluded: "The whole secret of Argentine ability to produce grains cheaply lies in the low scale of living of those connected with agriculture."[9] The fact that there were those who would live under such conditions and still consider themselves fortunate permitted Argentina to prosper from wheat production, despite backward techniques, a lopsided land-tenure system, governmental apathy, and the indifference of the landowner.

[9] Reprinted in *Review of the River Plate*, March 2, 1902, p. 601.

v. THE GROWING OF WHEAT

Wheat is not a difficult plant to raise. It grows in almost all climates and soils of the world and requires little agricultural skill. Indeed, it was these very conditions that made it such an enormously popular crop in Argentina and encouraged its extensive cultivation after 1890. The crop was doomed to be raised by farmers who knew little or nothing about scientific agriculture and who had little incentive to improve their methods. As has previously been pointed out, everything drove the farmer to plant one crop, to plant it on as much land as he could possibly plow, and to trust nature to do the rest—until harvest time.

Agriculture had remained a mere appendage of the Argentine economy for so long that few were interested in its condition, techniques, or advancement. The *Anales de la Sociedad Rural* succinctly commented in 1905: "Agriculture—and it almost seems incredible—being the activity of more people than any other in this country, is the one which is most poorly performed. While the cattleman has advanced, the *chacarero* [cultivator of a small farm] has merely marked time."[1] More than three decades earlier, *La Nación,* reporting on an impressive show of agricultural machinery in Córdoba, stated: "A landowner will spend 20,000 pesos for a prize bull or 200,000 pesos for a flock of fine sheep, but where agriculture is the concern, everything is left to fate. And if the harvest is lost, it will not be blamed on the fact that there were no machines, or canvas to cover the grain, or sheds, or even carts, but just because the harvest is always a risky time."[2] Behind such ignorance or improvidence lay more basic factors

[1] Manuel Bernárdez, "Literatura de chacra," January 1905, p. 62.
[2] *La Nación,* November 11, 1871, p. 1.

already suggested in the preceding chapters. Agriculture had entered Argentina by the back door. Even when demonstrating its economic vitality, agriculture remained subservient to pastoral and landed interests.

Land, labor, and capital determined the method and extent of wheat production. The land has already been introduced in Chapter ii: a soil and substratum of great depth composed of mixed alluvium and loess, sand and clay; a level, treeless plain; a temperate climate; sufficient rainfall for agriculture on the eastern portion of the pampas; occasional severe winds, thunderstorms, and hailstorms; and, at mid-century, deserted grasslands inhabited only by horses, cattle, Indians, gauchos, and wildlife. There was no question that this land was fertile. The contrast with tiny, often rocky, always intensively worked plots in Europe was striking. One of the first letters home to Switzerland from the newly established colony at Esperanza marveled: "Two feet of black dirt, then forty feet of sandy soil, and one reaches moist sand from which rises the water for the wells we have dug. There are no rocks or anything of the sort. Nothing has to be broken up or leveled. All is a beautiful meadow where the only thing required is plowing; once the land is cultivated, it will be truly a paradise."[3]

The fertility of this soil puzzled experts. In 1883 a French agronomist sounded a feeble warning after a visit to the Santa Fe colonies, where he had been amazed to see lands that had been cropped continuously since 1858. His experience in France told him that even new land should require some sort of fertilizer in its second year: "Despite the surprising results that I have seen, I cannot do less than express my fears for the future; the land is a capitalist which rich as it may seem must in the end exhaust itself if one always takes away and never returns anything."[4] Startling examples continued to be cited, such as the lands near Marcos Juárez in Córdoba or Sastre in Santa Fe, which had been cultivated for twenty years and still produced a better yield than virgin soil. Yet it finally became evident that even the pampas' rich gift could be exhausted. It was noted how the lands around Chivilcoy had run out by 1872 so that wheat hardly could be found within twenty miles of the town. In Entre Ríos in

[3] Jakob Huber, July 15, 1856, in Juan Schobinger, *Inmigración y colonización suizas en la República Argentina en el siglo XIX*, p. 196.
[4] Alfred Martin, "Informe del inspector agrónomo en su visita técnica a las colonias de Santa Fe," *Boletín del departamento nacional de agricultura*, 1884, p. 63.

1885 it was recognized that the yield from overworked soil had declined to one-third of what it had been thirty years before. The wheat crisis of 1895–1897 in Santa Fe and Entre Ríos and the competition of virgin soils in southern Buenos Aires and La Pampa irrefutably demonstrated the dangers of soil exhaustion.

The climate was less generous to Argentina's agriculturists than the soil. The amount of rainfall, as has been pointed out, varied from year to year, and certainly the timeliness of the downpours was totally a matter of chance. Wind and hail were constant dangers. If killing frosts were rare (except along the western and southern limits of the humid pampas), temperature fluctuations during the growing season vitally affected the harvest. The colonist or tenant farmer plowed and planted as much land as he and his family possibly could during May and June. The next five months were a torment of hope and frustration, for he had nothing to do except watch his crop develop or go to ruin. If the winter was too mild, the plants came up quickly and went to straw, a calamity which largely accounted for the poor harvest in 1914. If the spring was hot and dry, the young wheat shriveled as it came up. If the weather remained too damp, rust and blight set in. Once the heads of wheat began to develop, dangers seemed to multiply: winds could flatten the crop; rains could beat it down; frost, blight, rust could make the grain valueless; hail could chop the heads to ribbons.

After 1900, when wheat growing had reached its natural boundaries in the pampas, encompassing a six-hundred- by four-hundred-mile rectangle, the vagaries of climate rarely ruined the whole harvest. Yet the destruction of the crop on one farm, or in one colony or one province, while not a national calamity, was nonetheless a complete disaster for those involved. The average farmer could expect only one harvest out of three to give him good results. If he was lucky, the others covered expenses; otherwise, they brought serious losses. The fickleness of weather conditions cannot be captured in tables of total wheat production or by climatic records. It can be better understood from the newspapers, if studied over a period of years around the time that the crop was maturing—September to December. The prognostications of superb harvests, the fluctuating forecasts by regional reporters, and the despair caused by hailstorms, frosts, and heavy rains finally make the reader realize the truly unpredictable nature of the climate. The following items are indicative: October 1894—crop estimates radically altered by the effect of frost and rain, rust appearing on wheat heads; February 1896—crop estimates slashed by hail during growing season and rains during threshing; December 1896—severe storms caused widespread destruction throughout the littoral and virtually eliminated Entre Ríos' crop; September 1897—untimely frosts cut previously optimistic estimates of crop in Córdoba and Santa Fe; March 1899—extraordinarily heavy floods in Santa Fe destroyed stacked wheat; October 1900—terrible floods in Buenos Aires inundated all the southern part of the province; October 1901—drought and heat wave shriveled the crop in northern Santa Fe, Córdoba, and Entre Ríos; July 1905—frosts killed young wheat; October 1908—severe frosts and snow in some areas of the wheat belt; July 1909—drought in Santa Fe and Buenos Aires; December 1909—frost damage in Buenos Aires ruined 10 per cent of the crop; June 1910—drought so serious that throughout the littoral the ground could not be broken by plows; December 1910—starvation in La Pampa due to drought; December 1911—torrential downpours damaged cereal crops ready for harvest. And so it went. What the disasters of the wheat field meant to the individual farmer was captured by one traveler to Bahía Blanca in 1908:

Further on we are shown a stretch of land upon which a shower or two of hailstones have lately fallen. They have threshed the corn [wheat] almost clean. There is a loss of 80 percent and the remainder would not pay for the harvesting. It was sown by a man who died as the head was filling. His widow and children are there to do the sorrowing. . . .

We hear of a stalwart colonist who had his photograph taken last month to send to Europe. A week later he was seen at the railway station a wreck. The high winds of the New Year had shed his crop and sickness had overtaken him. His machines and peones [sic] were ready to go out harvesting when a Nor'easter snorted down upon him and saved him the trouble. . . .

They point out a hilarious person at one of the stations who has several inches of drink in his system over and above his carrying capacity. Three weeks ago he came in to indulge in the luxury of a shave and a hairclipping before beginning his harvesting. He had $50,000 [pesos] saved and his men and machines were ready for the wheat. While he was attending to the hair-cutting and shaving an alliance of wind and hail visited his chacra and swept his crop away. He has been drowning care ever since.[5]

Yet the conditions of the soil and climate were not unfavorable to wheat growing. Most of the shortcomings which occurred were caused, or at least aggravated, by improvidence or ignorance.

[5] *Review of the River Plate,* January 17, 1908, pp. 165, 167.

A more serious handicap was the locust. Long before wheat had become a vital commodity for Argentina those brown invaders, a couple of inches long, descended in enormous sky-filling clouds from their mysterious winter breeding grounds located somewhere in the interior of the continent. Anytime from August through May they might appear, a winged horde which destroyed virtually every green thing in its path. Once they descended on the land, there was little possible defense. They could pile up a foot deep even on the railroad tracks, delaying trains for hours and forcing continual sanding of the tracks so the locomotives could move. During the particularly bad 1896 invasion, one could read:

> On Monday afternoon [September 1] at two o'clock the city of Santa Fe was almost plunged in total darkness by an immense cloud of locusts which passed over it from east to west. The swarm took one and a quarter hours in passing over, and millions of the pests fell into the streets. . . .

And a month later:

> With our own eyes we have seen, a few weeks ago, the camps between San Nicolás and Baradero, and between Arrecifes and Pergamino, so covered with locusts, as far as the eye could reach on both sides of the railway, for a distance of 15 to 20 kilometres [10 to 12 miles], that nothing was visible but a glittering brown mass of moving insects.[6]

Even the cattleman hated the locusts. They stripped his *monte*—the trees and garden around the *estancia* headquarters. They ate his alfalfa pastures. Their bodies polluted the livestock's waterholes. But, depending on the month, their visitation to a *chacra* could spell disaster, not just inconvenience. For the wheatgrower, the critical time lasted until the grains were fully formed and hard, sometime in November; for the corn farmer, vulnerability lasted through the harvest in February or March.

Most dangerous, especially for late-developing corn, were the locusts which hatched from the land itself. The early clouds of locusts often descended merely to deposit eggs several inches under the surface of the ground. Against these offspring something could be done, and first the farmer's feeble hand and then that of the government went into action. Checking the voracious appetites of the "hoppers," which turned into "flyers" within a matter of weeks, was the only salvation for the harvest. Methods varied: the eggs could be

[6] *Ibid.*, September 5, 1896, p. 18, and October 10, 1896, p. 5.

dug up, exposing the cocoons to the sun; the baby locusts in their first week of life could be attacked with rollers, wet bagging, or sprinkled with kerosene and water; the hoppers could be knocked off the plants into huge wooden troughs and dumped into waiting graves; the hoppers could be driven into similar graves; or they could be heaped together on hard-packed roadways and flocks of sheep run back and forth across them. But such methods never exhausted the billions of insects, and more than once, after tons of eggs or hoppers had been destroyed, it seemed that it "was like trying to empty the [River] Plate with a cup."[7]

The 1896 descent which stripped trees in the Plaza de Mayo in Buenos Aires finally awoke national legislators to the dangers of the locust, and gradually official aid was extended to the farmer. These efforts (further explored in Chapter viii) culminated with the establishment of the Comisión de la Defensa Agrícola shortly after the turn of the century. The only practical deterrents which emerged, however, were the purchase of locust eggs and the use of galvanized iron fences. The government systematically bought the eggs, thus encouraging farmers and laborers to dig them up and destroy them. Threatened fields were often saved by erecting temporary walls of zinc sheeting to keep out the hoppers.

Labor was another major facet of wheat production and in many ways the most important since it put both land and capital to work. As with land, the question of labor has already been introduced: it consisted largely of immigrants, especially the rural peasants of northern Italy, who served Argentina's pastoral interests, and colonists or tenant farmers, submerged in the isolation and transiency of life on the pampas and driven to extensive agriculture.

Argentina's agriculturists had grown up in Europe, where labor was cheap and plentiful and land was scarce. They were accustomed to tenant farming or to infinitesimally small private properties. There the harrows and plows were primitive and barely scratched the surface of the soil. Much of the land was worked with mattocks or hoes. Artificial fertilizer was virtually unknown and the only means of rejuvenating the soil was to let it lie fallow for a year. Rotation was practiced but it was guided by tradition rather than by scientific principles. There was little effort to select good seed. Reaping was often done by hand with sickles and threshing by oxen or mules treading

[7] *Ibid.*, October 23, 1897, p. 27.

out the grain on a barn floor. Any notion of bookkeeping or accounting was totally absent.[8] During these years at the end of the nineteenth century very little scientific knowledge of soil conditions, techniques, or principles of agriculture filtered down to the peasants of Italy or France. Nevertheless, in their homelands these farmers possessed a considerable store of practical agricultural knowledge, born from centuries of experience with the soil, climate, and crops.

In Argentina the European peasant found himself completely disoriented: here even the very seasons were reversed; the soil, rainfall, and temperature conditions were totally different; land, though largely unavailable for his ownership, was plentiful; and labor was scarce. The new country dwarfed his previous experiences. Where before he had cultivated a few acres, he now was faced with hundreds. Where before a mattock had sufficed, he now needed gang plows, harrows, seeders, reapers, threshers, and teams of animals. Where before he had lived in a village environment perhaps a few miles from his markets, he now found himself removed from everything. In such perplexity, he had nothing to turn to except his own experience, conservatism, and ignorance. What is surprising is not that he was a poor agriculturist but that he did as well as he did.

The soil looked rich—"two feet of black dirt." There was no one to tell the farmer what crops would prosper in the different kinds of soil. He had to raise a crop which needed little care, and which yielded a nonperishable product that could be easily transported. Wheat answered these requirements, and it made little difference that much of Santa Fe was subsequently discovered to be submarginal for wheat cultivation. Actually, it took economic pressures, soil exhaustion, and the wheat crisis of 1895–1897 to push wheat southward into the zone best suited for its cultivation.

The farmer knew or cared very little about seed selection. Frequently he either sold the best of his harvest to secure a good price and saved the most inferior grains for the following year's seed, or sold his whole harvest and bought cheap wheat for seed. Just as damaging was his refusal to recognize the perils of seed degeneration. Despite extensive experiments and propaganda by the Ministry of Agriculture, rarely did he take the simple precaution of securing seed from a different wheat zone or province. Similar ignorance inflicted heavy losses from carbon smut, a disease which could be controlled

[8] Robert F. Foerster, *The Italian Emigration of Our Times,* pp. 81–82, 115–116.

merely by soaking the seed in a solution of copper sulphate. It seemed only reasonable to blame the blackened heads of grain on the weather, a wet season, or a hot sun in the early morning.

The agriculturist was no better prepared to handle the problem of soil exhaustion. Fortunately Argentina had an abundance of land, and in the pastoral areas the problem of land was not serious. Tenancy lasted from three to five years, and then the land was turned over to grazing—an ideal means of returning fertilizer to the soil. When Santa Fe and Entre Ríos finally began to show the effects of repeated crops of wheat and corn, wheat moved south and west into Buenos Aires, Córdoba, and La Pampa. In the face of such virgin frontiers and the appeal of the extensive one-crop gamble, the rational solution advocated by the Ministry of Agriculture—that a cover crop be plowed under for one or two years—made no headway. The use of artificial fertilizers was not even to be considered. "Rotation," meanwhile, meant only that the farmer planted corn first, followed by wheat, wheat, and more wheat, occasionally interspersed with a crop of flax.

Argentina's system of extensive agriculture as well as the ignorance of the farmers hardly permitted thorough preparation of the soil. The susceptibility of the entire cereal zone to drought, especially along the western edge of the humid pampas where average annual rainfall dipped to twenty inches, made the application of some dry-farming techniques desirable, the object being to conserve moisture in the soil. Deep plowing, twelve to fourteen inches, in the fall, followed by a second plowing and repeated harrowings, pulverized the dirt particles and created a dust mulch which reduced surface evaporation. Yet the desire to break up a few more acres almost always overrode the wisdom of careful plowing and harrowing. The Ministry of Agriculture recommended two plowings in the fall to a depth of eight or nine inches, followed by harrowing. Slightly deeper plowing was suggested for the western zones. But in 1914 an agronomy dissertation published in Buenos Aires concluded that the techniques of plowing were uniformly bad.[9] In Buenos Aires, one plowing to a depth of from four to six inches was customary, although in the south and west two shallow plowings with harrowing were more common. In Santa Fe the standard was two plowings to a depth of four inches. In Entre Ríos farmers plowed only once because it was felt that with

[9] Pedro Beco, "El trigo en la República Argentina," *Revista zootécnica*, Vol. V, 1914, p. 562.

3. A Typical North Italian Colonist Family in Argentina around 1910. Photograph from *Argentine Plains and Andine Glaciers* by Walter Larden.

4. The Main Street of Azul in the Province of Buenos Aires around 1910. Photog reproduced by permission of Dodd, Mead & Company from *The Real Argentin* J. A. Hammerton. Copyright 1915 by Dodd, Mead & Company.

5. A Typical Rural Town in the Cereal Zone, Melincué in Southern Santa Fe. Photograph from *Argentine Plains and Andine Glaciers* by Walter Larden.

6. A Typical Oxcart Used in the Argentine Cereal Zone. Photograph reproduced by permission of G. P. Putnam's Sons from *To The River Plate and Back* by William J. Holland. Copyright 1913 by G. P. Putnam's Sons.

the likelihood of rain two plowings would cause the wheat to go to straw. Córdoba and La Pampa, the areas most liable to drought, plowed once to a depth of less than four inches. Not until after the turn of the century did the rising value of land and the resultant need for its more intensive use finally teach farmers around Esperanza and some of the other Santa Fe colonies that plowing a couple of inches deeper increased the yields. It was patently hopeless to expect the wheatgrower in Córdoba, Buenos Aires, or La Pampa, with the limitless horizon surrounding him, to listen to such counsels.

Sowing and cultivation suffered from the same deficiencies as the preparation of the soil. The drill seeder, probably the most efficient method, required careful plowing and harrowing and remained virtually unknown outside of southern Buenos Aires. Although broadcast seeders increased rapidly in popularity and use after 1900, hand sowing remained dominant in northern Buenos Aires, Córdoba, and La Pampa. As for cultivation, "such labors are an enigma to our *chacareros*. Once the seed is in the ground it is abandoned to its fate. In Córdoba, Buenos Aires, Entre Ríos, Santiago del Estero, Jujuy, and La Pampa any labors between the sowing and the harvest are completely unknown: in some parts of Santa Fe, the wheat field is rolled in the late winter."[10]

The primary objective during plowing and planting was not thoroughness but extensiveness, to cultivate as much land as possible even if poorly done. Little outside labor was used. Usually the farmer relied on himself and his family to man the plows, harrows, and seeders. Yet this very extensiveness caused agriculture's most serious problem—a desperate demand for harvest labor. If the wheat survived all the perils of weather, disease, and locusts and reached maturity in mid-December, the farmer faced a Herculean task which had to be accomplished in a matter of weeks. What had been planted with family labor could be harvested only with the help of hired hands.

The wheat harvest consisted of three main operations: reaping, stacking, and threshing. The time for reaping was, of course, determined by the ripening of the heads of grain. In the northern cereal areas of Santa Fe, the heads began to ripen in mid-November; by mid-January they were ripe in the southern zone around Bahía Blanca. Once ripe, the wheat had to be reaped immediately or lost. The individual farmer had, at most, a few weeks in which to cut the

[10] *Ibid.*, p. 572.

grain, tie it in bundles, and stack it. Unless he had a very large family, he needed outside help. The sheaves had to be brought to some central location for threshing and stacked into piles for protection from the elements. He could easily lose a year's work to the rains if he was unable to secure labor to pile the sheaves or if the stacks were poorly made. Furthermore he had no control in determining when the grain would be threshed. The colonist or tenant farmer might own plows, harrows, and reapers, but not threshers. These were rented or contracted from the colony, landowner, local shopkeeper, or from private enterprises which followed the harvest southward. The agriculturist, therefore, was at the mercy of the availability of equipment as well as of labor. Threshing operations frequently continued through the end of March, increasing the danger of total loss from poor stacking and heavy rains.

Harvest labor came from three sources: the *golondrinas* from southern Europe, peons from the interior provinces, and, least important, urban workers and railroad gangs. All were attracted by wages five and even ten times above the norm for the rest of the year.[11] During the 1890's, Europe supplied an average of fifty thousand migrant harvest laborers a year, a figure which doubled in the early years of the next decade. After 1900, seasonal migrations from the northwest of Argentina also increased markedly. Compulsory military service, initiated in 1901, transplanted men formerly isolated in northern Argentina and opened their eyes to what they could earn during a few months in the littoral. To encourage this internal migration the national government distributed special posters advertising harvest-labor opportunities and secured from the railroads reduced rates for harvest labor. The yearly exodus of peons from provinces such as La Rioja, Catamarca, Santiago del Estero, and Tucumán increasingly supplemented the *golondrinas*.[12] When a dispute with Italy over technicalities of health standards temporarily cut off Italian emigration to Argentina in 1911–1912, the local labor-force expanded sufficiently to avert the expected harvesting crisis. Three years later hardly a shudder passed through the cereal zone when the Italian reservists were called back to their country. Yet

[11] Great Britain, House of Commons, *Sessional Papers*, 1895, Vol. 102, p. 32, Reports on Subjects of General and Commercial Interest, Miscellaneous Series, No. 369, "Report on the Agricultural and Pastoral Condition and Prospects of the Argentine Republic."

[12] *La Agricultura*, July 15, 1904, p. 376.

there never was a surplus of labor in the wheat belt, and partly for this reason, the harvest remained a crucial and often a disastrous experience for the wheatgrower. Harvest labor costs constituted the largest production expense and ate deeply into any profits which the plowing and sowing of additional acres might bring. The charge for hired help to reap and stack and for the machinery and gang to thresh amounted to more than 60 per cent of the average farmer's production costs.[13] Moreover, these were fixed costs and they did not decrease appreciably if rain damaged the harvest or the yield was poor. Consequently in bad years these labor charges magnified losses.

Ignorance and lack of foresight also contributed to the uncertainties of harvest operations. Improper stacking or failure to stack at all accounted for heavy losses. Green weeds, cut with the wheat and bundled into the sheaves, encouraged rotting or sprouting of stacked grain. Many a farmer, in hopes of duping buyers, tied up the riddles of the thresher to let through dirt and chaff and thus secure greater bulk. Most serious was the lack of adequate storage for the threshed grain. While waiting for cartage to the railroad station, the 160-pound bags of wheat were frequently left in the open without even a canvas to cover them.

Many of the problems encountered by labor in wheat cultivation were directly related to the third element in the production picture: capital. Agriculture developed in Argentina without the benefit of extensive capital investment. Argentine capital concentrated itself in cattle raising and sheep raising and in real estate. Foreign investment underwrote the railroads, industries, and commerce. Credit for the production of wheat came largely from the commercial grain interests but as such, it was limited to the actual process of planting, harvesting, and marketing the grain. Any capital improvements, such as sheds, housing, and even machinery, had to come from those least able to provide them, namely, the colonists and tenant farmers.

Since the agriculturist was almost by definition a man who came to Argentina without capital, he inevitably needed credit to back him until the harvest. At first the colonizing companies had provided food, seeds, animals, and machinery against promise of repayment. Gradually their place was taken by the rural storekeeper and the local merchant, who in turn received their credit from commercial houses

---

[13] Calculated from data in Ricardo J. Huergo, *Investigación agrícola en la región septentrional de la provincia de Buenos Aires*, p. 183, and Frank W. Bicknell, *Wheat Production and Farm Life in Argentina*, p. 62.

and cereal firms in Buenos Aires or Europe (discussed in Chapter vi).

One important effect of this credit system was to encourage the substantial mechanization of Argentine agriculture, ultimately amortized from the limited profits and savings of the colonists and tenant farmers. In the early days of colonization the farm plots were small and the equipment needs of farmers were still modest. The native, or *criollo,* plow, "a large log of wood with a piece of pointed iron at one end," soon gave way to plows hammered out in the smithies of the colonies—the "Taberning," made in Esperanza by a master blacksmith from the Tirol, gained particular fame.[14] The scythe and later the reaper were used to harvest grain. Farmers continued to rely on a centuries-old system of threshing: galloping mares over the sheaves of grain on hard-packed ground. The wheat was winnowed by tossing it into the air on a windy day.

In view of the scarcity of labor, such techniques and equipment would hardly have permitted Argentina to become an important producer of wheat. Mechanization was the answer. Modern agricultural equipment made extensive farming possible and helped to increase the size of farms from eighty acres to five hundred. Improvements evolved in England and in the United States rapidly found their way to Argentina. Steel-faced moldboards and chilled-iron and finally steel plows spread throughout the wheat zone. Sulky plows and gang plows further speeded the farmer's work and enabled him to cut several furrows at once. By 1900, in addition to locally produced plows, Argentina annually imported fifty thousand from the United States and England.

Cost and unsuitability kept some equipment out of Argentina. The steam plow, although it could do the work of fifty yokes of oxen, represented an enormous capital investment, burned imported coal, and required capabilities, talents, and resources beyond those of the tenant farmer and colonist. The tractor made its first appearance in Argentina in 1907, but for a number of years it could not compete with animal power. Since the agricultural immigrant did not at first raise horses or become a horseman, oxen for a long time provided the main source of locomotion and power. Oxen did not need selective fodder or oats and could do the heavy work for which the light

[14] Seymour, *Pioneering in the Pampas,* p. 166; Juan J. Gschwind, *Historia de San Carlos,* p. 114.

Argentine horses or ponies were totally unsuited.[15] Not until 1910 did the heavy Percheron breed begin to replace oxen in plowing and reaping operations.

The scarcity of harvest labor stimulated even greater interest in the mechanization of reaping and threshing operations. The first improvement imported from the United States was a platform behind the reaper which carried two or three peons to tie the sheaves by hand. The reaper-binder, at first using wire and later twine, dispensed with the need for those peons. Even more rapid was the header, which, pushed by horses, cut a wider swath and took only the heads of grain. But the lack of adequate protection for the grain heads from rain largely limited the use of headers to the more arid zones of Córdoba. After 1900 the reaper-thresher, or combine, was introduced, but the necessity for expert handling and perfectly ripe grain largely restricted its use.

The first thresher in Argentina was put into operation near Rosario in 1858, and the Santa Fe colonies rapidly abandoned threshing with mares in favor of this clean mechanical method. Enormous straw-burning steam threshers, moved by a team of twenty oxen and operated by twenty to thirty-five men, soon took over the field. Such a large capital investment forced the average farmer to rely on rented or contracted threshing units.

Both reapers and threshers had to be imported, at first primarily from England but after the turn of the century increasingly from the United States. The initial objection to United States equipment— that it was too complicated to be run by ignorant laborers and would not thresh wet or dirty grain as well as the sturdier and simpler British models—faded as wheat growing spread southward and agricultural techniques improved. These imports accurately reflected the fortunes of Argentina's wheatgrowers (Table 8). A peak of 9,000 reapers and 1,500 threshers was reached in 1894 only to dwindle to practically nothing in the ensuing disastrous years. In 1899 another peak was reached with 11,000 reapers, and the upward trend was resumed again in 1903 and 1904. By 1910 Argentina was importing annually 20,000 reapers and 1,000 threshers.

Up-to-date mechanization thus became an integral part of the Argentine agricultural scene. Yet, at the same time that it permitted

[15] Eduardo T. Larguía, *La economía rural en la provincia. El trabajo*, pp. 36–61 *passim*.

cultivation of extensive tracts of land, it reinforced the hold of tenant farming on the pampas. The acquisition of equipment was not merely a sacrifice for the agriculturist; it completely exhausted his limited savings and profits. The reduction in the number of *medianeros* in comparison to *arrendatarios,* it will be remembered, was in large measure due to the landowner's reluctance to risk his capital in agricultural machinery. The burden of investment, and consequently of risk, came to rest on those who tilled the land. A few figures illustrate the cost of mechanization. At the turn of the century, wheat sold for approximately 1.5 pesos a bushel. Yields ranged from 5 to 20 bushels an acre; the national average for the decade 1900–1910 was 11 bushels an acre.[16] At this time the minimum equipment for a small wheat farmer was a riding plow, a rake, 4 pairs of oxen and 4 horses, harnesses, and a reaper-binder—an investment of 1,200 pesos. Under ideal conditions, double the average yield, a low rent of 12 per cent, low transport and labor costs, a tenant farmer could net from 400 to 500 pesos from eighty acres.[17] But it must be remembered that such conditions were far from normal and that the farmer, even with luck, could hope for a bumper crop not oftener than once every three years. Since agricultural machinery was essential to wheat growing in Argentina, the commercial interests advanced the credit to buy equipment and the farmer devoted his small profits to repaying this loan. There was, obviously, little surplus left over either to buy land or to make capital improvements on the land.

Fencing was the only capital improvement which had been the agriculturist's responsibility and which in the late 1880's began to pass to the landowner's or cattleman's account. The open range had always been the rule in Argentina. The colonies in Santa Fe, though not located in a pastoral zone such as Buenos Aires, had to protect their crops against roaming cattle and horses. Ditches, hedges, and wire fences long remained costly necessities for agriculturists. In Argentina there was no conflict between the "cowman and the farmer." The farmer, as we have seen, was a transient tolerated by the pastoral and landed interests, never a competitor or rival. Although Santa Fe took a few hesitant steps in the 1870's to instruct cattlemen to restrict their animals and to respect the rights of agri-

---

[16] Argentina, Ministerio de agricultura, *Memoria, 1907–1910,* p. 8.
[17] Huergo, *Investigación agrícola . . . de Buenos Aires,* p. 210; Eduardo S. Raña, *Investigación agrícola en la provincia de Entre Ríos,* pp. 115, 131.

culturists, the end of the open range came only when the cattlemen began to recognize the value of fencing as it affected their own industry. One could not allow blooded stock to roam freely as the scrawny herds of former days had done. Cattle for on-the-hoof shipments and for packing plants had to be fat tame animals. To obtain tenant farmers to plant the needed alfalfa pastures, fields had to be enclosed. As the pastoral industry evolved, the landowner and cattleman began to purchase and build wire fences. The imports of fence wire increased from a yearly 5,000 tons in the 1870's to 20,000 tons in the 1890's and to 60,000 tons by 1910. By that year the era of the open range, at least in the humid pampas, had ended. But its end came as a result of the pastoral needs and not because of any conflict with agriculturists. The farmers, nevertheless, had won a victory in a sense, for it was cattlemen who from now on built and maintained these enclosures.

Responsibility for another important improvement fell squarely on the shoulders of the agriculturist and consequently, because of his limited resources and capital, was almost totally neglected. The colonist or the tenant farmer hardly ever built a shed or a barn. In view of his own poor housing and the transiency of his existence this is not surprising. His animals in a temperate climate needed no shelter and he did not realize the damage that exposure could do to his equipment. But Argentine agriculture paid dearly for this improvidence when it came to the bags of threshed grain. Every year rains spoiled several million pesos' worth of wheat still in the farmers' possession. After the particularly disastrous loss of thirty-two million pesos in 1915, resulting from damage to the harvested corn crop, *La Prensa* commented editorially:

In the way in which agriculture is now carried on, it is constantly necessary that a benign Providence should intervene not only during the period of germination, but also to arrange that the rains should be timed as though by a water-tap, the rainfall ceasing absolutely when the crop is collected. . . . A farmer of central Europe would be astounded if he was told that there is a certain very fertile country, of magnificent soil, where, when a large harvest has been obtained, it is lost by leaving the grain to the mercy of the weather, owing to lack of granaries in which to store it. One excuse advanced for the existing state of affairs is the lack of density of population to enable a grain shed to be erected. . . . The reason is much simpler. This rudimentary warehouse is not erected because the landlord acknowledges no improvements and because the tenant, with a lease so short, is unable to amortize during his tenure the cost of any installation of a permanent character on the property.[18]

Since March was the month of heaviest rainfall on the humid pampas and threshing often lasted through the end of that month, it was evident that Nature could not be counted on to protect the yield. Nowhere was the relative lack of capital for agriculture so evident as here. The credit advanced by the commercial grain interests enabled the farmer to plant and harvest his crop, but no more. The landowner or cattleman had no interest in providing capital improvements for such a transient enterprise as agriculture. The farmer, hard-pressed to pay for necessary machinery, had no surplus to expend for improvements that could not be taken with him. So the rains soaked the unprotected bags of wheat, and the farmers continued to regard harvest as "a risky time."

Fertile soil and temperate climate, hard-working and frugal European immigrants, and a relatively small capital investment, therefore, produced Argentina's bumper wheat crops. Wheat growing provided an income for the landowner and a method of improving pasturage for the cattleman. It brought millions of acres under cultivation and supported thousands of immigrants. It stimulated a wide-flung commerce in grains, a flour industry, and imports for agriculturists. Yet the interrelationships of the principal production factors—land, labor, and capital—reflected agriculture's peculiar role in Argentina. The growing of wheat on the pampas did little to erase rural isolation, transiency, lack of capital, and the poverty of the farmer. The primary interests of the nation were focused on pastoral and commercial activities, on sheep and cattle, and on the cities. To the Argentine mind, if not to the national economy, tilling the soil was a marginal occupation to be left in the hands of the ignorant tenant farmer.

Argentine wheat growing took the world by surprise. The crops of 1893 and 1894 led the Argentine press to exult that the nation would soon become the breadbasket of the world. In the United States, *Harpers Weekly* observed: "The Argentine Republic promises soon to become the greatest wheat producing country in the world."[19] The

[18] *La Prensa*, April 12, 1915, p. 5.
[19] *Harpers Weekly*, November 3, 1894, Vol. 38, p. 1035.

following decade saw the partial fulfillment of these prophecies. After 1900 Argentina ranked behind the United States, Russia, France, India, Austria-Hungary, and alongside Canada, Italy, Germany, and Spain as a world producer. But since less than one-half of the average crop was needed for local consumption, Argentina became the world's second- or third-largest exporter of wheat, surpassed only by the United States and sometimes by Russia.

Argentina's exports supplied Europe's mills and bakeries. The principal variety of wheat grown was Barletta, greatly sought after by Brazilian and European millers for its high gluten content. It was a grain originated in Italy, similar though slightly softer than the Turkey red, or hard winter, wheat of Kansas. It was particularly suited to Argentine farm conditions: it resisted drought, rust, frost, and extreme heat; it did not degenerate as quickly as other varieties; and the heads of grain did not shell out if left standing for several weeks after ripening. Russian and Hungarian wheat were two other popular and hardy varieties, but their grains fell off easily when ripe and consequently could not be left standing in the field when harvest labor was in short supply. Macaroni, or Candeal, wheat—a reflection of the country's increasing Italianization—was widely planted in Entre Ríos but consumed entirely within Argentina.

As we have seen, several factors affected Argentina's position as a producer of wheat. Argentine wheat growing was more extensive, at least in terms of equipment and manpower per acre, than that of other countries. The Argentine farmer did little more than scratch the surface of 250 or 500 acres. Understandably the national yield—11 bushels per acre for the period 1900–1910—was below the United States average of 14 bushels and did not compare with the results of intensive agriculture, such as 20 bushels in France and Italy or 29 bushels in Germany.[20]

A great deal of land was cultivated with a minimum of labor and capital. The predominance of the family-unit farm, colonist or tenant, precluded the expensive, large-scale equipment used on United States or Canadian bonanza farms. At the same time, Argentina did not have the peasant masses of Europe or India to overcome with sheer weight of manpower low yields and backward techniques. But it did have extensive lands and, even more important, immigrant

[20] United States Department of Agriculture, *Yearbook* (1911), pp. 530–531.

farmers who accepted a "low scale of living," isolation, transiency, and poverty.

Argentina's role as an exporter was based on these same factors of production. But further questions concerning the commercial aspects must be asked to complete this picture. What railroad and port facilities were available to transport the wheat? How was the grain handled? What was the relation of Argentina to European markets?

vi. THE COMMERCIAL ASPECTS

The growing of wheat was a credit operation, requiring an investment in seed, equipment, time, and labor to garner the results of the harvest. Since colonists and tenant farmers lacked capital of their own, everything had to be advanced to them. Capital, as has been noted, did not flow readily into agricultural activities. Landowners were willing to expend large sums to improve stock, to build fences, and to beautify their rural residences—but not to support agriculture. National and provincial banks did not even consider extending loans to wheat farmers until after 1910. Cattlemen, large landowners, even land speculators could benefit from the Banco Hipotecario Nacional and its several provincial replicas or from the Banco de la Nación, but the lowly colonist or tenant farmer never entered their portals. Agricultural cooperatives spread very slowly and by 1915 numbered only thirty scattered institutions. Consequently Argentine farming was financed by the country storekeeper or local merchant, who in turn received credit from the urban commercial and cereal houses. Charging usurious rates, at least partly justified by the risk of decamping farmers, these commercial interests advanced all necessities on the promise of the crop.

The farmer had already acquired land on credit against a percentage of his future crop. He turned to the storekeeper for seed, for agricultural machinery and repair parts, for binding twine and bags; for dried beans, hardtack, occasional stew meat, and even, incredibly, for flour; for shoes, for coarse work clothes, or for bits of finery to sport on Sundays. All this was sold him at highly inflated prices on the promise of cash payment with the harvest. When the harvest was a partial or total failure, the storekeeper inevitably had to carry forward the farmer's debts, for he was far less likely to collect than the hired hands, the threshing gang, or even the landowner. But when the harvest was good, the storekeeper was at the farmer's door, clamoring for payment of all the long-pending I O U's.

The wheatgrower's most pressing need at harvest time was cash. Even before the harvest drew to a close, he needed money to pay the hired hands and to rent a threshing machine. The local merchant extended just enough credit to get the crop grown and no more. Ironically, the very excellence of a harvest closed further credit to the farmer; his backers wanted payment and saw no reason for not getting it. The distant and inscrutable forces of the international market were not taken into consideration in determining the agriculturist's position. Bumper crops might have been harvested in France, in Russia, in Rumania, in the United States, or in India, affecting the price of wheat in Liverpool or Chicago, but these subtleties carried no import for the farmer. All he cared about was the price offered by the purchasing agents at the local railroad station, the impatience of his creditors, and the imminence of black rain clouds looming on the horizon.

This combination of factors went hand in hand with transportation problems, the virtual absence of storage facilities, and the method of sale.

Since most of the wheat was sold at the local railroad station or had to be delivered there, the farmer was faced with carting the bags of grain from farm to depot—no small problem in view of the deplorable state of Argentine country roads. An agricultural study in 1904 concluded that wheat *chacras* were limited to a distance of eighteen miles from railroad stations; beyond that, transport costs became prohibitive.[1] In actual practice, the maximum distance was closer to ten miles. Rural routes had never received the attention of commercial interests, entrepreneurs, or public authorities. Argentina passed from colonial trails to railroads without undergoing any intermediate development of roads. After 1870 the federal government placed primary emphasis on railway construction and neglected road building, a situation wholly satisfactory to the British companies that built and operated the railways. There was no national highway legislation. Landowners ran their fences as close as possible to the ruts which represented roads, and irrigation and drainage

[1] Carlos D. Girola, *Estudio sobre el cultivo del trigo en la provincia de Buenos Aires*, p. 11.

ditches were built with little regard for the public thoroughfare.[2] Provincial and municipal administrators felt no more responsibility than national authorities toward rural roads over which few people traveled, and most of these on horseback. Taxes were duly paid on carts, but not a solitary centavo found its way into road repair in country districts. Grading and paving were nonexistent.

The result was that the farmer remained isolated. The peculiar native carts with their two eight-foot wheels, pulled by three or four yokes of oxen, might get through the dust or mud or even the rippling ponds and frightful potholes which constituted much of the roadbed, but they hardly improved the condition of the road. Heavy rains cut the Argentine countryside off from everything except the mounted traveler. Each harvest season witnessed periodic shortages of wheat or corn in the market, invariably caused by the impossibility of moving the produce from farm to station in face of rain and impassable roads. In 1907 the national government made a first feeble attempt to come to the rescue of the farmer: the Mitre Law exempted railroads from taxation if they contributed 3 per cent of their profits to the construction and maintenance of approaches to their stations. The legislation gave employment to more than one thousand workers, and almost a thousand miles of road were annually repaired or built. But such paltry measures did little more than call attention to the decrepit state of rural transportation. From the heart of the wheat zone, at Juárez, Buenos Aires, came this report in 1915: "The greatest difficulty to be contended with is the lack of roads. There are farmers situated only three miles from the station who are nevertheless unable to transport their cereals there. The roads could not possibly be in worse condition."[3]

Another problem for the wheatgrower, already mentioned, arose from the absolute lack of storage facilities available to him. The absence of barns on the individual *chacras* combined with his need for cash to make long storage periods impossible. As a result, he was forced to dump his stocks on the market at the very time when the realization of the harvest had caused prices to tumble to an all-year low. In the United States and Canada the construction of small grain elevators at all local railroad stations had largely solved this problem. But in Argentina a combination of prejudices, lack of interested

[2] *Anales de la Sociedad Rural*, 1899, pp. 37–39.
[3] *La Nación*, January 29, 1915, p. 8.

capital, and market conditions conspired to prevent any spread of country elevators until after the First World War, and then only to a limited extent. To be successful, the grain-elevator system required that the farmer surrender his grain for cleaning, classification, and bulk storage in return for a "warrant," a negotiable paper indicating the quantity and quality of his grain. The farmer then had, in effect, a bond which he could endorse at any time to a wheat merchant or exporter for outright sale, or a document on which he could borrow money. In Argentina, however, the suspicion of the individual farmer toward an operation which forced him to surrender his own wheat before he had sold it, as well as the widespread acceptance of bagged rather than bulk wheat shipments, worked against the system. In addition, Argentine markets, unlike those in Canada and the United States, were not located in the interior of the country but rather at the ports. The principal need was to get the wheat from the thresher to the mills of Rosario and Buenos Aires or into the hold of an outbound ship as quickly as possible. In this situation, the complex cleaning and storage facilities of the small rural elevator appeared useless. Tarpaulins or sheds sufficed to cover bags and frequently even the existing elevators at the ports were used merely as storage depots for grain awaiting shipment.[4]

As a result, the elevator-warrant system was never used to the benefit of the Argentine wheatgrower. Several concessions for the construction and operation of local grain elevators were granted, but the only results were a few corn elevators. A similar fate awaited the warrants. At the end of the nineteenth century the government had passed several inconclusive laws authorizing their use. Not until 1914 did satisfactory legislation emerge from congress, and even then only the sugar producers took advantage of it.[5]

Local marketing procedures were just one more vise which held wheatgrowers after the harvest. As long as wheat growing remained a small-scale operation catering to the internal market, the commercial houses of Buenos Aires and Rosario, the local millers, merchants, and rural storekeepers could provide sufficient credit for agriculture. But by the time production reached the dimensions of the export market, the credit needs of agriculture exceeded the capabilities of

[4] *Anales de la Sociedad Rural,* August 31, 1904, pp. 338–341; *Review of the River Plate,* March 31, 1905, p. 631.

[5] Rodolfo Medina, *Warrants. Datos sobre su legislación en la República Argentina y el extranjero,* p. 3.

the local merchants. The establishment of Argentina's two major wheat-exporting firms—Bunge y Born and Dreyfus—dated from the late 1880's. These large companies, in reality branches of powerful European commercial interests, acted in the absence of local capital and government and bank credit to underwrite Argentine wheat expansion. The market and credit structure extended from their offices in Rosario and Buenos Aires, through several levels of *acopiadores* (from *acopiar,* "to gather or to amass"), who might be agents of the export firms, cereal merchants, millers, local storekeepers, or small-scale independents, and finally reached the *chacarero* with advances for seed, implements, and food.

Such a marketing system met the peculiar needs of Argentine wheat expansion, but it exacted its toll. In the ports it hardened into a highly organized, virtually monopolistic structure of the "Big Four" —Bunge y Born, Dreyfus, Weil Brothers, and Huni y Wormser— closely linked to the world market. In the country zones, the farmer received the necessary credit to plow, sow, and reap, but he was forced to deal with a market advised by, and indirectly controlled from, the ports. Ignorance prevented him from taking any effective action on his own: cooperatives were almost a complete failure in Argentina prior to the First World War. Totally untutored in foreign-market maneuvering, he continued to fall back on the same procedures which had served him when he had produced for an internal market. In face of the seasonal drop in wheat prices at harvest time, he attempted to hold his stocks as long as possible in hopes of a price recovery—this, despite pressing debts and lack of storage facilities. He wrangled with the *acopiador* but merely on the basis of his natural bargaining instincts and without any relation to the realities of a distant market. Not until 1908 did the Ministry of Agriculture, in combination with the railroads, provide meager assistance in the form of a daily posting at local stations of the cereal quotations from the Buenos Aires and Rosario markets. Inevitably the *acopiador* and in turn the export firms emerged victorious from such a tug of war with the wheatgrower. By April or May few indeed were the farmers who could hold off their creditors any longer or compete with the *acopiadores* in their knowledge of market conditions. The result was that if there were any profits to be made, the wheatgrower was certainly the last to reap them, and most of the time profits simply did not reach that far.

Despite the centralization and efficiency of the wheat market at the ports, many primitive local marketing practices remained to affect the quality of the grain received by exporters. Contracts between *acopiadores* and growers stipulated the "sound, clean, and dry" average of the crop for delivery. To an ignorant farmer, however, it was a temptation to mix in inferior grains, to use chaff and dirt for increased weight, and to resort to any stratagem to cheat the buyer. Such sharp practices could cut both ways, however, and frequently an *acopiador* who had contracted for a standing crop rejected bag after bag at harvest time on the basis of inferiority. The farmer, threatened with an awesome lawsuit, was then easily driven down on the contracted price.[6] In the last analysis it was the reputation of Argentine wheat abroad, and consequently the wheatgrower himself, that suffered. Everyone connected with the grain trade soon learned to allow generous margins—inevitably chopped off the price offered the farmer—to cover the eventual discounts for inferiority when the grain reached Europe.

At the railroad station the *acopiadores* inherited the headaches of storage and transportation, since few growers achieved the financial stature to merchandise their own grain. As the season advanced, the probabilities of rain increased. Yet here the same short-range view already depicted on the *chacra* hindered protection of the bags of grain. The *acopiadores* and grain agents were frequently on the move and had no incentive and often no opportunity to build permanent sheds. A tarpaulin sufficed to protect grain from average rains. If torrential downpours occurred, if the canvas rotted or disappeared in the night, if the grains sprouted or molded, the calamity was considered merely a typical misfortune of the trade which might ruin an occasional *acopiador* or cause a still larger margin for loss to be allowed in future dealings with the farmer. Railroads had no financial interest in protecting grain, and for a number of years they successfully resisted the annual outcry of the public and press against them. Not until 1903 did national legislation force them either to build sheds or provide sufficient rolling stock to move the harvest immediately after its arrival at the station. The resultant storage facilities were little more than galvanized iron roofs resting on four corner posts, but they did reduce some of the loss previously caused by the elements.

Carrying problems, meanwhile, were complicated by an Argentine

[6] *Review of the River Plate*, November 29, 1911, p. 861.

7. Threshing Wheat on the Pampas around 1910. From *Anales de la Sociedad Rural* (November–December 1910).

8. Loading Bags of Cereal at a Station of the Southern Railroad around 1910. From *Anales de la Sociedad Rural* (November-December 1910).

9. Bagged Wheat Awaiting Shipment at a Station of the Southern Railroad. From *Anales de la Sociedad Rural* (November-December 1910).

10. Loading Bags of Wheat by Chute at the Port of Rosario around 1900. From *Wheat Production and Farm Life in Argentina* by Frank W. Bicknell.

peculiarity of the trade—the persisting use of bags as the sole means of transporting grain. To the farmer, bags provided a manageable way of handling the relatively small unit of his crop. Bagged grain in commerce had been logical in the days when it was stacked along with bales of wool and hides in freight cars and holds of ships. But by the 1890's, with the increased volume of wheat production, the continued use of bags presented difficulties. As will be seen, worse problems occurred in the ports, where handling of the individual 160-pound bags of wheat, requiring a sizable labor force, brought about high costs and much wasted time during the crucial post-harvest season. Even in railroad stations, shipment by bags resulted in lost time and money: twelve hours and thirty peons were needed to load a train with six hundred tons of bagged wheat as contrasted with two hours when a small elevator was used.[7] Nevertheless, experiments with bulk carload shipments conducted by the railroads in 1907 proved unsuccessful. As long as the cleaning and classification services of local elevators were unavailable and there were no fixed standards of quality, each shipper wanted to keep his stock intact and separate.

As if the inefficiency and added costs caused by bagged shipments were not enough, the bags themselves were inordinately expensive. Until 1912, finished bags were virtually excluded from the country by prohibitive tariffs, while the components of the bags—the precut pieces and twine—were imported duty free. These were sewed together in several Buenos Aires factories employing slightly more than two thousand workers and sold at the highly inflated price allowed by the tariff barrier. Congress finally passed legislation authorizing duty-free importation of bags when the price of the domestic product reached a certain level; thereupon the industry conspired to hold prices down until the harvest months of December and January. Then increases of as much as 300 per cent could be made without fear that imports would arrive from abroad in time for the harvest. It was a significant index to the standing of agriculture that this small artificial industry could secure such exaggerated protection contrary to the interests of farmers who needed fifty million bags a year.

The high cost of bags, which amounted to 4 per cent of the farmer's total production costs, resulted in their constant reuse. Bags which might barely hold together for the trip to the railroad station—

[7] *Ibid.*, May 11, 1906, p. 1083.

but which were certain to split during the several handlings in transit to the port—became the despair of grain merchants and exporters. Prior to 1900, when most wheat still went to Europe in bags, such containers did not further the reputation of Argentine wheat abroad. To counter this unfavorable impression, leading grain exporters in Buenos Aires announced in 1892 that they would pay ten centavos more for wheat delivered in a new, heavy-duty bag. Although such efforts were periodically repeated, farmers were unable to keep up with prices which climbed to thirty-five centavos a bag by 1905.

Railroads were the only means of transporting the crop to a port. It was the potential of Argentine pastoral and agricultural expansion that had attracted British capital to build these railways, and transport of rural products now furnished satisfactory profits. Cereals, however, in spite of being an important part of this freight, created special problems. Since there were no barns on the *chacras* or elevators at the stations, the grain demanded rapid and immediate handling by the railroads. This meant, in turn, that just as the farmer had been forced by circumstances to unload his harvest as soon as possible at the local station, so now the *acopiadores* and agents wanted immediate transit for the piles of wheat stacked along the sidings. The railroads were expected to supply enough freight cars to handle the entire wheat crop (plus corn and flax) within the four months of January, February, March, and April; sufficient cars, in other words, to compensate for bag rather than bulk shipment and the consequent pile-up of cars at stations and ports. Yet this rolling stock lay virtually idle during the remainder of the year when the railroads carried only a normal load of wool, cattle, and consumer goods.

The production of wheat spread so rapidly after 1890 that for more than a decade the railroads were unable to keep up with this highly seasonal demand. The resultant shortages of freight cars and the damage to grain stocks stored in the open or under canvas aroused a public hue and cry. Newspapers and public officials rarely lost an opportunity to appease the newly apparent and blatant spirit of nationalism with attacks against "foreign" shortcomings which threatened Argentina's wealth. Repeatedly it was pointed out that despite their high freight rates, the railroads were derelict in providing sufficient rolling stock. Not until 1904 did a Ministry of Agriculture study admit what one defender of the railroads, the British *Review of the River Plate,* had pointed out ten years earlier: that the real problem was not lack of rolling stock but inefficient port facilities which tied up freight cars for days awaiting unloading.[8]

Handling and storage at the ports were acute problems. If hand loading a string of freight cars on some rural siding represented misused energy, the waste was magnified tenfold at the accesses to the ports. Rosario was best equipped to unload trains because its port facilities had almost kept pace with the rising production of the colonies. Grain elevators and warehouses had been built there in the early 1880's. But in the bumper year 1894, it was observed: "In Rosario there are deposits for about 100,000 tons, but that quantity is about ten days' work of shipping, and so great was the crush this year that in the busy months one railway alone had 1100 wagons for a considerable time blocking up their Rosario station, not to speak of many loaded wagons waiting at up country stations."[9] Buenos Aires was less prepared for the sudden rise of production in that province and for the increasing pressure of railroads and commercial interests to make it a major wheat port. As late as 1900 there were no storage facilities at Buenos Aires, and the wheat had to be loaded directly from trains onto ships. The heavy bags, therefore, had to be carried from the freight cars on stevedores' shoulders, up the gangplank and into the ship's hold—a slow, laborious process which immobilized not only the freight cars and siding but also the dock area and the ship for several days. Under these conditions, a train with six hundred tons of bagged wheat took three or four days to unload.[10] In turn, Bahía Blanca experienced the same problems. In 1905 the shortage of storage space and the inability to load more than five thousand tons per day (out of an estimated million tons of harvest in the Bahía Blanca area) blocked rail lines for months.

As the center of wheat production moved southward, so did the problems. The difficulties which had faced the Central Argentine and the Buenos Aires-Rosario lines in the 1890's became those of the Southern and Western railways after the turn of the century. By 1910, however, the period of rapid wheat expansion was over, and subsequently the railroads were able to meet the demands of shippers. Yet a certain vulnerability remained. Beginning with the harvest of 1904, railroad unions chose the harvest months for their strikes, and

[8] *Ibid.*, August 18, 1894, pp. 5–6; *Boletín del Ministerio de agricultura,* Vol. I, Nos. 4–6, pp. 479–499.

[9] *Review of the River Plate,* August 18, 1894, pp. 5–6.

[10] *Ibid.*, November 26, 1896, p. 5.

after the particularly bitter fifty-one-day strike in January and February of 1912, it took the railroads three months to return to normal
service.

Freight rates caused as much criticism of the foreign-owned railroads as seasonal shortages of rolling stock. The local press was fond
of recalling that these enterprises always recorded a profit. More
recent critics have noted that these rates, supervised by the national
government after 1896, deliberately favored the port of Buenos Aires
to the disadvantage of competitors such as Rosario and La Plata.[11]
Others contended that the lack of reasonable long-haul rates imposed
limits on the expansion of cereal growing in Argentina. One Ministry
of Agriculture study pointed out that the costs of railroad transportation prevented wheat from being grown farther than two hundred
miles from the coast.[12] An impartial and well-documented study of
Argentine and United States transport costs, appearing in the *Journal
of Political Economy* (Chicago) in 1902, concluded that if short-haul
(under one hundred miles) charges were far lower in Argentina,
those over two hundred miles were indeed more expensive.[13] The
division of responsibility between railroads and nature, however, was
a finely drawn one. It is true that circles with radii of two hundred
miles traced from the ports of Bahía Blanca, Buenos Aires, and
Rosario did in effect comprise the zone of actual wheat production,
but subsequent studies by the Ministry of Agriculture have shown
this very area to be virtually the climatic limit of profitable wheat
cultivation.

Despite the contemporary and subsequent accusations hurled at
the railroads, it must be admitted that they made possible the rapid
expansion of wheat production in Argentina. They tapped not only
the cereal zones of the Santa Fe colonies but enabled wheat to move
southward as well. Wherever rails penetrated, the colonist and the
tenant farmer could follow, assured that their crops could be moved
to market. The cars carried a highly seasonal freight with considerable efficiency and at a charge of 10 per cent of the wheat farmer's

[11] Ricardo M. Ortiz, *Historia económica de la Argentina, 1850–1930*, I, 261–
262, 266–267.
[12] Emilio Lahitte, *La producción agrícola y los impuestos en las provincias de
Buenos Aires, Santa Fe, Córdoba y Entre Ríos*, p. 2; repeated in Julio López
Mañan, *El actual problema agrario*, pp. 23–25.
[13] Robert R. Kuczynski, "Freight Rates on Argentine and North American
Wheat," *Journal of Political Economy*, Vol. X, No. 3, June 1902, pp. 333–360.

total production costs.[14] The railroads may have brought some unfortunate side effects: isolation to the countryside by discouraging or bypassing a system of rural roads; a yearly tribute in profits paid to London because national capital was insufficient or unwilling to build railroads; an obvious and often irritating target for Argentine nationalistic susceptibilities. The railroads, nevertheless, supplied the country with a transportation system which it could not have otherwise acquired. They funneled wealth to the coast, thus stimulating rapid commercial, industrial, and urban development, and they showed a sense of progress and adaptability not often demonstrated by either the wheatgrower or the Argentine government.

Until the 1890's Argentina produced wheat primarily for the internal market, for though wheat production was rising steadily, so was internal consumption. Then, in less than a decade, production far overshot local needs. After 1892 more than half of Argentina's harvest went abroad each year, in amounts ranging as high as 70 per cent (Tables 2 and 6). Simultaneously wheat rose to first place among Argentina's agricultural exports, contributing from 15 to 30 per cent of the total national exports (Table 7). Wheat's effect on Argentina's balance of payments was particularly noticeable with regard to England. For years England, a source of much of Argentina's consumer goods, capital, and shipping, had bought little in return, but beginning in 1895 a new era, marked by grains and meat, promised to create a favorable trade balance for Argentina.

In the face of this sudden shift from an internal to an international market and of the tremendously increased value of trade, the structure of grain commerce in Argentina underwent substantial change. During the 1870's and early 1880's, while Argentina was still attaining self-sufficiency in wheat, marketing procedures were simple. The colonists of Santa Fe or the farmers of Chivilcoy sold their crops directly to local millers or shopkeepers. Wheat, along with innumerable other agricultural and pastoral products, entered the large produce markets in Buenos Aires, Rosario, Santa Fe, and other coastal cities. Transactions there registered a daily average price per hundred kilos, varying according to quality and source. The demand for wheat and flour was well known and stable. Bakers

[14] Ministry of Agriculture figures quoted in *Review of the River Plate*, November 3, 1904, p. 476.

might force prices up slightly with year-end purchases; otherwise, the needs of the urban population, just beginning to expand with immigration, could be accurately predicted. Supply, therefore, was the primary determinant of price. Shortages, real or forecast, in the local harvest or in imports of wheat and flour sent prices upward; the arrival of Chilean or United States flour brought them down again. Unless the season was a complete disaster, the harvest from the Santa Fe colonies and northern Buenos Aires resulted in lower prices at the beginning of each year. Developments in the international market naturally were known locally, but the changes had to be drastic before their effects were felt in Argentina. Even in mid-1870, when it was noted that bad harvests in France, Italy, and Spain combined with the probability of a Franco-Prussian war had resulted in a world price-rise, local Argentine prices responded only slightly. And this response was due mainly to internal factors, since stocks were low and the next harvest was too far away to promise an adequate supply.[15]

The first lots of Argentine wheat to enter the world market were shipped along with regular consignments of wool, bones, meats, and hides. These shipments were commercial ventures made by established export merchants in Santa Fe and Rosario. Since the Argentine harvest was coincident with Europe's winter months, the lots arrived in March and April, when European stocks were low and prices were rising. The result was a happy one for the shippers, and profits were considerable.

Such haphazard commercial arrangements could continue only so long as the bulk of wheat was produced for internal consumption. As previously mentioned, the establishment of the wheat-exporting firms of Bunge y Born and Dreyfus in Argentina in the late 1880's opened a new era in the commercialization of grains, brought the local market into close contact with world conditions, and eventually created a virtual monopoly in the export trade.

It was logical that the increased volume of wheat exports should bring specialization. Credit was the crying necessity of all agricultural ventures, the more so when Argentine wheat was largely grown by penniless Italian colonists and tenants. Neither the country storekeeper and local miller nor the existing commercial houses possessed sufficient resources to finance an expanding internal market as well as export production. Consequently foreign capital and foreign com-

[15] *Revista económica del Río de la Plata*, August 7, 1870, pp. 13–14.

panies entered Argentina to provide the needed credit and specialization. The complexities and risks of international trade and the need
for established credit and large capital reserves limited the export
trade to a few hands. Bunge y Born and Dreyfus were never shaken
from their dominant position in the Argentine market, although by
1900 the common usage of the term the "Big Four" indicated that
Weil Brothers and Huni y Wormser had joined the leaders. Approximately a dozen small export firms hung on the fringes of the trade, a
shifting group which was constantly pruned by the risks of speculation in such a highly organized market.[16]

The structure of trade that emerged after the turn of the century
was not achieved without serious conflict.[17] It must be remembered
that although the export market suddenly became very vital to Argentina, there already existed an important domestic market with its
own procedures. The produce market at Plaza Once in Buenos Aires,
for example, had gradually evolved from a mere gathering place for
carts bringing wool, hides, fruits, and vegetables to the city, into an
organized body of merchants specializing in grains. The change was
crystallized in 1898 with the formation of the Bolsa de Cereales to
supervise and control grain transactions. Three years later its own internal legal machinery was created with the Tribunal Arbitral to
settle commercial differences between members. The Plaza Once
market, subsequently the Bolsa de Cereales, was primarily oriented
toward the internal market. Here the stocks of grain sent by the
country storekeepers and *acopiadores* were handled and sold by cereal merchants *(consignatarios)* to the millers and seed merchants of
Buenos Aires. Similar markets, though not formalized with the title of
Bolsa de Cereales, existed on a smaller scale in Rosario and Santa Fe.

The export firms, on the other hand, rarely tapped these internal
markets and then only to secure a certain quality or quantity of wheat

[16] Emilio A. Coni, *El mercado ordenado de trigo argentino*, pp. 89–102.

[17] There is little published material on these developments. The account given
here has been reconstructed from interviews with cereal merchants, millers, and
members of the Bolsa de Comercio and Bolsa de Cereales who were active during this decade; from articles in *La Agricultura, Review of the River Plate, El
Diario, La Producción Argentina*, and *La Semana Rural;* from Gert Holm, "Mercado de Cereales a Término de Buenos Aires," *The Standard*, special centennial
issue, August 1916, p. 156; from *La cámara gremial de cereales de la Bolsa de
Comercio en su cincuentenario, 1905—26 de mayo—1955* (Buenos Aires, 1955),
*La Bolsa de Comercio de Buenos Aires en su centenario, 1854—10 de julio—
1954* (Buenos Aires, 1954), *Revista de la Bolsa de Cereales*, special centennial
issue, 1954, and Fernando A. Bidabehere, *Bolsas y mercados de comercio en la
República Argentina.*

to complete a shipment. Their transactions were usually carried out directly with the *acopiadores,* country storekeepers, or millers, many of whom became, as already pointed out, virtual agents of the export houses in Rosario and Buenos Aires. From Bunge y Born and Dreyfus came the funds which enabled the *acopiador* or storekeeper in turn to advance money or goods to the farmer long before the harvest. These advances of credit represented only part of the exporters' power to exercise control over the market. The system of contracts based on the contemporary practice, *a fijar precio* (to fix the price), provided a further control. For example, if one hundred kilos of wheat was delivered by a farmer to an *acopiador,* or by an *acopiador* to an export house on a day when the market price was ten pesos, the receiver would advance 80 per cent of that price. The one who had delivered the wheat then had the option of selecting the actual day when he would sell the wheat to the receiver, but in the meantime he remained liable for storage, interest, and deterioration charges for which the 20 per cent margin had been withheld. The system operated in the receiver's interest whenever the price of wheat fell. The deliverer then was obligated to repay funds to maintain the proportion of 80 per cent of the advanced value, a payment which he rarely was in position to make. The receiver consequently could choose his day to foreclose on the farmer or *acopiador.* This mechanism gave rise to frequent accusations that export firms combined in May or June to bring about an artificial drop in the price of wheat in Buenos Aires and Rosario and thus to force stocks on the market at values profitable to them.[18]

Although the export firms rarely secured their stocks in the Bolsa de Cereales of Buenos Aires, they were inevitably members of the Bolsa de Comercio, which had united the principal commercial and financial interests of Buenos Aires since 1854 and of Rosario since 1884. On the floor of the Bolsa de Comercio, particularly of the Rosario exchange, sizable grain transactions were concluded.[19] To take care of matters related to the grain trade, special arbitration committees (Comisión Arbitral de Cereales) within these exchanges had been formed: in Buenos Aires in 1883 and in Rosario in 1899. The main functions of these committees were to settle any commercial disputes arising from sales of wheat for export and to fix the daily market

[18] *La Agricultura,* June 8, 1899, p. 459.
[19] Bidabehere, *Bolsas y mercados de comercio,* pp. 127–137.

quotation for grains. Logically in this latter activity they were strongly influenced by the export firms.

The export and the internal wheat markets in Argentina had thus developed somewhat individual characteristics and practices. The two markets were closely linked in prices and competition since they drew their stocks from the same source: the storekeepers and *acopiadores*. Both the export firms and the cereal merchants served as credit institutions that underwrote the rapid expansion of the export and internal markets. In Buenos Aires participants in either market might well be members of both the Bolsa de Comercio and the Bolsa de Cereales. But each had its own organizations for dealing in wheat, its own arbitration committees or courts to settle internal disputes, and, as competition for profits grew keener, its own interests to defend.

For a decade or more at the turn of the century, occasional indications of a now-forgotten struggle within the various grain markets broke through to the surface in the daily press. The export houses, resentful of the chain of *acopiadores* through which their stocks frequently had to pass, resorted to establishing their own offices and agents in the wheat zone to contract shipments directly from the local storekeeper. The volume of their shipments fostered cooperation with the railroads. Not only were rebates secured, but the local station manager often became the best source of information for the "Big Four" on immediate conditions of supply and demand in the far-flung rural districts. As their operations expanded, the exporters moved into allied fields, such as flour milling. At the same time, the independent *acopiadores,* particularly the cereal merchants established in Rosario and Buenos Aires, became distrustful of the increasing strength of the export firms. They felt that the virtual monopoly of the export trade enabled the "Big Four" to depress the local market artificially and thus reap the benefits of European price changes for themselves alone. Unable to break into this monopoly, the cereal merchants sought an alternative—to structure the market so as to share in those profits.

The struggle was not serious in Rosario, where by tradition the local grain merchants were firmly entrenched. In Buenos Aires, on the other hand, where the rise of wheat production had been more recent and more rapid, the exporters provided a large portion of the advances to farmers. The grain merchants, largely limited to Plaza Once and since 1898 to the Bolsa de Cereales, felt their participation in the export market curtailed and resented the increasing power of the large export firms. As a result they began to press for the establishment of a futures market where grain contracts could be made for delivery and sale at a fixed price on a specified future date. Only thus could their grain operations be covered: for when a shipment of wheat, *a fijar precio,* was received it could be guaranteed against loss if a similar quantity was simultaneously sold in the futures market. Initially the large export firms opposed the establishment of a futures market on the grounds that it would introduce speculation into operations. In reality, because of their large capital reserves and their ability to cover operations in the futures markets of Europe, they had no need for a local futures market. Indeed, they opposed the creation of a yardstick of grain values which might threaten their virtual monopoly of the export market.

The logical institution to support a futures market would have been the Bolsa de Comercio, but in grain matters it was largely controlled by the exporters. Consequently, as early as 1903, a group of *acopiadores* and cereal merchants in Buenos Aires formed the Asociación de Cereales with the purpose of fostering a futures market. The difference of opinion between exporters and cereal merchants was emphasized in 1906 when the export firms of Buenos Aires and Rosario formally declared their opposition to a futures market and agreed among themselves not to participate in the informal futures buying which had developed.[20] The Asociación de Cereales continued to press for its objective, and in March 1908 the first Argentine futures market was opened under its auspices in Buenos Aires.

During this struggle the exporters lost some of their control over the Bolsa de Comercio. Cereal merchants and *acopiadores* within that exchange had been working to secure outright approval for a futures market. As a result, when the futures market was established, the Bolsa de Comercio announced it would recognize the transactions although it would not permit them on its premises. The following year the Bolsa de Comercio moved to take over the futures market, only to have the national government, under pressure from the "Big Four," disapprove the necessary statutes and regulations.[21] Finally, in 1910, the Bolsa de Comercio incorporated the futures market within its structure (Mercado a Término de Cereales de Buenos Aires); the Asociación de Cereales, having won its point, dissolved.

20 *Review of the River Plate,* June 15, 1906, p. 1433.
21 *Ibid.,* March 19, 1909, p. 769.

That same year, a futures market opened in Rosario on Bolsa de Comercio premises. The former opposition by the export firms to the futures market rapidly faded. For several months its "rings" were boycotted by the exporters, but when it became apparent that the market did not threaten the virtual export monopoly held by the "Big Four," the exporters began to support such trading in Argentina. In effect, the principal result of these developments was to bring the internal and export markets into close contact with each other and to confirm the predominant influence of the "Big Four" in Argentine cereal commerce.

These changes in the structure of the grain trade as well as increasing exports brought Argentine prices closely into line with international exchange quotations in grain. The time lag between purchases in Argentina and sales in Europe always introduced a certain speculative risk: European conditions of supply could change markedly before the grain was delivered. This was well illustrated in 1892, when rain delayed the harvesting of the Argentine crop. Shippers who had had to place their orders for tonnage early were then forced to buy wheat at high local rates. By the time these shipments reached Europe—a month later—the market had collapsed with the promise of an abundant United States harvest. The thorough organization of the Argentine market by export interests and the spread of futures markets lessened the likelihood of such occurrences. The Argentine markets became increasingly sensitive to developments abroad and the grain exchanges at Chicago, Liverpool, and London began to watch the progress of the Argentine crop rather closely. Some items from market reports in the 1890's indicate the effect of world production on Argentine prices: June 1894, some recovery of the market because of drought in the United States and untimely rains on the Continent; January 1895, sharp fall due to United States production estimates; January 1897, rapid rise with loss of crops in Australia, India, and Russia as well as poor Argentine harvest; April 1898, speculative rise due to the outbreak of the Spanish-American War. In the following decade excerpts from the British *Corn Trade News* reflected the attention paid to the Argentine harvest: November 1904—"The market at present is nervous, owing to the critical state in which the Argentine crop now is"; November 1906—"The wheat market remains in a state of suspense over the result of the approaching harvest in Argentina, as so much depends upon the size of this crop, for Europe is looking for something like 9 or 10 million quarters [from 2 to 2.2 million tons] of Wheat to come from that quarter of the globe during the first seven months of the new year"; October 1908—alarmists and speculators exaggerated reports of frosts in Argentina and estimated a 25 per cent crop loss (actual loss was in the vicinity of 11 per cent). Speculator interest in the Argentine crops of 1905 and 1906 was particularly notable. Certain groups in Liverpool and Chicago did their utmost to raise prices by having their Argentine agents deliberately cable alarming messages. Every drop of rain was magnified into a deluge. One cable to Chicago went so far as to announce that half of Argentina's wheat crop had been destroyed by rust.

In a single decade Argentina shifted from home consumption of the entire wheat crop to the export of more than half the annual harvest. European capital flowed into the country to finance this expansion. Export firms provided credit to the *acopiadores* and storekeepers who in turn passed on the credit to colonists and tenant farmers. Market operations became highly organized. The "Big Four" developed and controlled the export market and strongly influenced local markets. The change, therefore, brought Argentine grain commerce into close contact with world prices and the world wheat trade.

Rosario, Buenos Aires, and Bahía Blanca were the principal ports that fed Argentine wheat into the world markets. The first exports left from Colastiné, port for the city of Santa Fe and consequently for the first colonies in central Santa Fe. After the completion of the Central Argentine Railroad and with the rapid expansion of wheat production along that line, Rosario emerged as a major wheat port. Although located on the broad, winding Paraná River two hundred miles above Buenos Aires, Rosario could be reached by ocean steamers and sailing ships, possessed excellent natural loading facilities, and was the terminus of the only railroad from the interior. The river had cut a channel close to shore. Ships anchored alongside the high bank and received bagged or bulk grain by means of long wooden chutes. In 1881 Argentina's first major grain elevator improved on these natural facilities by providing storage for seven thousand tons of wheat and a loading capacity of sixty tons per hour. Rosario's commercial interests continued to champion bulk shipments of grain and subsequently constructed several more elevators. But the farmers' predilection for bags was not easily overcome, and until 1900 bagged wheat accounted for three-quarters of the port's exports.

New port facilities built by French capital were completed in 1902. The timing of this grandiose project—new wharves, warehouses, elevators, and railroads—was unfortunate, for the 1895–1897 wheat crisis had cut deeply into the prosperity of the province. The amortization of this investment resulted in higher port charges and drove some shipping to the smaller river ports and even to Buenos Aires. At the same time, national authorities tended to favor Buenos Aires' predominant commercial position. Dredging of the Paraná channel was neglected and vessels frequently ran aground off Rosario. After 1900 the British railroads also began to build more and more lines to connect the wheat-producing areas of Córdoba and southern Santa Fe directly with the port of Buenos Aires (Map 5). Rosario remained a major wheat exporter, but its share dropped from two-thirds to one-third of total wheat shipments.

As Santa Fe's proportion of total production began to decline in the 1890's, Buenos Aires and then Bahía Blanca handled a rising share of the exports (Table 9). Buenos Aires, despite its importance as Argentina's principal port and seat of the country's economic and political power, possessed incredibly poor docks and shipping facilities until the very end of the nineteenth century. The main channel was several miles offshore and the approach to the docks was very shallow. Only small ships could reach the Riachuelo estuary on the city's southern limits. Most freight and passengers had to be transferred from the ocean-going vessels in the main channel to lighters and sometimes to high-wheeled carts before reaching shore. The violence of the occasional pamperos added danger to the inconvenience and expense caused by such a lack of protected anchorage and adequate docks. In the 1890's the volume of trade and the agitation of commercial interests resulted in the construction of modern concrete ship basins alongside Buenos Aires' waterfront connected to the main channel by dredged canals. With the completion of the Madero docks (Dársena Norte) in 1897, ocean-going vessels could tie up in close proximity to the railhead at the city's northern side. Several years passed, however, before facilities were added to handle the province's increasing grain production efficiently. In 1904, elevators were inaugurated which could store 76,000 tons of wheat and load at the rate of 900 tons per hour.

For a brief period in the 1890's the port of La Plata, twenty-five miles south of Buenos Aires, gave promise of becoming a major grain-exporting center. Its natural facilities, similar to those of Rosario, were far better than those of Buenos Aires, and it was closer to the rapidly developing southern portion of the province. In 1896 it handled more than one-third of the grain exports from the province of Buenos Aires. La Plata was too close to Buenos Aires, however, to emerge as an independent commercial center, and ships preferred to land their cargoes at Buenos Aires and load return cargoes at that same port. The completion of Buenos Aires' docks consequently checked La Plata's rise as a wheat exporter. In addition, the railroads conspired to centralize commerce in Buenos Aires by providing rebates on shipments direct to the produce markets of Buenos Aires or to the Madero docks.[22]

Bahía Blanca, which exported no wheat in 1890, two years later supplanted Santa Fe as a major wheat port, and by 1905 accounted for one-quarter of total national exports. The railroads, particularly the Southern, took advantage of Bahía Blanca's location on a broad, sheltered bay. By 1908 an 8,000-ton elevator was in operation and several others were being constructed.

Slow, clumsy, and costly handling long handicapped Argentina's grain trade. Until the turn of the century only a few shippers at Rosario and some of the smaller river ports sent wheat in bulk cargoes. In the new elevators built on Buenos Aires' Madero docks in 1904, 47,000 tons of the 76,000-ton storage capacity was allotted to bagged wheat. The volume of trade, however, finally forced a transition, and by 1906 from one-half to two-thirds of the shipments left Argentina in bulk.[23] Despite extensive elevator construction, many bulk shipments were merely the result of emptying the bags into the hold of the ship or onto a conveyer belt. There certainly was nothing in Argentina comparable to the 60,000- or 100,000-ton terminal elevators of Chicago or New York.

The lack of adequate storage facilities at the ports went hand in hand with the unsatisfactory handling of grain. Any complication—

---

[22] Argentina, Ministerio de agricultura, *Memoria, 1904–1905*, p. 91.

[23] The shift to bulk from bagged exports of wheat, taken from data published in the *Boletín mensual de estadística del Ministerio de agricultura* is as follows:

Year	Total Bagged Tonnage	Total Bulk Tonnage
1903	1,357,519	314,714
1904	1,412,657	929,227
1905	1,447,402	1,447,083
1906	848,818	1,511,900

an unusually good harvest, a strike of stevedores or cartmen, inefficiency on the part of the port authorities—could make a shambles of Rosario, Buenos Aires, or Bahía Blanca. Thousands of freight cars would be immobilized, *acopiadores* could not move their shipments, and the resultant problems reached all the way back to the *chacra*. Neither entrepreneurs nor government demonstrated any effective interest in these difficulties. The railroads and the "Big Four" were practically the only ones to build elevators and warehouses, but capacity never caught up with production. As a result Argentina as a nation was in the same situation as its farmers—forced to liquidate its stocks in the world market because there was no place to store a surplus.

Argentine wheat had to contend with other problems in world trade. One complaint which had caused grave concern to the Department of Agriculture in 1880—"the bad odor of mares' urine persisting even in the flour made from our wheat"[24]—disappeared with the abandonment of ancient threshing methods in favor of the steam thresher. Other defects, however, more deeply ingrained in Argentina's production and marketing habits, caused European buyers to be wary of Río de la Plata products. Since there were no standards of quality in the local markets, the variation within lots and even within bags was enormous. Shippers and exporters, at least in the early days, did not prove much more scrupulous than the colonist who tied up the riddles of the thresher. In turn they tried to pass on the product to unwary buyers, and it was soon discovered that all Argentine wheat had to be cleaned upon arrival in Europe. The complete lack of attention to quality of seeds, methods of agriculture, and bagging caused depreciation and deterioration of the product. Characteristic was the complaint voiced by one British minister in a report to his Foreign Office: "Not long ago a cargo of maize left here with sprouts a foot long growing outside of the top tier of bags, and promised before arrival to furnish a second crop in the interest of the shipper."[25] While it was acknowledged that the Diamante region in Entre Ríos and the southern portion of the province of Buenos Aires produced some of the world's finest wheat, for many years the general run of

[24] *Boletín del departamento nacional de agricultura*, 1880, pp. 150–151.

[25] *Sessional Papers*, 1892, Vol. 81, p. 13, Diplomatic and Consular Reports on Trade and Finance, Annual Series, No. 983, "Reports for the Year 1891 on the Agricultural Condition of the Argentine Republic."

grain in the Río de la Plata area did not meet the standards of European markets.[26]

Another detrimental factor to Argentine shipments was their literal shortness. Shiploads invariably arrived at least 1 per cent under bill-of-lading weights and sometimes the shrinkage rose as high as 8 to 10 per cent. Part of the reason was that ships coming downstream from Rosario and Santa Fe frequently had to shift their cargoes to lighters in order to cross over the Martín García bar near Buenos Aires. Not only was grain spilled from rotten bags in the process but a considerable volume disappeared in organized thievery to which the lighter captains were no strangers.[27] The Argentine minister to Berlin in 1901 pointed out a further danger: the deceitful practices of some exporters who had only immediate profits in mind. He warned his government that several large German houses planned to terminate their trade with Argentina because they had repeatedly received shipments inferior to the samples on which they had based their purchases.

After 1900 control of the export market by the "Big Four" tended to remedy many of these deficiencies. The large commercial houses had reputations to safeguard. Lack of uniform standards in bagging and grading of wheat might still make purchase of Argentine wheat somewhat a gamble, but the short-sighted marketing practices of the 1880's and 1890's became the exception rather than the rule.

England was the principal purchaser of Argentine wheat. This was a satisfactory arrangement for Argentina, since England had furnished and continued to furnish the great bulk of capital, shipping, and goods for the Río de la Plata area. With the advent of the meat-grain era at the turn of the century, the balance of trade tipped in Argentina's favor, the peso valued at forty-four centavos gold became one of the world's soundest currencies, and Argentina embarked upon a period of rapid economic development.

From 1900 to 1905, according to Board of Trade figures, Great Britain absorbed 44 per cent of Argentine wheat exports. Germany, Belgium, and Holland divided the rest among themselves. Other consumers could not be considered consistent buyers. France, despite high tariffs on wheat imports, periodically took a portion of the exports when its crop failed. Spain, Portugal, and Scandinavia also placed occasional demands on the Argentine supply. There were even

[26] *La Nación*, January 3, 1890, p. 1.
[27] *Review of the River Plate*, February 6, 1892, p. 5.

11. The Riverbank at Buenos Aires around 1880, Prior to Construction of the Docks. Photograph reproduced by permission of A. & C. Black, Ltd., from *Argentina, Past and Present* by William H. Koebel. Copyright 1910 by A. & C. Black, Ltd.

12. Grain Elevators of the Central Argentine Railroad at the Port of Buenos Aires. Photograph reproduced by permission of Cassell and Company, Ltd., from *The Amazing Argentine* by John F. Fraser. Copyright 1914 by

some unique exports, such as twenty thousand tons to Australia in 1903 and again in 1915, and three thousand tons to Russia in 1907, in response to crop failures and famines in these world breadbaskets.

Argentina's rapidly expanding population also consumed increasing quantities of wheat. The influx of Europeans in the 1880's and during the first decade of the twentieth century transformed Argentina into a wheat-eating country. During the 1880's the individual consumption of wheat in the province of Buenos Aires increased from a yearly 260 pounds (180 pounds of flour) to 460 pounds (320 pounds of flour).[28]

The increasing demand for flour resulted in the rapid development and improvement of Argentina's milling industry. Flour ceased to be the high-priced luxury noted by a British consul in 1871, when Argentine wheat prices were equivalent to England's but bread was three times as expensive.[29] The small water- or animal-powered mill gave way to steam mills in Santa Fe, Rosario, and the colonies of Esperanza and Casilda. In 1889, sixty-three of Argentina's one hundred thirty steam mills were located in the province of Santa Fe.

By the end of the century the city of Buenos Aires began to emerge as the center of the flour-milling industry. The wheat crisis of 1895–1897 and taxation of the industry in Santa Fe contributed to the southward move, and by 1908 Buenos Aires or Córdoba flour was underselling the Santa Fe product in its own province.[30] Rebates and differential long-haul railroad rates further encouraged the centralization of the industry in the nation's capital. Illustrative was the fact that it cost 2.06 pesos to ship a bag of flour from Buenos Aires to Salta; a competing bag of flour shipped from Córdoba to Salta—half the distance—was charged 2.53 pesos.[31] The construction of modern milling plants on the very docks of Buenos Aires and the purchase by Bunge y Born of competing mills provided further efficiency and centralization. In 1914 the third national census showed that the city and province of Buenos Aires controlled 55 per cent of Argentine flour production. Santa Fe had slipped from 25 per cent in 1895 to 17

[28] Fliess, *La producción agrícola y ganadera*, p. 187.

[29] "The Conditions of Industrial Classes, and Emigration to the Argentine Republic," Phipps, enclosure from Macdonell to Earl Granville, July 15, 1871, Great Britain, Public Record Office, Foreign Office Records, General Correspondence 6, Vol. 304, No. 79.

[30] *Review of the River Plate*, June 26, 1908, p. 1625, and July 10, 1908, p. 85.

[31] Ortiz, *Historia económica*, II, 102.

per cent, while Entre Ríos accounted for 6 per cent and Córdoba 17 per cent.[32]

Flour exports never acquired the importance of wheat in Argentine trade. During the 1880's approximately five thousand tons a year were exported, but even after the bumper 1893 crop, flour amounted to only 5 per cent of the grain export of wheat (Table 2). Aside from handicaps such as weevils and other impurities in the flour, the export was limited by international competition with nations that protected their own milling industry by tariffs or possessed cheap combustibles or water power near their coasts. Argentine mills produced, three-fore, for markets close to their shores, namely, the domestic market and Brazil, where freight charges worked to their advantage.

Indeed, the story of Argentine flour exports after 1890 became that of a struggle to develop and maintain the Brazilian market. At the very moment that the milling industry began to look for a foreign market, the Brazilian–United States commercial agreement of 1891 threatened to eliminate the most likely buyer. The volume of coffee taken by the United States forced Brazil to give preferential treat-ment to United States flour. In addition the Brazilian government had been angered by Argentine protective tariffs on tobacco, *yerba mate*, and sugar. Diplomatic negotiations removed the discrimination against Argentine flour in 1895, but lack of standardization and the bad faith of Argentine shippers determined a Brazilian preference for the North American product. Five times as much flour was sent to Brazil from the United States as from Argentina.[33]

The flood of articles appearing in the Argentine press from 1899 to 1901 demonstrated concern with this state of affairs. Associations of millers, formed in 1899, pledged to sell only standardized brands. In 1900 *La Molinera Argentina* and *La Industria Molinera* made their appearance as spokesmen of the milling trade. In January 1901 the Minister of Agriculture called a conference of millers in Buenos Aires to formulate improvements in the industry. Gradually the quality and reputation of the Argentine product improved and, favored by the closeness to its market, flour from the Río de la Plata area began to gain on United States competition. Proof of this was the fact that the United States felt called upon to aid its own flour industry: in 1904, under diplomatic pressure, the Brazilian government announced a 20

[32] Emilio Lahitte, "La industria harinera," in *Tercer censo nacional de la República Argentina*, Vol. VII, *Censo de las industrias* (1917), p. 498.
[33] *Anales de la Sociedad Rural*, 1899, p. 184.

per cent tariff reduction on United States flour in return for preferential treatment of Brazilian coffee. Still Argentine flour gained. By 1907 the United States product could find a market only in the northernmost ports of Brazil, where it was favored by transport cost. The roles had been reversed, for Argentina now exported almost five times as much flour to Brazil as did the United States.[34] Consequent pressure by the United States in 1910 further extended the tariff reduction on its flour to 30 per cent but without noticeable effect on the trade.

The problem of Argentine flour exports, meanwhile, had taken on another aspect which in the long run would prove decisive. Brazil as well as some European countries deliberately began to develop and encourage their own flour industries by the simple expedient of lowering tariff barriers on wheat and raising them on flour. This form of discrimination barred Argentina from expanding its own milling industry through the export trade. By 1903, 50 per cent of Brazilian needs were supplied by mills in São Paulo and Rio de Janeiro. Although the Argentine product, favored by low freight costs, continued to enter the Brazilian market, the milling interests of Río and São Paulo blocked any significant increase. Under such conditions, Argentine flour exports stabilized in the vicinity of 100,000 tons yearly—taken mostly by Brazil. In practical terms, therefore, the flour industry was largely restricted to the domestic market, which consumed approximately 700,000 tons a year. In growth, the development of the industry had paralleled that of wheat: from village economy, to the Santa Fe colonies, and finally to centralization in Buenos Aires. But in trade, flour, unable to overcome tariff barriers or the sometimes cheaper and better milling facilities of Europe, remained a home-consumed product.

The handling and marketing of the wheat crop stretched from the *chacra* to Europe. Within a decade Argentina became an important world producer and reaped enormous economic benefits from the wheat trade. But degenerate seed, rotten bags, mud huts, sweating stevedores, and dirty grain remained to cast their shadows over the country and to reflect the shortcomings of the Argentine landholding system, of the farmers who were attracted to Argentina, and of the attitude of a government and a people.

[34] *Review of the River Plate,* February 26, 1909, p. 575.

vii. GOVERNMENT POLICIES

Land, Immigration, and Tariffs

Government attitudes and policies had a crucial effect on late nineteenth-century Argentine economic development. The dominant liberal economic tenets discouraged any active direction or control of the economic structure by the government. National and provincial authorities did little to intervene in the booms of 1882–1889 and 1904–1912 or their subsequent depressions. Yet the tradition of authoritarianism and even paternalism reaching down from the colonial period did not allow the government to disavow its influence on the economic scene. Often the very lack of action or the failure to establish rules and procedures had as immediate an effect as the mercantilist regulations of a previous century or the exchange controls of a later generation.

Aspects of the Argentine attitude toward land have already been set forth in the preceding chapters. The public domain had traditionally been surrendered to private ownership before there was the remotest possibility of its utilization or occupancy. If any practical consideration underlay this action, it was that Argentina's future rested solely on its pastoral industries—the pampas occupied by vast herds of cattle, sheep, and horses, and few men.

Ever since the permanent settlement of Buenos Aires in 1580, land had represented the only disposable form of public wealth in the coastal area. First the Crown and later the early provincial and national governments had drawn upon this apparently inexhaustible reserve to reward officers, political leaders, and entrepreneurs. But the land itself had so little intrinsic value that the units, for grants or sale, had to be enormous. The smallest unit of the pastoral enonomy was the *suerte de estancia,* measuring almost seven square miles or forty-five hundred acres, equivalent economically to a few acres in an agricultural zone. In the eighteenth and early nineteenth century, the most optimistic carrying capacity of such a unit was nine hundred head of cattle, which in turn could be expected to produce ninety hides a year, a very insignificant income.[1] When to this was added the lack of transportation, the urban orientation of the Hispanic population, harassment by hostile Indians, and the backwardness of pastoral exploitation, only the owner of hundreds or even thousands of square miles could hope to survive economically. And let us recall that there was little incentive to settle these lands. At best, private owners populated them only with cattle and sheep.

Throughout the nineteenth century the pastoral orientation of Argentina's coastal economy continued to foster the transfer of huge chunks of the public domain, both within and beyond the Indian frontier, to private individuals. Only for a moment in the 1820's did Rivadavia's administration in Buenos Aires attempt to lease rather than to sell public lands. Such far-sighted proposals were promptly overturned by the frankly pastoral interests of the Rosas government, and although political authorities changed at mid-century, the land policy remained bound to pastoral traditions. Poverty and lack of revenues reinforced the attitude that public lands were to be used to secure funds or to reward politicians. It was no accident that the important political and military figures of these years were landowners such as the López family in Santa Fe, the Urquizas of Entre Ríos, the Taboadas of Santiago del Estero, the Rosas and Fernández families and the Anchorenas and Álzagas of Buenos Aires.

As Argentina's economy began to show signs of change in the 1860's, some protests against the reckless alienation of the public domain were heard. Yet despite the efforts of national presidents like Bartolomé Mitre, Domingo F. Sarmiento, and Nicolás Avellaneda or governors such as Patricio Cullen and Nicasio Oroño in Santa Fe to reverse the traditional land policies, few among the elite wanted to change practices which had brought them wealth and power and which promised even greater returns in the future. Indicative of this attitude was the unenthusiastic reception of agricultural immigrants and their relegation to marginal or frontier zones. Even with the experience of the Santa Fe colonies at hand, warnings that provincial governments must no longer squander their land reserves went un-

[1] Giberti, *Historia económica de la ganadería argentina,* p. 47.

heeded. Not until 1875 did a Minister of Interior send a circular to provincial authorities encouraging them to make lands available to immigrants. The response was significant: Mendoza and Corrientes— the only provinces to answer—set aside lands on their remote and unprotected Indian frontiers.[2]

The contemporary discussion in Buenos Aires concerning United States homestead legislation most clearly expressed the Argentine attitude toward land policies. Just as with colonization ventures, journalists and politicians applauded the idea in its theoretical aspects. The new Department of Agriculture published its first annual report in 1872 with this summary:

Among those measures adopted [in the United States] for the benefit not only of the immigrant but for those in even worse straits, the Homestead Law has given excellent results, bringing population into vast areas which only a few years ago were completely deserted. That law grants ownership of 160 acres (40 *squares*) to every citizen or prospective citizen for the insignificant cost of title registration. Such a measure applied to our situation and needs would undoubtedly bring the same beneficial results which are developing that great Republic of the North.[3]

Nine years later an article in the *Anales de la Sociedad Rural* went to great pains to point out that Argentina should be able to apply homestead legislation with even greater benefit than the United States since its lands were cheaper and closer to the cities.[4] And from that same journal: "Ownership of the land by the small proprietor is our present necessity, and it will become an essential in the very near future."[5] Yet advocating homestead legislation and applying it to the Argentine scene were quite different matters. When the national congress finally passed a "Homestead Act" in 1884, its provisions were limited to grazing lands south of the recently conquered frontier of the Negro River. Citizens could secure fifteen hundred acres if they occupied and made improvements on the land within five years. The legislation apparently aimed at transforming the vanishing gaucho into a landowner. But fifteen hundred acres was too small a unit to support sheep grazing on the barren Patagonian coast, and although the law was not repealed until the turn of the century, few applied for homestead concessions.

[2] *El Plata Industrial y Agrícola*, May 10, 1876, p. 9.
[3] *Informe de 1872*, p. lxvi.
[4] *Anales de la Sociedad Rural*, April 30, 1881, pp. 99–101.
[5] *Ibid.*, December 31, 1884, p. 585.

The best of intentions were repeatedly warped to fit the interests of Argentina's political and landholding elite. The first comprehensive national land legislation dated from October 1876.[6] On paper the law appeared a model of wisdom. It had been drafted under the supervision of President Avellaneda, a man who had written his law thesis on the subject of public-domain legislation and who had constantly demonstrated his concern for immigration and agriculture. National lands were divided into sections of one hundred thousand acres and further subdivided into lots of two hundred fifty acres. Eight lots in each section were reserved for a town and town lands. The first one hundred lots in each section were to be distributed free to immigrants, while the remainder were to be sold (a maximum of four lots per person) at a flat rate payable in installments over ten years. To handle administration the Office of Lands and Colonies was created under the Ministry of Interior. Since colonization, immigration, and the public domain were closely linked in the philosophy of the law, every facility was given to colonization projects. Provinces were encouraged to cede lands to the national government for colonization. Special provisions enabled private colonizing companies to select, survey, subdivide, and colonize lands on their own account. But speculators used these provisions, especially the last one, to make a mockery of the Avellaneda law. During its twenty-five years of existence, only fourteen of two hundred twenty-five colonizing companies that received land grants complied with the requirements for subdivision and settlement.[7] Typical was the attitude of one concessionaire who petitioned congress in 1889 that, in place of the two hundred fifty families he was supposed to have settled on his land, he be permitted to introduce some cattle.[8]

The Conquest of the Desert—Roca's military expedition against the pampean Indians in 1879–1880—doubled the size of the province of Buenos Aires and added vast areas to the national public domain south of the Negro River. This new-found territorial wealth was disposed of in the traditional manner: sold or granted to established

[6] The classical work on land legislation still is Miguel A. Cárcano, *Evolución histórica del régimen de la tierra pública, 1810–1916.* Valuable summaries are also contained in Ramón M. Bóveda, *Legislación rural argentina,* and José P. Podestá, "La pequeña propiedad rural en la República Argentina," in *Investigaciones de seminario de la facultad de ciencias económicas de la Universidad de Buenos Aires,* III (1923), 3–144.

[7] Argentina, Ministerio de agricultura, *Memoria, 1901–1902,* p. 86.

[8] *El Diario,* September 26, 1889, p. 1.

landowners or speculators in huge lots for the mere pittance that it was worth at that moment. Bonds redeemable in public lands within five years underwrote much of the military cost of the expedition. As surveying advanced with the frontier, the holders of these bonds chose their lots, at the cost of one bond or four hundred silver pesos per square league—almost ten square miles. When lands were offered in public auction in November 1882, each buyer was theoretically limited to one hundred thousand acres, currently worth only a few centavos an acre, but speculators used agents or fictitious names to circumvent even this limit.[9] The economic boom of 1882–1889 merely speeded alienation of the public domain. Commercial groups in Buenos Aires, foreign investors, and speculative interests acquired enormous tracts of land not only on the pampas but also in Patagonia, Misiones, and the Chaco. By 1903, when congress finally passed comprehensive and effective land legislation to classify the public domain as to grazing, farming, or forest use and to provide for its systematic rental or sale, the damage had been done. The whole area of the pampas had long since passed into private hands, to be held for speculation, investment, or prestige—but not to be owned by those who cultivated the land.

By the end of the century it was beyond the power of national authorities or the coastal provinces to create a land policy suited to the needs of the immigrant or the small farmer. The governments no longer possessed lands in the agricultural zones. At the same time, agricultural and improved pastoral techniques now made the pampas valuable. The landowner was unwilling, at least at the price which a poor immigrant could amortize, to part with any of his large holdings. Subdivisions of estates did occur in the early twentieth century in response to the continued rise of land prices. But such subdivisions merely created smaller holdings to be bought by city men, by investors and speculators, and to be rented to the agriculturist. The rise of the tenant farmer was the direct heritage of these traditional land policies.

The graveyard of abortive land laws was as significant as the laws actually sanctioned. The political power of the Argentine landowner had, if anything, expanded since the days of Rosas and Urquiza, and his interests were immediately aroused whenever congress or the politicians ventured into the land problem. Even that enlightened body of cattlemen, the Sociedad Rural, closed ranks against proposals by President Sarmiento to expropriate and distribute lands suitable for agriculture. Legislation to make small lots available for farmers from provincial public lands died an equally swift death in the Buenos Aires legislature in 1875. Not until 1887 did that pastoral-minded province, in a law of Centros Agrícolas, take the agriculturist into consideration. And even then those who benefited from the law were not the farmers but the landowners. Its provisions permitted the owner to secure credit from the official banks on the promise to subdivide and colonize a portion of his lands. Very few landowners actually established the promised colonies. Bad faith, difficulties in execution, and the depression accounted for the all-too-frequent scene painted by a British traveler in the early 1890's:

> This same spot I had noted down as one of the places on which a large advance had been made by a Mortgage Bank under the Centro Agrícola law. I examined carefully the site of the supposed agricultural centre, and the portion allotted to the township, of which I had seen a very fine survey on paper before leaving Buenos Aires. The result of my investigations was to discover here and there a few pegs in the ground that had been placed there when the land was surveyed, but beyond this no sign was visible of any endeavour having been made to carry out the conditions on which the money had been advanced.[10]

The British minister in Argentina concluded: "The principle of the law and the advantages it offers are undisputable. Unfortunately, it served as a means to obtain money under false pretenses. The history of these agricultural centres is a history of fraud, false statements, over-valuation, and non-fulfilment of contract."[11]

During the 1890's, when the value of the immigrant and of agriculture to Argentina had already been clearly proved, congress, provincial legislatures, and newspapers debated how to utilize the rapidly vanishing agricultural portion of the public domain. A profusion of ideas, pamphlets, and speeches resulted, but no practical measures emerged from the torrents of eloquence. A project to recast and

[10] Akers, *Argentine, Patagonian and Chilian Sketches*, p. 59. Also see Buenos Aires, Province of, *Memoria del Ministerio de obras públicas, 1894–1895*, pp. xi–xvi, for further comments on the failure of this law.

[11] *Sessional Papers*, 1895, Vol. 102, p. 34, Reports on Subjects of General and Commercial Interest, Miscellaneous Series, No. 369, "Report on the Agricultural and Pastoral Condition and Prospects of the Argentine Republic."

strengthen the provisions of the 1876 Avellaneda law was introduced in congress in 1896 only to be defeated after long discussion. Rejected even more quickly was a proposal to place a progressive tax on idle or unexploited tracts of land of more than twenty-five thousand acres.

The efforts of the national government to establish farmers on public lands were few and universally unhappy and helped to bring almost total repudiation of official colonization measures. Legislation in 1875–1876 permitted provinces to turn over colonies or colonizing lands to the national authorities. Depressed economic conditions in Argentina in those years caused several marginal colonies—General Alvear and Villa Libertad in Entre Ríos and Sampacho and Caroya in Córdoba—to pass to the vague supervision of authorities in Buenos Aires. Official colonization, however, even under the 1876 Avellaneda law, was largely restricted to the national territories and little affected the agricultural or wheat zone. This very remoteness permitted the Office of Lands and Colonies in Buenos Aires to amass for itself a monumental reputation for red tape and corruption. In 1899 the *Review of the River Plate* exposed the unsavory activities of certain bureaucrats and politicians:

> In theory, any new settler can get a grant of land, and if he were to go to the land office, and find an official who spoke his language, he would be greatly impressed with the liberality of the Argentine government. But when he came to test this liberality in practice, his opinions might undergo a most disagreeable modification. After wasting an incredible amount of time and patience, he would probably take advice from some friend, and buy or acquire land from some private holder rather than hang about the government office to no purpose. We know, as a matter of fact, that it has required two or three years to obtain from the government the right to rent land for which there was no competition and this although the services of an agent learned in government *trámites* [bureaucratic procedures] have been employed.[12]

These conditions grew steadily worse until scandal exploded in October 1910. A full-scale parliamentary investigation revealed that the bureaucrats in the Office of Lands and Colonies had neutralized whatever small benefits national laws might provide for the immigrant or farmer. The primary concern of the officeholders had been to continue the tradition of transferring huge concessions of the public domain to private ownership and at the same time fill their

---

[12] *Review of the River Plate*, June 17, 1899, p. 7.

own pockets. Typical was the case of the German-Argentine Society, which had requested six thousand square leagues, or thirty-seven million acres, in the southern territory of Santa Cruz. At first the petition had been brusquely denied. Then the usual intermediary appeared, in this case an intimate associate of President Figueroa Alcorta, and informed the company that everything could be arranged for the slight consideration of one hundred thousand pesos.[13] The only immediate benefit of the scandal for the small farmer was the creation of regional land-offices in the territories, in La Pampa, Río Negro, Neuquén, Chubut, Santa Cruz, and Misiones. He still needed to use an intermediary but at least he did not have to rely on one in far-distant Buenos Aires.

The agricultural immigrant and the small farmer thus found little encouragement in Argentine land policies and legislation. Land was the country's basic wealth, but the incompetence of governments and the rapacity of politicians and speculators had turned this potential over to private ownership when it was practically valueless. The majority of landowners assumed a passive role toward their possessions and often left them totally abandoned. They waited for the government to remove the Indian menace, for British capital to construct railroads, for Irish or English managers to build up their pastoral stock, for Italian sharecroppers to harvest crops. Their wait was hugely rewarded, for the value of their enormous estates climbed from several pesos per square mile to values counted in the hundreds of thousands, or even millions, of pesos within half a century. By the time agriculture had proven the value of these lands, the agriculturist could not afford ownership. There were honorable exceptions to this tradition of unproductive landed aristocrats: farsighted leaders of the pastoral industry clustered in the Sociedad Rural; conscientious leaders in government; dedicated men in commerce and journalism. But it was the nation's loss that these men were unable to impose their views in time and that instead economic evolution rewarded the owners of huge, unoccupied expanses on a distant frontier.

Immigration policies in Argentina evolved as did land policy: under the impact of rapid economic development and the impossibility of imposing long-range measures on a liberal, *laissez-faire* economy. Just as there had been no end of publicists and statesmen to point out that a nation of small landowners would mean prosperity

---

[13] *Ibid.*, November 25, 1910, pp. 1369, 1411.

and democracy, so there were legions who preached the necessity of immigrants to fill the empty wastes and dilute the barbarism of the Argentine interior. All politicians after the fall of Rosas at mid-century accepted this need as axiomatic. Yet practical efforts to attract immigration lagged far behind the ideals, the projects, and the oratory.

The modern era of Argentine immigration, a cultural revolution of the coastal area, began in 1870 (Table 1). Prior to that date there had been a steady flow of individual Europeans into Buenos Aires, the abortive colonizing ventures of Rivadavia, and the Swiss establishments in Santa Fe, but the immigrant had failed to fill the wastelands. By mid-century nearly 45 per cent of the inhabitants in the port of Buenos Aires were foreigners, and there was a sprinkling of foreigners in other coastal cities. But anarchy, insecurity of life and property, hatred of the gringo, lack of economic opportunities, and loneliness all served to keep the foreigner who ventured to the Argentine shore in or near the city of Buenos Aires, where those disadvantages, if not completely absent, were at a minimum.

Compared with previous decades the 1870's favored immigration. The end of the Paraguayan War, increasing trade, rising foreign investments in railroads, commerce, industry, and lands, and consolidation of a national government under Buenos Aires' hegemony all tended to attract a small part of the flood of emigrants pouring out of Europe to the United States and to Australia.

Argentina, nevertheless, failed to direct or stimulate immigration during this decade, and the country had to await the economic boom of 1882–1889 before the composition of the coastal provinces began to change radically. Immigration agents in Europe were increased from five in 1869 to thirteen in 1870 to twenty in 1871. Few were of the caliber, however, of the colonizer Beck-Bernard, who had returned as agent to Switzerland. Most of them succumbed to a system that rewarded them according to the number of immigrants they supplied. In this they were admirably assisted by the Italian, Spanish, and English governments, which were only too glad to subsidize the export of their undesirables.[14] Argentina, for several years, became a dumping ground for beggars and cripples. A report to the British Foreign Office stated that the net effect of immigration policies had

[14] *La Nación*, January 6 and 14, and December 25, 1872, p. 1.

been to transfer the dregs of the large Italian cities to the streets of Buenos Aires.[15]

There was no official agency responsible for immigration, although general supervision fell upon the Minister of Interior. A board of private citizens, first appointed as an immigration commission in 1863, struggled valiantly with the myriad problems. Its reports repeatedly emphasized the danger of permitting new arrivals to remain in the cities, encouraged the establishment of immigrant hotels in provincial centers, argued for free transportation of immigrants to agricultural colonies, and pleaded for a homestead law. Yet the commission could make no headway even on the simple question of the reception of immigrants. Indigent arrivals were put up for one week in the Immigrant Asylum, a filthy, unventilated horsebarn, located in the very center of Buenos Aires on Calle Corrientes. Then they were turned out to crowd the city's slums and *conventillos*. Repeated proposals for a new asylum were rejected by the government, and charity proved insufficient to make up for the official negligence: when the commission appealed to 900 leading *porteños* for contributions, it was able to add only 100 names to its former list of 100 subscribers.[16] During the severe cholera outbreak of 1871, national authorities failed to provide medical or quarantine facilities for arriving immigrants. At the end of 1873, ten years after its establishment, the commission resigned, unable to stir the government into action despite the impending arrival of 15,000 European immigrants and the threat of a second cholera epidemic. At the same time, repercussions of the world crisis of 1873 spread to the area of the Río de la Plata, and the balance between immigration and emigration figures dropped from 58,000 in 1873 to 16,000 in 1875, 17,000 in 1876, and 18,000 in 1877. With little official direction or assistance to put them on the land, immigrants stagnated in Buenos Aires and eked out a meager existence as fruit vendors, bootblacks, porters, or beggars.

The economic boom of the eighties provided the impetus for immigration that the Argentine government had previously been unsuccessful in supplying. Labor was needed to build railroads and houses, to load trains and ships, to work in industry, to harvest crops.

[15] "The Condition of Industrial Classes, and Emigration to the Argentine Republic," Phipps, enclosure from Macdonell to Earl Granville, July 15, 1871, *loc. cit.*

[16] *La Nación*, August 4, 1870, p. 1.

The Labor Office, which had been founded in 1872 as the government's only concession to the immigrant problem, raised the percentage of immigrants placed outside the city of Buenos Aires from 10 per cent in the early seventies to 40 per cent by 1889.[17] Until 1888 annual government expenditure on immigration remained the same as in the 1870's. Yet the balance of immigrants over emigrants climbed from 28,000 in 1878 to 43,000 in 1882, 79,000 in 1886, and 107,000 in 1887. In the last two years of the boom—1888 and 1889—the national government succumbed to the enthusiastic demand for more and more laborers and spent 5,500,000 pesos for 125,000 prepaid passages.[18] Immigration responded and reached a net of 220,000 in 1889.

The decade of the eighties added 846,000 immigrants to the population and the 1895 census showed one-quarter of Argentina's 4,000,000 inhabitants to be foreign-born. Immigration in the 1890's did not compare, however, with the previous decade of economic boom. In the crisis year of 1890 the yearly balance dropped to 30,000, and the following year showed a net outflow of 30,000. Wages lagged far behind the cost of food and shelter. By 1895 real wages had declined almost 50 per cent from those of the previous decade.[19] Although, as we have seen in Chapter iii, these conditions did not curtail agricultural and wheat expansion, the high cost of living in the coastal cities did reduce net immigration to a yearly average of 50,000. Letters from established residents and newspaper reports turned many a prospective immigrant in Italy, Spain, and England away from the Río de la Plata area and helped to account for twelve times as much immigration to the United States as to Argentina.

During the slack period of the 1890's, Jews provided an important and unique addition to the immigrant and agricultural scene. In 1891 Baron Maurice Hirsch had founded the Jewish Colonization Association, a philanthropic institution to provide emigration possibilities for Russian Jews. With the substantial capital of £ 2,000,000 and the decision to concentrate efforts on agricultural colonies in Argentina, the association introduced paternal protection and guidance totally lacking in private, company, or official immigration schemes. Colonies were systematically planned and established in Santa Fe,

[17] Calculated from statistics in Juan A. Alsina, *Población, tierras y producción,* p. 48.
[18] Juan A. Alsina, "Inmigración—Colonias," in *Segundo censo de la República Argentina de 1895,* I, 649.
[19] *Review of the River Plate,* August 3, 1895, pp. 5–6.

Entre Ríos, and Buenos Aires. The prospective colonist received land to be purchased in installments over twenty years. He secured all advances of equipment, seeds, and food; rented threshing equipment; made all purchases and sold all crops through the association. In many cases supervision extended to instruction of what and when to plant. Rather than entangle themselves with Argentine law courts, all civil disputes were settled by a board of arbiters in Paris. In a decade 17,000 Russian Jews entered Argentina, the great majority under the auspices of the association, and were settled on the land. The creation of such culturally isolated communities in the Argentine countryside was severely criticized in the national press. But in view of the abject poverty of these colonists and their total ignorance of agricultural matters, the paternal guidance of the association was a blessing not only for them but also for Argentina.

Even after the turn of the century immigration figures lagged behind the expectations and hopes of Argentine authorities. The Argentine bureaucrat, businessman, or landowner, especially those of immigrant origins themselves, welcomed the European peasant as a necessary tool to build Argentina's economic greatness. Yet they could develop little feeling or understanding for the dirty, ragged, illiterate, and apparently stupid masses that poured off the ships. All projects, discussions, and legislation relating to immigrants amply reflected this spirit. In 1896 congress seriously debated, and the *Anales de la Sociedad Rural* publicized, a prize of twenty thousand pesos for the design of a ship which could carry live cattle on its European run and immigrants on its return.[20] In 1903 the fear of anarchist agitation caused congress to pass a Foreigners' Residence Law, which provided for the arbitrary expulsion of any gringo displeasing to the authorities. The fact that the small agriculturist had to content himself with tenancy rather than ownership, the heavy and inequitable taxation of small properties, the lawlessness of rural authorities (further explored in Chapter ix), all were a further reflection of national attitudes. Since the immigrant's primary motivation in coming to Argentina was economic gain, such attitudes did not discourage new arrivals in prosperous times. But during periods of crisis or of moderate development, net immigration figures reflected the European awareness of greater opportunities in Brazil, Canada, Australia, or the United States, and resentment against restrictive measures such as the Residence Law.

[20] *La Agricultura*, August 20, 1896, p. 620.

A second economic boom lasting from 1904 to 1912 revived Argentine immigration. Its effect on net immigration was almost twice that of the expansion in the eighties. In the decade 1904–1913, more than 1,500,000 Europeans were added to the population, and by the 1914 census nearly a third of Argentina's 8,000,000 inhabitants had been born overseas. Once again, however, the national authorities had little influence on this tide of European labor. In 1898 an Immigration Office, under the newly established Ministry of Agriculture, had taken over the duties of the former Labor Office. Handling of the harvest influx of *golondrinas* was streamlined: laborers, landed from the ships in the morning, were quickly processed and before the day was over had been loaded into boxcars or flatcars for the free and relatively short ride to the wheat fields. The Immigration Office also administered the Immigrants' Hotel, served as a clearing house for employment opportunities, and routed new arrivals to jobs throughout the country. But despite the admirable work of its director, Juan Alsina, which made the Immigration Office the most efficient department in the government, basic attitudes toward immigrants changed little. Even the construction of a new and badly needed Immigrants' Hotel in Buenos Aires had to wait until 1910—a full five years after congress had given its approval. Plans for a similar hotel in Rosario were repeatedly postponed, and the only reason Bahía Blanca secured one was that a private citizen, Ricardo Rosas, built it at his personal expense and turned it over to the Immigration Office in 1911.[21] Economic depression starting in 1913 and the outbreak of the First World War cut immigration to one-half and then one-quarter of the boom's record figures, and for two years the recall of Italian reservists contributed to a net loss of more than 60,000 annually.

As frequently happens in countries formed by immigration, the foreigner at first remained outside the national culture. During much of the nineteenth century, foreign citizenship and even the vague protection of a foreign flag were distinct advantages, eagerly sought after and retained. Immigrants came to make money, to work, not to become embroiled in the local scene. Transiency reinforced this aloofness. Few immigrants came to Argentina with any intention of remaining there. Even those who were not *golondrinas* hoped to make a small fortune and at the end of several years return to their homeland.

In terms of religion, language, dress, and food, the largest immi-

[21] *Review of the River Plate,* November 10, 1911, p. 1241.

grant groups—the Italian and Spanish—had little cultural adaptation to make. Indeed, the Italians eventually changed Argentine habits: added macaroni, spaghetti, and vermicelli to the national cuisine; put Italian expressions and words in the spoken language; created *lunfardo,* a dialect of the slums and underworld of Buenos Aires; and revolutionized urban architecture. Yet in the cities the foreigners, the Italian and Spaniard as well as the Frenchman, German, and Englishman, formed their own groups, clubs, schools, had their own newspapers. They clustered together with their countrymen in the *conventillos* or appropriated certain sections for their own. La Boca, the port area on the south side of Buenos Aires, became a wholly Italian district. British merchants and businessmen turned Hurlingham, a suburb to the west of Buenos Aires, and Belgrano to the north, into English villages. Basques, Catalans, Italians, and French united in mutual-aid societies. The Germans, British, Spanish, and French each had their own hospitals to care for their nationals. Germans and British maintained their own school systems, albeit under the remote control of the Ministry of Education. Swiss shooting clubs, German singing clubs, Garibaldi Associations were found in all the major coastal cities. By the end of the century, each major immigrant group had at least one daily newspaper.

Strong as the self-isolation of these foreign groups was, it melted with the second generation—the immigrants' children who grew up on Argentine soil. At least in the cities the educational system fostered assimilation. After 1896 all school instruction had to be given in Spanish, and even in the Swiss or German colonies the spectacle of Argentine children unable to speak a word of Spanish quickly disappeared. Still more effective was the psychological need of these second-generation Europeans to prove themselves more Argentine and more nationalistic than the established Argentines. Considered citizens by the fact of their birth in the country, they violently rejected anything that threatened their claim to unadulterated "Argentinism." Often they refused to speak their parents' tongue. They shed all cultural traits that could link them to the foreigner. Since the parents had usually arrived penniless and illiterate, the children were not educated to appreciate European traditions. Only those who had economic and cultural security assured—such as English and German technicians, managers, or merchants—could maintain cultural isolation through ensuing generations and create a separate community like that of the Anglo-Argentines. However, it was not these small, aloof groups that built modern Argentina, but the children of Italians and Spaniards attracted by the economic booms of the 1880's and the 1900's. When these generations reached maturity in the government posts, the legislatures, the schools and universities of the 1920's, 1930's, and 1940's, they in turn imposed new values of nationalism on the country.

In the countryside the immigrant could not form a cultural or social group with his countrymen as he had in the city. Most of the colonies were economic ventures and only occasionally, as with the early Santa Fe colonies or the Jewish Colonization Association, did they provide religious and cultural unity. Extensive tenant farming did not permit even accidental unity or contact. The very isolation and transiency of the agricultural immigrant's life retarded his assimilation into the national culture, not because he formed groups outside that culture but because he himself was so remote. Schools and the cult of patriotism often did not reach his children, and the violent embracing of Argentine nationalism so evident in the urban second-generation Europeans was not apparent in rural districts.

In view of the immigrants' tendency to hold on to European origins, it is not surprising that few became Argentine citizens. For this, the national authorities were also responsible. If anything, the foreigner was rewarded for remaining one: "In no country in the world does the foreigner enjoy more personal liberty than in Argentina. He comes and goes, establishes his business, buys land, forms his home, enjoys all the freedom that an Argentine possesses, and more, for he has not to serve in the National Guard, nor to fulfil a single civic duty."[22] In some provinces, notably Buenos Aires, the foreigner could even vote in municipal elections. The procedure for becoming an Argentine citizen was simple enough. It required no more than a few years' residence and a declaration to that effect before a local justice of the peace. Yet rather than making the acquisition of citizenship desirable enough to strive for and placing some handicap on those who remained foreigners, Argentine politicians argued that the process of naturalization must be made still easier. A project in 1895 would have automatically naturalized all foreigners with ten years' residence in the country unless they took deliberate action to maintain their foreign citizenship. Another in 1904 suggested lowering this residence period to five years, and still another in 1908 proposed only two years if the foreigner was married to an Argentine. That

[22] *Ibid.*, July 24, 1897, pp. 4–5.

lawmakers did not have to concern themselves more with this problem was due to the fact that children of these immigrants soon outdid long-established Argentines in the expression of nationalist sentiments.

During the nineteenth century, government policy with regard to tariffs was never clearly defined. It appeared that public authorities, unwilling to intervene or to direct economic development, responded only to the immediate demands of well-organized and powerful pressure groups.

Local industries in the interior provinces had long advocated tariff barriers to protect their products. The concept of protectionism, however, was not applied to the Argentine tariff structure until the 1870's and then only in limited measure. Prior to that decade, tariffs had been levied for revenue and had indeed provided most of the income for provincial and national governments. Until 1869 a flat 18 per cent ad valorem had been charged on imports and 6 per cent on exports; in that year the mounting costs of the Paraguayan War forced an addition of 5 per cent and 2 per cent, respectively. Then in 1870, 20 per cent was established as a standard import duty; a second category of 25 per cent was levied on alcoholic beverages and tobacco; and two remaining categories—10 per cent and free—were provided for goods considered essential to the national welfare.

As Argentina approached self-sufficiency in wheat and flour, protectionist advocates supported tariff barriers to stimulate production of those items. A proposed customs-union with Chile foundered on the suspicion that it was designed to flood the Argentine market with cheap Chilean wheat and flour.[23] In September 1875, Carlos Pellegrini introduced in congress a tariff measure to protect wheat and flour. After sharp debate the suggested 40 per cent ad valorem charge was replaced by an equally stiff charge of 4 silver pesos per hundred kilos of flour and 1.60 pesos per hundred kilos of wheat.[24] At the same time, export of these items was encouraged by placing them on the free list. Only after Argentina became a major exporter of wheat was protection removed: for wheat in 1891 and for flour in 1893.[25]

[23] La Nación, January 18, 1871, p. 1.
[24] Argentina, Cámara de diputados, Diario de sesiones de 1875, II, 1123–1140, passim.
[25] Argentina, División de comercio del Ministerio de agricultura, Cuadro sinóptico de la ley de aduana en los años 1883 a 1906 (Buenos Aires, 1906), pp. 22–23, 36–37. Technically wheat and flour were not placed on the free list until

Although wheat production was undoubtedly encouraged by protection in the 1870's and 1880's, tariffs eventually worked to the detriment of agriculture. A new tariff law was enacted each year near the
close of the congressional session. Immediate needs for revenue and
pressures from organized industries rather than any over-all policy for
economic development determined rates. Thus several Tucumán
landowners who controlled the sugar mills were able to exact protection which made sugar one of the most high-priced items of daily
consumption and protected it not only from the competitive West
Indian but even from the closer Brazilian product. The grape and
wine industry of Mendoza enjoyed equally high protection from
European competition. The pastoral industries secured some recip-
rocal trade benefits and the favorable admittance of materials necessary for the elaboration of their products. As a result, the difficulties
that Argentine flour encountered in the Brazilian market first grew
out of resentment toward Argentine barriers against tobacco, *yerba
mate*, and sugar, and only subsequently from the development of the
Brazilian flour industry. Likewise French tariffs against Argentine
wheat and corn not only sought to protect French production but also
to retaliate against Argentine taxation of French sugar and wines.[26]

The effectiveness of organized pressure on congress was even more
striking in the protection afforded certain industries in the city of
Buenos Aires. Meat-salting and meat-packing plants, flour mills,
washing and baling plants for wool obviously needed no protection.
But there were in addition a vast number of small factories that had
begun to emerge during the rapid economic growth of the 1880's: dis-
tilleries and breweries; industries to produce food products such as
biscuits, preserves, candy, and macaroni; and plants to assemble items

---

1913. The specific duties were removed, but they were not listed as free articles
and consequently fell under an over-all coverage of 27 per cent ad valorem. The
question did not arise until 1913, when Argentina wished to take advantage of
recent United States legislation granting free admittance of wheat, corn, flour,
and semolina (used for making macaroni and similar edible pastes) from countries levying no duties on those products. A study of the Argentine legislation
by the Commerce Department in Washington, D.C., revealed the discrepancy.
Congress hastily amended the Argentine tariff provisions and specifically placed
those products on the free list.
    [26] Francisco Seeber, "Argentina, Canadá, Australia. Lecciones de progreso
comparado. Inferioridad relativa de la Argentina," *Anales de la Sociedad Rural,*
1908, pp. 97–101; Emilio Frers, *El prohibicionismo y la política comercial argentina. Cartas de un hombre de estado.*

manufactured abroad. These factories had a very active interest in protection, for often tariffs provided the sole basis for their survival. There was, as a result, a concentration of lobbying pressure on congress which the vastly more important but unorganized agricultural interests of the country could not match. A case in point has already been noted: the bag industry, which gave employment to some two thousand workers stitching together imported, precut pieces of burlap with imported twine. Despite the annual outcry from wheat-growers at the high cost of these "Argentine" bags and the protests of exporters against the consequent use of the poorest and most rotten bags, congress continued for years to protect this artificial industry. An investigation and report, highly unfavorable to the bagging companies, made by the chief of the commercial section of the Ministry of Agriculture in 1905 had little effect against the organized interests of the industry. As mentioned earlier, legislation to permit free entry of foreign bags when domestic prices rose above a certain level was frustrated by collusion among the companies: prices were merely kept down until it was too late for imports to reach Argentina by harvest time. How profitable these arrangements were, was amply shown by the 15 and 25 per cent dividends annually declared by the two largest bag companies.[27] Almost identical was the case of the galvanized iron industry. Ordinary iron sheets were imported and then corrugated and galvanized in Argentina. A 25 per cent ad valorem duty protected the so-called "Argentine" product. Although sheeting became a vital item in restricting the ravages of locusts and also in providing roofing for sheds and ranchos throughout the littoral, agricultural interests were once again subordinated to the more immediate pressures of a small local industry.

An examination of the broad policies toward land, immigrants, and tariffs shows that the Argentine government had little lasting or effective interest in the country's agricultural development. It had failed to adopt a rational land policy before the usable public domain passed into private hands. It had failed to stimulate immigration beyond that which naturally resulted from the economic booms of 1882–1889 and 1904–1912. It had failed to provide attraction or opportunity for the immigrant to settle on the land. And by its tariff policy it had favored other agricultural products and even pseudo-

[27] *Review of the River Plate,* October 18, 1912, p. 977.

industrial products to the direct detriment of wheat and flour. In this, the national authorities followed the general attitude of the landowner and pastoral interests. Agriculturists and immigrants were accepted as servants to build Argentina's greatness. They were not, however, primary concerns of the nation.

viii. GOVERNMENT POLICIES: *Agriculture*

The same indifference toward agricultural matters that permeated government policies and the attitudes of pastoral groups applied to questions directly related to agriculture. Public employees and agronomists, many of them truly devoted to the improvement of Argentine potential, struggled against monumental indifference toward their department, their ministry, or their activities. The official accomplishments in the field of agriculture emerged, as in the case of Juan Alsina in the Immigration Office, as the fruit of heroic personal endeavors rather than of government policy.

The creation of a separate division under the Ministry of Interior to take care of agricultural and pastoral matters was proposed in congress in 1870. The following year a formal project was introduced and passed, and a Department of Agriculture came into existence at the beginning of 1872. Ernest Oldendorff, the first director, and his four employees faced a virgin field. Any government action in Argentina's major economic pursuits was a novel concept. The founding decree had vaguely indicated that statistics might be useful, but the sole requirement had been that an annual memorandum of accomplishments be presented. Oldendorff, a man of imagination, immediately launched an extensive correspondence with the provinces, attempted, with very scattered results, to collect statistics of areas sown and production, and established his office as a clearing house for seeds and for information on agricultural techniques and machinery. Good relations were fostered with the Sociedad Rural, the recently established association of the country's most progressive cattlemen. In order to disseminate information and arouse interest in the Department's work, Oldendorff started publication in early 1873 of the *Anales de Agricultura,* a semiofficial bulletin appearing twice monthly.

Whatever headway might have been made was cut short as the depression of 1873 spread to the Río de la Plata area. The *Anales* collapsed when the government subsidy was withdrawn in 1875. Only its spirit was kept alive for the next two years by *El Plata Industrial y Agrícola,* which printed agricultural bulletins and correspondence. The Department's budget was cut by two-thirds, and at the same time the duties of the government's statistical office were assigned to Agriculture.[1]

In early 1877 Oldendorff resigned, leaving his secretary, Julio Victorica, in charge of a depleted department temporarily merged with the Immigration Office. The Department of Agriculture continued to receive an insignificant allotment of the budget, an amount "which the average man of means would spend on the care of his *quinta* [suburban home and garden]."[2] Thus hamstrung, the Department was unable to undertake any of its projects such as employing secretaries to collect information in the provinces or inspectors to investigate agricultural resources and techniques. Offices consisted of a cramped room in the Port Authority building. Victorica bitterly pointed to the difference between his annual budget of 9,000 pesos and the equivalent of 600,000 spent each year by the single state of Victoria in Australia.[3] Yet with the help of two or three clerks he attempted to distribute seeds and to arouse an interest in the Department's potential. In January 1878, he brought out the first number of a *Boletín mensual,* soon to become the *Boletín del departamento nacional de agricultura.*

Difficult times did not end with the booming eighties, but in 1881 Victorica moved his department to a new building and acquired several more employees. A 300 per cent increase in his budget enabled him to contract for an occasional foreign agronomist, to secure seeds for distribution, and to buy a small printing press. He was even able to revive a neglected experimental garden in the Tres de Febrero Park in Buenos Aires. The *Boletín* reflected this expansion. Its initial run of 500 copies had grown to 2,000 by 1884, and it boasted 752 paid subscribers. Nevertheless, the shortcomings were serious. Five major needs for any scientific study of agriculture—a chemical laboratory,

---

[1] Argentina, Departamento de agricultura, *Informe de 1876,* pp. xxxvi–xli.
[2] *El Economista,* December 15, 1878, p. 553.
[3] *Boletín del departamento nacional de agricultura,* 1879, pp. 222–224.

a library, a veterinary clinic, a meteorological station, and an entomology division—were completely lacking. Salaries were so low that only a combination of extreme patriotism and independent means permitted anyone to work for the Department.[4] The dangers of such official penuriousness were amply demonstrated when a national crisis almost occurred as a result of the ravages of plant lice (phylloxera) in the vineyards of Mendoza. The Department had no means to combat or even to study the plague.[5]

During the rapid agricultural expansion of the 1890's, the Department's poverty became even more glaring. The 1890 depression brought about austerities in government, and Agriculture had no powerful financial, commercial, bureaucratic, or military friends to protect its appropriations. The work of the experimental garden in Buenos Aires was paralyzed by a lack of funds. Plans for an agricultural museum had to be shelved. The library possessed only a few hundred out-dated volumes. The personnel, in addition to its director, consisted of a secretary, two agronomists, a gardener, a bookkeeper, three clerks, and two office boys. The annual budget of 9,000 pesos contrasted sharply with the equivalent of 1,950,000 spent in the United States, 2,850,000 in Germany, 4,000,000 in Austria, or 8,000,000 in France.[6] Even its administrative position, long under the Ministry of Interior, was jeopardized as ministry after ministry sought to rid itself of the headaches and heartaches of agriculture. It was merged with the Office of Lands and Colonies in 1892. Then in 1893 it was assigned to the Ministry of Finance—because lands and agriculture were closely connected to financial matters—and within a fortnight transferred to Foreign Relations—because it was so closely connected with immigration. It finally came to rest at the end of the same year in that catchall of Argentine ministries: Justice, Education, and Religion.

In the late 1890's the rising importance of agricultural products among exports and the live-cattle trade, now threatened by British and Continental regulation, won a begrudging acknowledgment in government circles. In 1896 a botanist, a veterinarian, and another agronomist were added to the Department's staff in Buenos Aires. And for each of the five experimental stations in the provinces—ex-

---

[4] *Boletín del departamento nacional de agricultura*, 1888, pp. 538–542.

[5] *La Nación*, February 1, 1890, p. 1.

[6] Gustavo Niederlein, "Reorganización del departamento nacional de agricultura," *Boletín del departamento nacional de agricultura*, 1891, pp. 97–100.

istent little more than on paper—an agronomist, a foreman, and four peons were assigned.

Two years later, with President Roca's expansion of the cabinet to eight posts, agriculture was raised to ministerial level. The United States minister, William I. Buchanan, who had been intimately connected with agricultural affairs in his own country, played an important role in convincing Argentine authorities of the wisdom of this change.[7] At least an administrative organization replaced the merges and shifts which had dominated agricultural matters previously. Four offices were opened within the Ministry: Commerce and Industry, Lands and Colonies, Agriculture and Livestock, and Immigration. Six subdivisions shared agricultural duties: scientific, including chemistry and meteorology; livestock and veterinary science; agronomy; zoology and entomology; agricultural education; and agricultural statistics and rural economics.[8] Emilio Frers, a prominent figure in the Sociedad Rural, was selected to preside over the auspicious beginnings of the new Ministry.

In less than a year Frers had resigned in a dispute over currency matters. The newspapers were filled with proposals to abolish the Ministry in the interest of economy.[9] Only after considerable delay did the Argentine minister to Washington, Martín García Merou, succumb to Roca's personal pressure and accept the post. The parade of ministers had only started. Within a year he also resigned after his complaints against protective tariffs and inadequate financial resources brought no response from the government. Ezequiel Ramos Mexía, president of the Sociedad Rural, was the next appointment, but despite his popularity with the livestock interests he lasted a bare six months. His successor, Wenceslao Escalante, though unconnected with agricultural or pastoral affairs, was an excellent financier. But he was able to accomplish little in the Ministry of Agriculture since he was simultaneously called upon to fill the exacting post of Minister of Interior. Indeed, it was not until the second term of Ramos Mexía from 1905 to 1907 and the appointment of Pedro Ezcurra from 1907 to 1910 that the Ministry enjoyed any continuous policy or supervision.

The political failure to provide systematic leadership for the new Ministry was further irritated by the continuing shortage of funds.

[7] *Review of the River Plate*, June 17, 1899, p. 7.
[8] This structure was altered slightly by decree, February 6, 1900, when meteorology was created as a separate subdivision and zoology and entomology passed under the scientific subdivision.
[9] *Anales de la Sociedad Rural*, 1899, pp. 255–258.

Each time the budget was brought up for discussion by the cabinet, there was an acrimonious exchange between the Ministers of Finance and Agriculture, quite often followed by the latter's resignation. As Escalante pointed out in his *Memoria* for 1901–1902:

It is absolutely impossible with the meager resources allotted to provide any effective stimulation for agriculture, livestock, colonization, or immigration; to carry out the survey and alienation of public lands; and to supervise agricultural schools, rural economics, the various industries, mining activities, and commerce, which are the responsibility of this Ministry according to its organic law.

The parsimony in allocation of funds and personnel which has been characteristic of the national budgets over the years reveals a total lack of comprehension or awareness of the transcendental importance of agriculture to the welfare of the nation.[10]

Agriculture's budget, which in round figures amounted to 1,700,000 paper pesos in 1899, had been gradually forced up to 2,800,000 by 1903. A request that year for an increase to 6,000,000 brought compromise—at 4,000,000. During the period from 1899 to 1910, Agriculture's share of the national budget fluctuated between 2 and 3 per cent. It remained one of the most poorly supported ministries, and its allocation contrasted sharply with the 20 per cent average spent on military appropriations. Characteristic of its plight was the situation created in 1906 when congress deliberately delayed approval of the budget for several months. The Ministry completely ran out of funds: publication of the statistical bulletin was suspended; payment of salaries was postponed; and the two most essential projects—the antilocust campaign and hoof-and-mouth inspection—had to be financed by emergency measures.

The general disinterest in agricultural affairs was logically reflected in the annual message of the president to congress. Whole chapters would be devoted to Interior, Foreign Affairs, Justice, Public Instruction, Armed Forces, Public Works, and Finance, but agricultural and pastoral matters were fortunate to receive a few sentences. Typical was Figueroa Alcorta's 1910 message in which he referred briefly to irrigation projects, railroad extensions, imports of seeds and implements, and added the erroneous statement that the import of pedigreed animals had increased. Even when unusual energy such as that of Eleodoro Lobos, another prominent figure of the Sociedad Rural

[10] Argentina, Ministerio de agricultura, *Memoria, 1901–1902*, pp. 4–5.

who occupied the Ministry in 1910 and 1911, forced a multitude of agricultural bills on congress, the projects were lost in committee, tabled, or held over for another session. In mid-1913, the Minister of Agriculture sent to congress an urgent bill that would have authorized the government to purchase burlap bags and sell them at cost to the farmers. Congress took no action, while local bag importers and manufacturers, fearing such competition, suspended their orders. Then, despite the reluctant sky-high prices of bagging and the forecast of a huge harvest, congress did not even include the matter on its agenda for the extraordinary session.

In the face of such political and national attitudes, the work which the Department—later the Ministry—of Agriculture did accomplish was all the more amazing. Within areas directly related to wheat cultivation, it engaged in several programs or projects to help the wheatgrower. Repeatedly during regional harvest failures it advanced seed to farmers. Within its very limited means it attempted to encourage the extension of credit to farmers and to build up among the farmers themselves the spirit of cooperatives. It attempted, once more against enormous handicaps, to collect statistics, establish crop forecasts, and raise standards of yield and export. It actively developed an antilocust campaign which at least managed to contain if not eradicate the plague. It established and expanded a modest program of agricultural education. And it provided the farmer with his only political advocate in the years when the *estancieros* had the Sociedad Rural and the manufacturers had their lobbying forces to represent them at court.

Structured as wheat cultivation was on a system whereby the wheatgrower supplied labor and implements but had to borrow everything else against the promise of a good harvest, the loss of a harvest seriously strained the lines of credit. The rural storekeeper had little choice but to carry the debt over for another year. The landowner would usually permit the agriculturist to try his luck again. But few were willing to send good money after bad by advancing seed to the farmer. In the early days of colonization, the company or provincial government often supplied a new stock of seed and food. With the spread of tenant farming, however, the wheatgrower lost even that limited support. As wheat production increased, losses also grew. Provincial governments could no longer meet disasters which wiped out production on thousands or hundreds of thousands of acres. Now the only resort was the national government.

At the end of 1896, with the third disastrous harvest in a row, a special commission came from Santa Fe to petition congress for help. The politicians in Buenos Aires responded with a four-million-peso grant for seed purchases and two projects to loosen bank credits. Part of these appropriations was used to mend political fences, for Santa Fe faced a gubernatorial election in early 1897 and a presidential election was in the offing. For a while the seed funds were even "lost" somewhere between the national government and the provincial authorities. Locally appointed committees in Santa Fe, Entre Ríos, and Córdoba reduced graft and waste, and soon the main criticism was merely that the supply of seed was insufficient to meet the demand of all the farmers. Additional funds answered that complaint in mid-1897, just before the planting season ended. Recipients of seed signed I O U's due the next harvest season, and by March 1898, nine thousand out of the eleven thousand advances had been repaid. The next appeal came from the flooded province of Buenos Aires in late 1900. Land taxes were suspended for three months and payment of land rents was postponed. An extension of the same disaster struck Entre Ríos, and three thousand tons of wheat seed was distributed among colonists who signed I O U's at 7 per cent interest on the Banco de la Nación. Again in 1902 Santa Fe and Entre Ríos were hard hit, and the national government opened small credits for the advance of wheat seed to farmers in the stricken areas. Thus the aid continued: dribbles which tided the farmer over to his hope in a new harvest, always extended as an advance to be repaid, and too frequently characterized by delay, red tape, and corruption. But at least the Ministry of Agriculture made an effort to provide the wheatgrower with seed for his next crop.

In the larger sphere of financial credit, the Ministry of Agriculture was less successful in helping the farmer. As seen in Chapter vi, the wheatgrower had no access to the banking structure. He relied on a credit system which extended from the *chacra* to the local storekeeper to the large commercial or export house in the ports. The agricultural banks which blossomed throughout the littoral in the 1880's and 1900's catered to the large, reputable landowner. As Emilio Lahitte, director of Statistics and Rural Economics in the Ministry and one of Argentina's leading agricultural crusaders, reported in 1907:

I have taken special pains to consult with the managers of branch and local banks in all the rural centers, and all of them without exception have told me that they are very careful not to make any loans to an agriculturist unless he is a landowner or businessman of well-established standing; it is too risky, they say, to lend to farmers or even to colonizing enterprises, when they have no other security to offer than the promise of a harvest, however bountiful it may be.[11]

When congress, in 1897, approved seed credits, it also appropriated six million pesos in mortgage bonds and opened the reserve of the Banco de la Nación for agricultural credits. No one, except a few politicians, came forward to receive the proffered aid.[12] Banks could not extend loans on conditions which the farmer could accept. The Banco de la Nación required a colonist—if ever he penetrated its august portals—to present two guarantors in order to secure the maximum credit available to him: a renewable ninety-day note. The charge was 8 per cent interest with a 10 per cent amortization rate. Banks could not afford to consider social benefits or long-range economic growth in their calculations. All too typical of this credit structure were cases such as that of a small Russian colony near Paraná, Entre Ríos, whose lands were sold at public auction in 1901 by the Banco Hipotecario Nacional when amortization and interest payments could not be met because of crop failure.

It was not until 1913, however, that Emilio Frers, the first Minister of Agriculture and now a congressman, introduced a project for a government agricultural bank. The proposal embodied long-term loans to farmers repayable in installments. The probability that the institution would be a "poor man's" bank was ruled out by the lack of a top limit on the amount of individual loans. Even under such conditions, congress demonstrated its customary indifference to agricultural matters. Although the measure reappeared the following year with government sponsorship, it met with no success and was finally crowded off the agenda by the Chamber of Deputies in 1916.

The cooperative, an institution whose success depended on the farmers themselves, was hardly more effective in meeting credit problems. The spirit of cooperation was notably weak among Argentine farmers. Their peasant origins gave them little experience or tradition in cooperatives. Ignorance, illiteracy, transiency, and isolation further

[11] Emilio Lahitte, *La situación agrícola. Sociedades cooperativas*, p. 8.
[12] *El Diario*, January 31, 1897, p. 1; *Review of the River Plate*, March 13, 1897, p. 17.

hampered the development of any cooperative movement in Argentina. And the very structure of wheat growing encouraged extensive one-man gambles. Indeed, the spread of cooperatives was limited to a few colonies: the first, an agricultural company in the Welsh colony of Chubut on the Patagonian coast in 1885; a hail-insurance company in the French colony of Pigüé in 1898; a farmer group in the Jewish colony of Lucienville near Basavilbaso, Entre Ríos, in 1900; and in 1904 several small colonist ventures in Entre Ríos, a second hail-insurance company at Juárez, and a mixed cooperative at Junín in Buenos Aires.

The Ministry of Agriculture, primarily under Lahitte's prodding, attempted to stimulate the cooperative movement. An agent was sent to Europe to study cooperatives in France and Belgium and their application to the Argentine scene. Circulars and a mass of propaganda went out to all correspondents of the Ministry in the provinces with full details on the organization and functions of cooperatives. During the prosperous harvest years of 1904 to 1907, informal groups of farmers began to club together to purchase machinery and equipment directly from the United States or England. In the Bahía Blanca area a few cooperatives undertook to cut out the grain agents and *acopiadores* from wheat transactions. But the movement did not prosper. Decamping treasurers forced a number of cooperatives out of existence. The constant shifting of the tenant farmer made membership and organization difficult. In a study on agricultural credit in 1912 Lahitte had to admit: "There is much talk of cooperatives in the rural centers; it is an idea which has aroused interest, but there is no definite purpose or orientation of this potentially powerful agent of rural credit."[13] Although government files showed sixty cooperatives in existence in 1912, investigation revealed that only thirty were in actual operation and their combined capital amounted to only five million pesos.

The total lack of agricultural statistics had been a prime reason for establishing the Department of Agriculture in 1872. Prior to 1870 there were no import-export statistics for the whole country. There existed only the vaguest ideas of areas sown and harvested, and there was no concept of forecasting labor and transportation needs or production estimates. With four employees and a budget that would barely keep a *quinta* in operation, the first director, Oldendorff, did what he could: he asked the provincial governments to supply sta-

[13] Emilio Lahitte, *Crédito agrícola,* p. 57.

tistics, hoping that their response would enable him to arrive at some estimate of the total area sown to wheat. The result was only a guess, rarely an educated one, by officials seated in some provincial capital. Entre Ríos, La Rioja, Catamarca, and Jujuy did not even submit replies. Only two provinces—Tucumán and Santiago del Estero—attempted to make a complete report on agricultural and pastoral production. The others submitted scattered fragments of information: Buenos Aires gave figures from several of its better-organized and better-surveyed districts; Córdoba and Salta left out entire departments; San Luis reported only on livestock.[14] With regard to wheat, few provinces even attempted a guess at total production. Yet from that survey emerged the first national estimate of total area sown—325,000 acres in 1873. Two years later the Department was able to estimate the production of the four wheat provinces at slightly over 75,000 tons.[15]

Oldendorff's hope for engaging agricultural secretaries to travel through the provinces and collect crop statistics was frustrated by the budget cuts of the mid-1870's, and any complete picture of Argentine agricultural production was postponed for more than a decade. In 1882 Victorica sent out a statistical questionnaire to the Department's honorary correspondents in the provinces, but the response was so meager that it did not even warrant publication. Only from Santa Fe was the *Boletín* able to secure fairly consistent reports of areas sown and harvested. But even here wide discrepancies often cropped up between these figures and those published in the *Anales de la Sociedad Rural*, in special reports on the colonies, or in provincial publications. Indifference, sloppy transcription, and careless proofreading often made a jumble of even reliable figures.[16]

During the eighties a growing concern with statistics began to fill a few of the gaps in the wheat picture. Santa Fe published a provincial census in 1887. Figures on area and production for 1884, and consistently after 1887, appeared in the *Anuario estadístico de Entre Ríos*. A few scattered estimates were included in a similar publication in Buenos Aires as well as in that province's censuses of 1881 and 1888. Yet not until 1891 did an annual estimate of total Argentine

[14] Argentina, Departamento de agricultura, *Informe de 1873*, pp. 299–301.
[15] *Ibid., Informe de 1875*, passim.
[16] Even the Department of Agriculture was guilty of these faults, as shown by the *Boletín del departamento nacional de agricultura*, 1888, pp. 182–183.

area and production emerge from the Department, and it was almost another decade before this estimate was broken down on a provincial basis.

A second national census in 1895 added impetus to the improvement of statistics. The work of Francisco Latzina, director of the National Department of Statistics, Alberto Martínez, head of the Statistical Office of the city of Buenos Aires, and Ricardo Pillado, head of the Commercial Section of the Ministry of Agriculture, raised standards and accuracy. In agricultural statistics, however, most of the credit was due to Lahitte, who introduced some accuracy into the relative guesswork of wheat figures. All threshing-machine operators received official booklets in which they were required to enter total areas harvested and quantities threshed from each *chacra;* a provincial tax paid on the machines was the only element of control over these reports. Lahitte himself was the first to admit the possibility for error even in this system:

. . . [the problems] can be judged by the following entries: a harvest of 300,000 kilos [11,000 bushels] from 4 hectares [10 acres]; one of 60,000 kilos from 10 hectares; and another which indicates 2,000 kilos from 40 hectares.

The majority of the threshers have failed to note the total area sown, and the figures have often been registered without any notion of accuracy.

In Santa Fe, the *quintal* [one hundred kilos] has often been confused with the kilo, and in many booklets it has been discovered that entries have been made without the slightest notion of their arithmetic value.[17]

In 1907, despite improved procedures and checks added to the system, he again complained: "The erroneous preoccupation of many of the threshers that the figures they supply will be used as a basis for taxation makes many of them refuse to fill out the booklets or causes them to record completely inaccurate figures . . ."[18] Yet the contrast with the methods used to secure the first estimate of 1873 showed how far agricultural statistics had advanced.

Rarely did the various compilers of statistics agree exactly in their results. Even in the relatively uncomplicated field of exports, some discrepancy was still evident in the 1900's. The year 1904, for example, registered:

[17] Argentina, Ministerio de agricultura, *Memoria, 1898,* p. 122.
[18] *Boletín del Ministerio de agricultura,* July-August 1907, p. 101.

National Statistics Department	2,304,724 tons
Ministry of Agriculture	2,341,884
Comtelburo Company (private agency)	2,345,544
Times of Argentina (shipping organ)	2,247,331
Review of the River Plate	2,405,117

In the vaguer realms of area and production, the range between national, provincial, and private figures varied from 20 to 30 per cent. By 1910, however, the Ministry's estimates, based on reports from some three thousand voluntary correspondents in the cereal zone, the threshing returns, and the constant checking and inspection by agronomists, were probably as reliable as those of any world wheat producer.[19]

Accurate forecasting of production was one of the goals that inspired the collection of agricultural statistics. A major service of the *Boletín,* despite its spotty sources, had been to estimate annually the expected harvest from Santa Fe and Entre Ríos. When the Ministry of Agriculture was formed in 1898, Lahitte took over this work, heading a special subdivision with increased personnel. Within a year the division started to publish the *Boletín mensual de estadística agrícola.* This and other special reports by the Ministry were watched with increasing interest in the wheat markets of the world, for they provided fairly reliable estimates of the crop situation at critical stages of its development. In 1910 Lahitte's division began to issue three official forecasts each year: one in September or October based on area sown; one in December with modifications caused by the growing season; and one in February or March as the harvest ended.

The problems arising from lack of classifications or standards in Argentine wheat have already been noted in Chapter vi. Although these conditions frequently depreciated the reputation of Argentine wheat abroad, the government proved unwilling to involve itself in commercial questions. An early decree of the Ministry of Agriculture did establish an inspection service at the major grain ports to place its stamp of approval on good-quality shipments. Such limited and purely voluntary inspection did not flourish, however, in a trade which was soon to be controlled by the major grain exporters. To European buyers, the seal of quality was the reputation of Bunge y Born or some other firm whose name had meaning, not the unknown standards of an Argentine grain inspector.

On the other hand, plagues, especially the locust, did furnish the

[19] *Review of the River Plate,* May 13, 1900, p. 1165.

government with an extensive area for action. Because of financial duress, early steps taken by the Department to combat locusts were restricted to printing an occasional news item on a current invasion in the *Anales, El Plata Industrial y Agrícola,* or the *Boletín.* Then, during the eighties, locusts mysteriously disappeared from the scene. But in 1890 the invasions recommenced in Santa Fe and Entre Ríos with renewed vigor. A provincial decree in Santa Fe that year established local commissions to supervise and coordinate efforts for eradication. Budgetary difficulties connected with the depression limited the Department of Agriculture to reprinting an article first published in its *Boletín* in 1878 entitled "The Natural History of the Locust and Methods of Destroying It" and to lamenting:

It is in moments such as this that the failure to provide this department with proper elements to undertake effective and prompt action on behalf of agriculturists is most disturbing. This office should have been established so that from the very first moment of the locusts' appearance it could have put into effect a well-coordinated plan of action combining the efforts of the government and of the citizenry.[20]

The following year, 1891, the government did take a few steps, limited largely to paper shuffling. A law at the end of August authorized the president to take joint action with the provinces to check the locust advance. A national committee, composed of Estanislao Zeballos, current president of the Sociedad Rural, Nicasio Oroño, director of Lands and Colonies, and Victorica, was appointed to coordinate activities, and a vague decree was issued ordering the destruction of the locusts. In 1892 the federal government extended some slight financial assistance to the provinces, characterized by one critic as ". . . as miserable . . . and unavailing as trying to extinguish a fire with a penny squirt."[21]

Such a state of affairs continued without effective national or provincial action until the alarming 1896 invasion, when locusts literally crawled down the necks of legislators sitting in Buenos Aires. Government measures then were at least extensive if not effective. One of the Department's agronomists was immediately dispatched to Santa Fe with fifty thousand pesos and authority to use national troops in the eradication work. Congress voted an appropriation of four million pesos for the campaign. The panicky decrees of the Santa Fe govern-

20 *Boletín del departamento nacional de agricultura,* 1890, p. 672.
21 *Review of the River Plate,* November 24, 1892, p. 9.

ment verged on the ridiculous: one ordered every citizen to bring in ten kilos (twenty-two pounds) of locust eggs; another required colonists to drop everything—just as the harvest season was beginning—and exterminate locusts. Another perennial problem was that government funds, both national and provincial, often found their way into pockets far removed from the locust area. *La Nación* noted the distribution of funds to provinces where locusts had not even appeared.[22]

A committee of grain merchants, fed up with official procrastination, set about looking for a scientific answer to combat the locust invasions. With the assistance of the United States minister, the committee secured the services of Lawrence Bruner, an entomologist with extensive experience in Canada, the United States, and Mexico. Despite a year of study, soon supplemented by the services of Jules d'Herculais, a government entomologist brought from Europe, no simple answer, such as parasites or disease, could be found to undermine the locust.

Although additional legislation in 1897 authorized the president to take all necessary measures to wipe out the plague and ordered everyone in the afflicted areas to participate in the campaign, official and public interest flagged as soon as there was a relaxation in the invasions. With the damp seasons and floods of 1899 and 1900 eggs rotted in the ground, reducing the numbers of locusts. Even in conscientious circles, questions about the wisdom of an all-out campaign began to be heard. The *estancieros* observed, with considerable justice, that eliminating the locust in a land as vast and unoccupied as Argentina, was an idle dream. After all, the plague did relatively little damage to pasture, except for alfalfa, and did not harm the cattle. In most years the wheat and flax crops reached maturity before the most dangerous stage—the hoppers—developed. Corn, therefore, was the only product seriously endangered. Its survival could rest on intensive cultivation and cooperation among farmers to ward off the hoppers by the only effective defense yet found—corrugated metal sheeting placed around the fields.[23]

Thus the campaigns continued, carried out by local committees with occasional appropriations from provincial and national governments. In 1901 the national committee was abolished and supervisory responsibility was assigned to the Agriculture and Livestock Section

[22] *La Nación,* January 31, 1897, p. 4.
[23] *Review of the River Plate,* February 18, and March 4, 1899, p. 5.

of the Ministry of Agriculture. Renewed agitation finally caused the Sociedad Rural and the Ministry of Agriculture to sponsor an agricultural conference in 1906, and from those sessions emerged recommendations subsequently embodied in a government decree. Comisión de la Defensa Agrícola, an autonomous, semiofficial body, was created to centralize the work of the local committees. The principal issue was how to keep politics and corruption from neutralizing the battle against the locusts. The grain trade led by Dreyfus forced the 1906 committee to resign under accusation of using funds for political purposes. Supposedly apolitical committees in 1907 and 1908, made up of leading merchants and railroad managers, attempted to remedy these difficulties. But the vastness of the work, the substantial funds now amounting to ten million pesos a year, the incompetence and overbearance of local officials, and the infatuation with bureaucracy continued to provide targets for a critical press.[24] Then when a dispute with the government over appropriations resulted in the committee's resignation in 1909, the national authorities merely refrained from appointing a new committee and its duties were taken over by a functionary in the Ministry of Agriculture. In a decade, administration of the antilocust campaign had come full circle and in 1910 officially passed to the control of the Ministry. From the political, commercial, and scientific wrangles, metal sheeting emerged as the only practical defense against hoppers; annual government purchases alone amounted to 12,500 miles of it. Thus, despite the politicians, the locust problem was held within bounds.

Bureaucracy and inefficiency frequently hampered efforts to combat other agricultural plagues. A general law in 1905 gave the president authority to take action against any plague or parasite and placed an obligation on the citizenry to cooperate in reporting and combating such plagues. The purpose was to free the government from the necessity of referring each and every occurrence of disease or parasite to congress before taking action. The authorization, however, did not seem to speed up the government's measures. A case in point was the hares of Santa Fe, Buenos Aires, and La Pampa. Having declared the hares a pest, the government took no further action to eradicate them. A project appeared in congress in 1908 to pay a bounty of ten centavos for each hareskin, but it met the fate of most

[24] *La Prensa*, October 21 (p. 5), 23 (p. 5), 24 (p. 9), 25 (pp. 7–8), 26 (p. 6), 1907; letter from an unidentified Santa Fe *estanciero* in *Review of the River Plate*, January 17, 1907, pp. 161–162.

agricultural projects. Newspapers sarcastically suggested that the new conscript army should be turned loose for target practice. Slightly more effective were the small demands of a local rabbit cannery and local hat manufacturers. Yet despite the petitions and complaints of farmers, the hares multiplied with no interference from the Ministry of Agriculture.

In a country where the general level of instruction of wheatgrowers was so pitifully low and where techniques of agriculture were virtually ignored, agricultural education would seem to have provided great possibilities. Nevertheless, higher institutes of agricultural science, practical agricultural schools, experimental farms and stations, foreign technical help, publications, expositions, and competitions suffered from the familiar shortcomings of lack of interest, funds, and continuity.

The experience of Santa Catalina in the province of Buenos Aires was indicative of the problems of formal agricultural education. The germ of an agricultural school had emerged in the provincial legislature in 1868 with prodding from Eduardo Olivera, one of the founders of the Sociedad Rural. Not until two years later were school lands (twenty-five hundred acres) secured at Santa Catalina, twelve miles south of Buenos Aires. Delay followed delay, but finally in September 1874 the school officially opened its doors. The visions of grandeur evoked on the floor of the Buenos Aires legislature had faded by now. Funds, enthusiasm, even students were lacking. Some old ruins had been patched up to serve as dormitories, a few fences had been put up, and two-thirds of the land rented out to provide a meager income. Twenty boys, aged thirteen to seventeen, were drafted from the provincial orphanage to form the first student body.[25] Two years later only two or three students remained, and the ambitious institute closed. In 1878 it reopened as a practical school for gardeners but again met with no success. The booming eighties provided a renewal of enthusiasm and, more important, of funds. In 1883 the Instituto Agronómico Veterinario de Santa Catalina was installed. A new two-story building housed seventeen students and under energetic direction enrollment rose to eighty by the second year. A school magazine, *La Revista Agrícola y Veterinaria,* made its appearance at the end of 1884, and two years later emerged under the more imposing title *Anales del Instituto.* The first class of eight students, most of

[25] Argentina, Departamento de agricultura, *Informe de 1874,* pp. 154–157; *Anales de Agricultura,* October 1, 1874, p. 183.

whom would leave their mark on the nation's agriculture as agronomists in the Department of Agriculture or the Ministry of Agriculture, was graduated in 1888. Finally, in 1890, the institute was raised to the rank of a faculty and transferred to La Plata. But the depression curtailed this expansion and not until 1906 was the faculty incorporated into the University of La Plata.

The national government was as negligent as that of Buenos Aires in supporting agricultural studies. In 1870 congress authorized the teaching of agronomy in the national secondary schools of Mendoza, Tucumán, and Salta. In the latter two provinces, programs never progressed beyond the planning stage. Only in Mendoza did the viticulture subdivision finally produce a graduating class after seven years and innumerable difficulties. In 1881 the Department of Agriculture assumed control over the only two national establishments for teaching or research: the viticulture school of Mendoza and the experimental garden in the Tres de Febrero Park of Buenos Aires. But there were no funds for their expansion or even successful utilization. Two experts were brought from France in the eighties to improve the vineyards of Mendoza, and a few Argentines were sent abroad on government grants to study agriculture in Belgium and Italy. The crisis in 1890 ended even these limited measures.

The budget of 1896 permitted the Department for the first time to make plans for agricultural stations. In cooperation with provincial governments, stations were immediately established in Entre Ríos and Córdoba and plans were drawn up for additional ones in Santa Fe and Corrientes. Officials in these stations quickly developed the more ambitious idea of turning them into agricultural schools. By 1903 two agricultural schools—in Casilda, Santa Fe, and in Córdoba —had an enrollment of ninety students, and another ninety students were scattered among the country's six "primary" experimental stations. Not to be outdone by the Buenos Aires government, the national authorities established the Instituto Superior de Agronomía y Veterinaria at Chacarita in the city of Buenos Aires in 1904, a forerunner of the agronomy faculty of the University of Buenos Aires. But a total absence of realistic planning, the tendency to rush headlong into exaggerated programs and to abandon them just as quickly when enrollment or interest lagged, and the lack of trained personnel within the country seriously hampered any national educational system.[26]

[26] "¿Porqué no progresan las escuelas de agricultura en el país?" *Anales de la Sociedad Rural*, June 30, 1904, p. 250.

In an effort to create a system out of chaos, a council on agricultural education was appointed at the end of 1907 to draw up an overall program. A subdivision of the Ministry assumed direction of rural education. Some schools reverted to experimental stations, although the Ministry admitted to a constant struggle with directors: "The agricultural army boasts many chiefs and officers, but there is a total absence of those who are willing to work with the masses."[27] Others became mere technical schools. Below the university level, secondary instruction was concentrated in three schools, Escuela de Vinicultura of Mendoza, Escuela de Agricultura y Ganadería at Córdoba, and Escuela de Arboricultura y Sacaritécnica in Tucumán. For a brief moment, it even appeared that there would be funds to make such a reorganization meaningful. Then the 1914 depression cut back budgets "until the allotments for institutions of agricultural education have reached a level where further operations are virtually impossible."[28] Yet even when rational measures could not be implemented, there was no end of ambitious or fanciful projects: a program of traveling professorships to carry instruction to the farms, or the creation of zones of technical education with inspectors to spread knowledge of the latest methods of cultivation and to establish cooperatives.

In the wider field of informal education, the very vastness of the problems conspired to defeat all efforts. The ignorance of the farmers, their poverty, their lack of any intellectual horizon, a system of land tenure which largely shut out hope of advancement, and poor communications combined with the forbidding distances in rural areas, all served to isolate them from the few sources of instruction available. The various *Boletines* and *Anales* hardly ever reached such an audience. The *Anales de la Sociedad Rural*, with its occasional treatise on wheat cultivation, commented in 1872: "We will not deny that an occasional large-scale wheat farmer will become excited when he stumbles onto a report on sowing, plowing, or threshing; but it is also undeniable that the benefits which the *chacareros* of San Isidro or even Chivilcoy derive from this journal is the same as if the *Anales* were published on the planet Uranus."[29] The early Rural Expositions of Buenos Aires in 1858 and 1859, after passing out a

[27] Argentina, Ministerio de agricultura, *Memoria, 1905–1907*, p. 96.
[28] Tomás Amadeo, *La enseñanza y la experimentación agrícolas en la República Argentina*, p. 11.
[29] "El desarrollo de la agricultura," *Anales de la Sociedad Rural*, December 31, 1872, p. 391.

few silver medals for wheat samples, had admitted to the same difficulties:

> If the Exposition is to serve as a school and a stimulus to agriculturists and is to provide the benefits which its efforts deserve, then the mass of farmers must not be excluded. One can be sure that out of every hundred, hardly ten know how to read, and even if the notice of the Exposition reaches them, an honorary prize without monetary value will certainly not stimulate their brains or their efforts to better production.[30]

Competitions and expositions continued to bypass the mass of farmers. A progressive Córdoba law in 1883 established agricultural prizes but required a minimum of from two hundred to three hundred cultivated acres for entry, at a time when the majority of farmers cultivated a maximum of ninety acres. In 1886 an International Rural Exposition, held in Buenos Aires under the auspices of the Sociedad Rural, brought forth the following participation: "In the first section, *cereals*, two samples of wheat, one of barley and one of corn submitted by a lone entry from the province of San Juan, and one of barley and one of corn from the province of Buenos Aires."[31] And that was all! The Sociedad Rural, which had with such excellent results undertaken to improve the pastoral industries since its first livestock show in 1875, attempted to infuse some of the same spirit into its first Agricultural Exhibition in 1903. But even the *Anales* had to admit that although such exhibitions were very important, they had none of the color or interest of the cattle shows. And it must be added that it was not the small tenant farmer or colonist, so desperately in need of encouragement and stimulation, who participated in these exhibitions, but rather the established, educated, and prosperous landowner. The government hardly did any better. In 1902 the Ministry of Agriculture established four wheat regions with the munificent amounts of one hundred, fifty, and thirty pesos as prizes for the best samples grown in each region. Such hollow honorary incentives could hardly be expected to affect, let alone break down, the extensive farming practices of Argentina's conservative and materialistic tenant farmers.

The shortcomings of the Department of Agriculture or the Ministry of Agriculture were no reflection on those agronomists and public

---

[30] *Exposición agrícola-rural argentina de 1859* (Buenos Aires, 1859), p. 25.
[31] *Boletín del departamento nacional de agricultura*, 1886, p. 300.

servants who labored to arouse a self-interested bureaucracy and an indifferent nation to an awareness of Argentina's rural potential. The problems of rural credit and cooperatives, statistics, antilocust campaigns, and agricultural education were vast and in some cases insoluble. The principal conclusion which emerges from an examination of government policy toward agriculture is that Argentina as a nation was not concerned with the condition of farming or of farmers. The wealth which wheat growing had brought the country was accepted in the same way as the wild cattle or the rich soil—a factor of the economy which needed or deserved no official attention. A few conscientious men, starting with Oldendorff, Victorica, Alsina, and Lahitte, struggled to improve the farmer's position in agriculture and in the nation. They provided, in the Department and the Ministry and in their publications, the agriculturist's only spokesman. But they could not change the thinking and attitudes of a nation. The *laissez-faire* spirit, pastoral industries, and commercial interests still dominated Argentina.

ix. POLITICAL IMPLICATIONS

The preceding chapters have indicated that the agriculturist in Argentina rarely possessed political power or influence. Only the large landowner with agricultural interests had any organization or lobby to represent him. The Sociedad Rural, though primarily a livestock organization, did have a peripheral concern with farming and was often consulted by the government on rural measures. From within the Sociedad Rural there emerged in 1900 a Sindicato de Consumos Agrícolas to speak specifically on farm issues. In 1892, certain large landowners and businessmen had formed the Sociedad Agraria to protect their mutual interests in a manner similar to the Sociedad Rural. These groups, however, were landowner organizations. They did not represent, and had little concern with, the colonist, tenant farmer, or rural laborer.

For many years, the small agriculturist was apolitical. Isolation, illiteracy, and transiency made political organization or action difficult, if not impossible. The agricultural immigrant tended to cling to his original nationality and to avoid entanglement in the treacherous and incomprehensible field of local politics. His main desire was to be left alone. By origin he was fearful of those in authority. He had come to Argentina to attain a material objective—to make enough money to buy a farm, to establish himself in a town or city, or to return to his homeland with a profit—not to reform or change the political structure.

As a result the farmer was remarkably unsuccessful in making his needs felt or in assuming any civic role in Argentina. The rare occasions when he did express himself were largely the result of a momentary reaction against unjust measures or taxation and lacked the continuity and force to create any permanent organization or interest. Such were the movements centered in the colonies of Santa Fe in the 1890's. A spontaneous agricultural congress convened in Esperanza in 1892 to discuss rural problems. After a week of conferences it dissolved without taking any action or providing for subsequent congresses. The following year the recently formed Radical Party (Unión Cívica Radical), an urban middle-class and professional movement, staged a military revolt against the national authorities in Buenos Aires and Santa Fe. The Radicals successfully enlisted the agriculturists' support, not because the farmers understood, or were even interested in, the political issues or personalities involved but because they were outraged at the corruption of rural authorities and at recent acts of Santa Fe's provincial government: the right of foreigners to vote in municipal elections had been withdrawn and a provincial cereal tax had been levied on farmers. The Swiss and German colonists consequently took up arms to overthrow the incumbents, and a unit of one hundred Swiss sharpshooters from Esperanza distinguished itself in a skirmish outside the city of Santa Fe, much to the discomfiture of the government forces. Although the Radical revolt was snuffed out within a month, the colonist centers of Santa Fe remained strongholds of Radical opposition, not, it is worth repeating, because of sympathy or understanding for this urban reform-movement but because of resistance to the existing provincial government. When the provincial governor attended a ceremony for the laying of a hospital cornerstone in Esperanza in 1895, "Hotels and shops were closed, no coaches were to be obtained for the party, and the whole function was gone through without the assistance or presence of any Esperancinos."[1]

The first successful organization of farmer sentiment falls outside the scope of this study. The so-called "Agrarian Problem" of 1912 was nothing more than the result of accumulated difficulties from bad harvests and excessive land rents.[2] But the problems were aggravated by the ensuing depression and served to consolidate the position of a farm organization, the Federación Agraria. Typical of areas where the land had become valuable and where too many tenants competed for holdings were the conditions described at Alcorta, Santa Fe:

The colonists [tenants] are paying the proprietor 33 per cent of the crop with selected grain, threshed, placed in bags and delivered at the

---

[1] *Review of the River Plate*, June 15, 1895, p. 29.
[2] Details of this movement are given in Plácido Grela, *El grito de Alcorta. Historia de la rebelión campesina de 1912.*

railway station; they are only allowed to thresh their crops with machines provided by the landlord, buy their bags from him, and unless with his consent cannot sell their crops to third parties but must sell it to him; they are only allowed 10 per cent of the camp rentage for pasturage purposes and they have to pay for this $30 [30 pesos] per square per year, and if they require more pasturage land they have to pay double the price. All their provisions have to be obtained from the store indicated by the owner. Of the four pigs which they are allowed to have, one has to be given to the owner; he making his own selection and with the guarantee that it shall not weigh less than 120 kilos. The colonists now demand that the rent be reduced to 25 per cent of the crop, and that they shall only deliver same at the foot of the thresher, ready bagged and of export type; that they may be allowed to sell their crop to whom they please giving preference to the owner under similar conditions, and that he has to receive same eight days after threshing. Liberty to buy bags where they please, and also all their store goods, and that they be given 6 per cent of the camp without charge for pasturage purposes.[3]

The farmers resorted to strikes and refused to plow or plant until rents were reduced. The representative of some of these farmers, a Rosario lawyer named Francisco Netri, organized the Federación Agraria to give unity to the movement. Initially the strikes were limited to the corn-growing areas of northern Buenos Aires, Santa Fe, and Córdoba, where, despite the higher yield of corn, rents could no longer be met. By 1913, high labor costs and further crop failures encouraged the movement to spread to the predominantly wheat-growing regions of southern Buenos Aires and La Pampa. Yet despite the Federación's call for a general strike in March 1913, most contracts were settled on an individual basis between tenants and landowners. The wheat failure of 1914 and the return of much land to pastoral use during the First World War encouraged many agriculturists to migrate to the cities and momentarily alleviated the "Agrarian Problem." The Federación Agraria remained, however, as an expression of farmer sentiment. And during the 1920's, with a new generation of immigrants' sons, the Federación and its newspaper, *La Tierra*, would provide the stimulus for political action and for some agrarian reform.

The attitude and actions of provincial authorities toward the agriculturist were yet another indication of the farmer's lack of political power or influence. If the national government had done little to

[3] *Review of the River Plate*, July 5, 1912, p. 15.

help the farmer, the provincial governments rarely hesitated to hound him with petty officialdom, to tax him, and even to persecute him.

The fiscal policy was probably the most irritating. All Argentine governments, especially those of towns and provinces, were constantly hard pressed for funds to maintain their expanding bureaucracy. There were few sources that could be taxed without arousing resentment and threatening the stability of the government itself. Thus when industrious colonists and tenant farmers—gringos without political influence or ambition—began to make profits from land which previously had only pastured scrawny cattle, the cupidity of local authorities was immediately aroused. Here, for once, was a source of income that could be tapped without fear of retribution. Municipal governments placed onerous demands on the farmer. Local taxes on produce, farm carts and animals, and on machinery added a burden which amounted at times to 12 per cent of the farm's gross produce.[4]

Nominal provincial *guías*, or taxes, had long been collected on pastoral products transported from one locality to another. This form of taxation had also been applied to cereals at the railroad stations. Then in 1891 Santa Fe, promptly followed by Entre Ríos, imposed a more severe tax on cereals: a charge of ten centavos on every hundred kilos of wheat or linseed produced. In Santa Fe the tax was sold for a lump sum to a local politician. Theoretically the tax was to be collected on the farm, but tax agents soon discovered that it was healthier not even to venture into the colonies. Consequently the tax was levied on grain merchants, who were less likely to resist by extralegal means. For more than a year the legality of the tax was debated in the courts, but in March 1893 the Argentine Supreme Court declared it constitutional. As wheat growing expanded, provincial governments became more and more dependent on cereal taxes for their income. In Santa Fe the proceeds from the cereal tax were nearly as much as the revenue from all land taxes.

At the turn of the century Emilio Lahitte concluded two studies of provincial and municipal tax policies which revealed that the fiscal demands made on the farmer were putting him out of business in the cereal zone.[5] The Buenos Aires legislature was so impressed that it

---

[4] Emilio Lahitte, *Los impuestos en la provincia de Buenos Aires. Apuntes estadísticos* (Buenos Aires, 1900), p. 22.

[5] Emilio Lahitte, *La producción agrícola y los impuestos en las provincias de Buenos Aires, Santa Fe, Córdoba y Entre Ríos* and *Los impuestos en la provincia de Buenos Aires. Apuntes estadísticos.*

promptly ordered municipalities to cease any further taxation of the farmer. Naturally nothing was done to reduce provincial taxes, and the municipalities turned a deaf ear to the instruction from the authorities in La Plata. The national government, however, was also impressed with Lahitte's conclusions. In January 1901 a national decree relieved the railroads of the responsibility of ascertaining whether goods they loaded had paid *guías*. A second blow fell in 1902 when the Supreme Court declared the *guías* of Corrientes, Santa Fe, and Buenos Aires illegal. Since farmers were still excellent sources for provincial revenues, it was merely a question of how such taxes would be collected. The Buenos Aires authorities evolved a "production tax," but in 1904 the Supreme Court ruled it unconstitutional. Finally in 1905 another version, different only in technicalities, withstood court scrutiny. Several other provinces replaced the *guía* revenues with new "production taxes," with land taxes, and with license taxes on employees of the grain firms. The man who ultimately paid was the farmer.

Just as the farmers were a logical source of money for budget officials seated in a distant provincial capital or for the more immediate municipal authorities, so they became the prey of the petty officialdom and even of the lawless elements of the Argentine countryside. The local *comisario* and the justice of the peace were constant villains in rural dramas which often reached tragic proportions. Rural officials were rarely of a benevolent or paternal disposition. They were usually illiterate, poverty-stricken, and lazy. Within their locality their appointment had elevated them to almost absolute powers. The abuse of these powers frequently led to incidents such as that reported in 1876 from San Carlos, Santa Fe, where a justice of the peace exceeded his jurisdiction and carried out the expulsion of a tenant family. In the process he shot the nonresisting father and son; the mother died of shock.[6] These officials also had little sympathy or understanding for foreigners who spoke a different language, who had different customs and often a different religion, and who were frequently better off than the mass of rural Argentines. Bribery and corruption, prevalent at the higher levels of government, were equally rampant here. Even the powerful landowner often bribed the local authorities rather than suffer the harassment and annoyance of their petty decrees, orders, and thievery. Indeed, the Sociedad Agraria came into being in 1892 largely because the *estancieros* felt the need to reform the appoint-

6 *La Nación,* January 28, 1876, p. 1.

ment and conduct of these rural officials. If the landowner felt this pressure, one can well imagine the burden which weighed on the colonist and the tenant farmer.

Occasionally the farmers, especially where they were banded together in colonies, took action. As pointed out already, the participation of colonists in the Radical Party revolt of 1893 was brought on largely by the corruption of rural government. Earlier that year local authorities at Bolívar had been fired upon by colonists in self-defense. At Humboldt the colonists had expelled the police picket. Such resistance was rare, however, and when it did occur, provincial and even national authorities were only too ready to interfere and prosecute the gringo (any foreigner) for meddling in politics.

Since the justice of the peace was the immediate arbiter of rural laws, the farmer rarely benefited from the high-flown phrases about equality and freedom set forth at a national level. A favorable sentence was almost invariably related to the bribe handed the judge. Indicative was the fact that the appointment was greatly sought after, ". . . and despite the miniscule salary, the holders always manage to live very well, and in the colonized regions, usually acquire a fortune."[7]

Hand in glove with such an attitude toward the law went the most lawless elements of the provinces. Cattle thievery, which affected the *estancieros,* had long been a complaint of rural districts, and quite often the rustlers connived with the local police. With the increased value of cattle after 1900 and the rapid development of new zones in the territory of La Pampa, rustling became an organized racket. *Estancieros* who failed to pay tribute were apt to find their stock disappearing at a rapid rate. The farmer also suffered from the spread of lawless bands. The colonist or tenant farmer did not use banks, and at harvest season he was almost certain to have a considerable sum of money around his person or his rancho. To attack, rob, and murder the inhabitants of an isolated farm was simple enough for a gang of armed men, and even if the act attracted passing attention in the press, the local authorities were unlikely to take the matter seriously. The public sense of justice was aroused only when the farmers took the law into their own hands. When two murderers

[7] Leopoldo Velasco, "El éxodo hacia Buenos Aires," *Revista Argentina de Ciencias Políticas,* XVI (1918), 347. *La Nación,* May 21, 1900, p. 3, and *El Diario,* December 30, 1903, p. 1, cited the lack of rural justice as the principal cause for Argentina's few immigrants in comparison with the number in the United States or Australia.

were caught and lynched in 1893 at Carcarañá, Santa Fe, twenty-two colonists were immediately arrested and the judge requested the death penalty for seventeen of them. Although the prisoners were eventually released, the concern of the provincial government was not the repression of crime. Indeed, many years were to pass before order and security began to penetrate the rural areas. When the Austrian colonists at Firmat, Santa Fe, complained to their representative in 1908 of the lawless conditions in the countryside and their protest was routed through devious diplomatic channels, the senator from their district gave them the frank advice that their only recourse was to go armed to their fields.[8]

Thus, the efforts of the provincial, municipal, and country authorities were directed not toward helping the farmer but rather toward discovering the most effective means to relieve him of his money. Lawlessness, thievery, and persecution by both petty officials and criminals added one more burden to the farmer's life in Argentina and made rural existence still less attractive to the immigrant and city dweller alike.

In the broadest sense, what did the development of Argentina's wheat economy mean to the country's political formation? What was the result of thousands of immigrants, of an export worth millions of pesos, of vast virgin lands brought under cultivation, and of the creation of new industries?

Just as few fresh elements had entered the Argentine economy prior to 1860, so had there been little fundamental change in the political structure since the colonial period. The economy rested on the native cattle; the government on a small elite of landowners, lawyers, and military leaders. The only significant adjustment of the early nineteenth century had been the increasing shift of economic and political power toward the coast and into the hands of the province and city of Buenos Aires.

The economic development of the late nineteenth century laid the basis for a new Argentina. But it was an Argentina of cities and especially of the city of Buenos Aires (see Map 3 for population shift between 1869 and 1914). The revolution on the pampas had created wealth and prosperity, but it was a wealth and prosperity which acquired reality only in urban surroundings. Tenant farmers labored on the pampas. They did not make homes. *Estancieros* refined their live-

[8] *Review of the River Plate*, January 29, 1909, p. 271.

stock, but they lived in Buenos Aires or in Paris. Cereal and beef came from the pampas, but socially and politically the pampas remained unconquered, unsettled, isolated, and remote.

Wheat growing served as an important catalyst in the economic transformation of Argentina. It provided a new use for the fertile plains extending back from the coastal cities. It attracted immigrants. It complemented the pastoral industries by refining pasturage. Yet whatever political impact this economic growth brought was registered not in the countryside but in the cities. In 1870 Argentina's total exports amounted to 30,000,000 gold pesos, almost 100 per cent pastoral. In 1890 exports totaled 100,000,000 gold pesos, of which wheat contributed 10 per cent. By 1910 the total had risen to almost 400,000,000 gold pesos, and wheat annually contributed almost a fifth of these exports (Table 7). It was the flow of this commerce through the coastal ports that stimulated the growth of Buenos Aires from 187,000 in 1869 to 1,577,000 in 1914; of Rosario from 23,000 to 223,000; of Santa Fe from 11,000 to 60,000; of Bahía Blanca from 1,000 to 62,000. And it is in this urban growth—not in the countryside—that the broad political implications of wheat growing must be sought.

After half a century of political struggle among landowner and military groups in the interior and coastal provinces, Buenos Aires finally imposed its hegemony on the country and achieved a national government in 1862. Four great presidents followed—Mitre, Sarmiento, Avellaneda, and Roca—all men of extraordinary culture and foresight. Yet as the threat of external and internal wars died away, as power became increasingly centralized in the hands of the national government, and as the nation began to expand economically, there developed a bureaucratic and economic monopoly over the processes of government. Politicians and landowners consolidated their control and emerged in the 1880's as the so-called "Oligarchy" of the new Argentina.[9] This decade also saw the expansion of other politically vocal elements of the population. The monopoly of government and the accompanying corruption aroused resentment among native Argentines, especially in urban middle-class groups, university students, merchants, businessmen, certain military officers, and professional men. Although the immigrants had not yet penetrated the political arena, they added to the spirit of economic and social fer-

[9] See Thomas F. McGann's excellent chapter, "The Generation of Eighty: Politics," in his *Argentina, the United States and the Inter-American System, 1880–1914*, pp. 20–34.

ment in the cities. Thus were the urban protest and reform movements formed: both the Radical and Socialist Parties were formally
constituted in the early 1890's.

The small middle-class groups that originated these reform movements might have accomplished little if it had not been for Argentina's rapid economic growth at the turn of the century. Although
initially attracted to Argentina by agricultural opportunities, the bulk
of European immigrants had settled in the coastal cities. Here they
or their children were able to obtain the property, security, sociability, education, or advancement so often denied them in the countryside. The list of urban employments created by the stimulus of agriculture was endless: stevedores, grocers, milkmen, mechanics, clerks,
tailors, bricklayers, bakers, cartmen, servants, office managers, fore-
men. As the cities spread out, especially with the growth of Greater
Buenos Aires after 1900, there was a decentralization of shops and
facilities and a consequent increase of jobs in neighborhood stores
and factories. Industry and construction provided extensive employment: for 102,000 workers, or 37 per cent of the active population of
Buenos Aires in 1895, and for 273,000 workers, or 43 per cent by
1914.[10] It was to these urban newcomers and especially to the sons of
the immigrants who had come to Argentina in the eighties that the
Radical and Socialist Parties increasingly appealed. The successes of
reform movements significantly occurred during the years when this
second generation came of age: the surrender of power by the "Oligarchy" with the Saenz Peña Law of 1912, which established secret,
compulsory male suffrage, and the election of a Radical, Hipólito
Yrigoyen, as president in 1916.

Although it was largely the stimulus which agriculture had given
to the cities that enabled these middle-class protest movements to
develop and finally to achieve power, neither the Radical Party nor
the Socialist Party ever secured a permanent agrarian following nor
did either evince a lasting concern with farm problems. Their contact
with agriculturists was limited to opportunistic appeals such as in the
1893 Radical revolution or in the 1912 Socialist agitation of the
"Agrarian Problem." In this they reflected both their urban orientation and the traditional Argentine lack of preoccupation with agricultural matters.

Thus the impact of Argentina's wheat economy on the political
structure was largely restricted to the cities. Commercial prosperity

[10] Aparicio and Difrieri, *Suma de geografía*, VII, 239–240.

and the effects of the revolution on the pampas attracted and supported hundreds of thousands of newcomers in the coastal cities.
Here, these immigrants gave rise to a growing middle class and to a
large labor force, and by the second generation had appropriated a
new and aggressive spirit of nationalism as their own. Their demands
for political emancipation gave strength to the reform demands of the
urban intellectuals and professional middle classes and finally ended
the monopoly of the "Oligarchy." But in this process of urban democ-
ratization no benefits filtered down to the shifting, disfranchised tenant farmers.

At the same time, wheat growing actually fostered the centralization of political and economic power in the coastal cities. The products of the agricultural and pastoral economy flowed toward Europe,
and whatever stimulus, commercial or industrial, these products
provided was concentrated in the ports which handled and processed
the raw materials. The interior, once so important for its textiles,
leather goods, and other local manufactures, had fallen far behind
the coast in population, culture, and opportunities. Even in the
coastal region, the transiency and isolation of agriculture encouraged
Argentines to look to the city and in particular to the metropolis of
Buenos Aires and beyond that to Europe. Man had not taken root in
the pampas. On the pampas there were no important towns, commercial centers, or industrial sites. There was no settled, prosperous
agrarian class to consume as well as to produce. Railroads provided
admirable transportation, but it was a one-way route—to draw the
wealth of the land to the ports. No one wanted to remain in the
countryside. The *estancieros* might build châteaus, but they spent
only a few weeks or weekends on their estates, and they were far
better acquainted with the streets of Buenos Aires or Paris and the
beaches of Mar del Plata than with the land that made them wealthy.
And so it was down the line, from the rural storekeeper, the country
priest, the local station manager, the miller, to the farmer. They all
aspired to move, and always toward the coast and toward the city.
For only there could be found what was so patently lacking in the
pampas: social institutions, people, economic opportunities.

This drive toward the urban centers had political results. Frequently the newly arrived immigrant never left the coastal city, or he
returned there as quickly as possible. The ambitious and the capable
from the countryside drifted toward the city. Inevitably the talents

and abilities of the nation were concentrated in the urban areas and especially in Buenos Aires. Rather than a frontier, Argentina had a city. Instead of turning the country toward its rural areas, agriculture had emphasized urban development.

POSTSCRIPT

By 1910 a revolution on the pampas had been accomplished. The haunts of wild cattle, Indians, and gauchos had been transformed into cultivated fields and rich pastures. A land that had produced only scrawny sheep and cattle was now one of the world's leading exporters of wheat, corn, beef, mutton, and wool. In fifty years Argentine exports had multiplied seventeen times in value. A country that had had only a sparse and scattered Spanish and mestizo population now boasted a metropolis of almost 1,500,000 and a population of 8,000,000, nearly a third of them born in Europe.

These were significant changes, and wheat growing had played a major role in all of them. The foundations of the present-day Argentine countryside as well as much of urban Argentina rested on the development of wheat-beef economy. Yet growth was not the only factor of change. The revolution on the pampas had introduced or reinforced certain other national characteristics: the *porteño* and urban domination of a government and an economy; the large-scale ownership of the land by those who rarely farmed it; the apathy of government and people toward their human and natural resources.

The rural scene which emerged as a result of this revolution did not change fundamentally after 1910. During the 1920's the farmer made his voice heard through the Federación Agraria and its newspaper, *La Tierra*. There were efforts toward land reform in Buenos Aires and an increase in the number of cooperatives and rural elevators. Wheat and cereals in general recovered from the recession of the First World War and once more overtook the pastoral industries. The 1930's brought overproduction, now made critical by a world depression, and, as a consequence, government controls of production and marketing. As wheat lost its dominant importance in the national economy, its place was taken by other farm products. But the increasing controls and the decreasing production of the next decades solved no problems.

The Argentina of today still reaps the fruits of its revolution on the pampas. Buenos Aires and the coastal cities, rather than the land, received the bulk of the population, commerce, and capital which an agricultural economy had attracted. Rural development fostered no independent political force or economic vitality to balance or complement the resultant dominance of the urban centers. Although private enterprise and unrestricted immigration had developed the wealth of the pampas in the early twentieth century without government assistance, public and official indifference toward rural affairs unfortunately continued into the more complex decades of world depression and subsidized industrialization. The conservative governments of the 1930's and the Peronista regime after the Second World War once more demonstrated both the dominance of certain urban groups or centers in policy decisions and the total absence of any agrarian consciousness in Argentina. As a result the tenant farmer today is the common denominator of rural Argentina. The farmer lives a miserable life, far removed from most benefits of society or industry. The influx of immigrants has all but ended, and their loss is compounded by an internal migration to the cities. And the government and the people remain tragically negligent of one of the nation's greatest wealths—its agriculture and its rural population.

TABLES

TABLE 1

Immigration and Emigration, Argentina, 1871–1910

Year	Immigrants	Emigrants	Balance
1871	20,933	10,686	10,247
1872	37,037	9,153	27,884
1873	76,332	18,236	58,096
1874	68,277	21,340	46,937
1875	42,036	25,578	16,458
1876	30,965	13,487	17,478
1877	36,325	18,350	17,975
1878	42,958	14,860	28,098
1879	55,155	23,696	31,459
1880	41,651	20,377	21,274
1881	47,484	22,374	25,110
1882	51,503	8,720	42,783
1883	63,243	9,510	53,733
1884	77,805	14,444	63,361
1885	108,722	14,585	94,137
1886	93,116	13,907	79,209
1887	120,842	13,630	107,212
1888	155,632	16,842	138,790
1889	260,909	40,649	220,260
1890	110,594	80,219	30,375
1891	52,097	81,932	(—)29,835
1892	73,294	43,853	29,441
1893	84,420	48,794	35,626
1894	80,671	41,399	39,272
1895	80,989	36,820	44,169
1896	135,205	45,921	89,284
1897	105,143	57,457	47,686
1898	95,190	53,536	41,654
1899	111,083	62,241	48,842
1900	105,902	55,417	50,485
1901	125,951	80,251	45,700
1902	96,080	79,427	16,653
1903	112,671	74,776	37,895
1904	161,078	66,597	94,481
1905	221,622	82,772	138,850
1906	302,249	103,852	198,397
1907	257,924	138,063	119,861
1908	303,112	127,032	176,080
1909	278,148	137,508	140,640
1910	345,275	136,405	208,870

(Figures from Ernesto Tornquist & Co., *The Economic Development of the Argentine Republic in the Last Fifty Years*, p. 15.)

TABLE 2

Wheat and Flour Exports and Imports, Argentina, 1870–1910
(in metric tons)

Year	Wheat Exports	Wheat Imports	Flour Exports	Flour Imports
1870	-------	3,903	-------	5,726
1871	9	1,524	17	5,681
1872	17	1,425	206	2,141
1873	5	1,055	122	1,017
1874	358	2,550	24	7,451
1875	-------	4,887	13	16,923
1876	21	335	353	3,130
1877	200	600	218	128
1878	2,547	10	2,919	6
1879	25,669	6	1,603	4
1880	1,166	18,581	1,428	1,265
1881	157	11,478	1,287	2
1882	1,705	200	549	unknown
1883	60,755	230	4,844	unknown
1884	108,449	0.1	3,734	117
1885	78,493	17	7,447	3
1886	37,864	4	5,262	14
1887	237,866	42	5,501	5
1888	178,929	88	6,392	12
1889	22,806	3,051	3,361	61
1890	327,894	1,306	12,018	22
1891	395,555	120	7,015	-------
1892	470,110	5	18,849	5
1893	1,008,137	95	37,921	0.2
1894	1,608,249	4	40,758	14
1895	1,046,000	3	53,935	2
1896	532,001	319	51,732	55
1897	101,845	14,406	41,443	356
1898	645,161	395	31,933	112
1899	1,713,429		59,464	184
1900	1,929,676†		51,203	17
1901	904,289‡		71,742	-------
1902	644,908		39,040	0.4
1903	1,681,327		71,980	
1904	2,304,724		107,298	
1905	2,868,281		144,760	
1906	2,247,988		128,998	
1907	2,680,802		127,499	
1908	3,636,293		113,500	
1909	2,514,130		116,487	
1910	1,883,592		115,408	

(Figures from Argentina, *Estadística general del comercio exterior.*)
† *Review of the River Plate* recorded 2,042,167 tons exported that year.
‡ *Review of the River Plate* recorded an export of 972,514 tons; the Ministry of Agriculture reported 973,000 tons.

TABLE 3

Expansion of Argentine Railroads, 1857–1910

Year	Total Mileage	Year	Total Mileage	Year	Total Mileage
1857	6	1875	1,220	1893	8,590
1858	11	1876	1,280	1894	8,690
1859	18	1877	1,380	1895	8,760
1860	24	1878	1,380	1896	8,980
1861	24	1879	1,380	1897	9,150
1862	29	1880	1,570	1898	9,600
1863	38	1881	1,570	1899	10,200
1864	58	1882	1,630	1900	10,300
1865	160	1883	1,960	1901	10,500
1866	320	1884	2,250	1902	10,800
1867	360	1885	2,790	1903	11,420
1868	360	1886	3,620	1904	12,050
1869	380	1887	4,140	1905	12,300
1870	460	1888	4,700	1906	12,750
1871	530	1889	5,070	1907	13,750
1872	580	1890	5,850	1908	14,620
1873	690	1891	7,800	1909	15,380
1874	830	1892	8,500	1910	17,350

(Based on Alejandro Bunge, *Ferrocarriles argentinos. Contribución al estudio del patrimonio nacional*, pp. 119–121.)

TABLE 4

Argentine Land Values in 1888 and 1911
(in gold pesos per hectare)

Province	1888	1911
Buenos Aires	19.35	44.70
Santa Fe	4.94	21.70
Córdoba	4.19	18.20
Entre Ríos	12.90	22.65
La Pampa	1.79	9.65

(Figures from Emilio Lahitte, *La cuestión agraria*, p. 16.)

TABLE 5

Areas Sown to Wheat

Year	Total Acreage	Santa Fe	Buenos Aires	Entre Ríos	Córdoba	La Pampa
		Percentage				
1872–1873	325,000	27	38	6	12	----
1887–1888	2,000,000	49	27	9	7	----
1889–1890	2,500,000	42	32	10	6	----
1890–1891	3,000,000	46	?	9	6	----
–1892	3,300,000	53	?	15	11	----
–1893	3,900,000	56	?	14	?	----
–1894	4,500,000	57	?	15	?	----
–1895	4,900,000	51	19	14	14	----
–1896	5,600,000	46	17	13	?	----
–1897	6,200,000	35	19	9	?	----
–1898	6,400,000	38	23	10	?	----
–1899	7,900,000	48	24	8	18	----
–1900	8,000,000	43	26	9	18	----
1900–1901	8,400,000	42	28	8	18	----
–1902	8,100,000	41	30	8	18	----
–1903	9,100,000	34	36	7	21	----
–1904	10,700,000	31	40	5	22	1
–1905	12,100,000	29	41	6	22	1
–1906	14,000,000	27	42	5	22	2
–1907	14,000,000	26	39	6	26	2
–1908	14,200,000	23	41	5	25	5
–1909	15,000,000	22	41	5	25	5
–1910	14,400,000	22	36	5	31	5
1910–1911	15,500,000	20	36	5	31	7

(Figures from *Anuario de la dirección de estadística de la República Argentina; Anuario estadístico de la provincia de Buenos Aires; . . . de Entre Ríos; . . . de Córdoba;* Ministry of Agriculture; Sociedad Rural Argentina; and *Review of the River Plate.*)

TABLE 6

Argentine Wheat Production, by Provinces, 1891–1911

Year	Thousands of Metric Tons	Millions of Bushels	Santa Fe	Buenos Aires	Entre Ríos	Córdoba	La Pampa
				Percentage			
1890–1891	850	31	59	14	15	7	----
–1892	1,000	36	59	?	18	?	----
–1893	1,600	59	?	?	15	?	----
–1894	2,250	82	53	18	16	8	----
–1895	1,650	61	42	26	12	15	----
–1896	1,250	46	40	29	8	19	----
–1897	850	32	35	38	4	19	----
–1898	1,450	53	49	23	16	8	----
–1899	2,800	105	40	33	7	17	----
–1900	2,750	102	40	33	7	16	----
1900–1901	2,000	75	35	37	4	20	----
–1902	1,500	56	23	63	4	6	----
–1903	2,850†	104	25	44	3	23	----
–1904	3,550	130	31	37	4	23	1
–1905	4,100	151	24	49	5	17	1
–1906	3,650	135	18	53	4	20	2
–1907	4,250	156	15	54	5	21	1
–1908	5,250	192	19	48	5	23	2
–1909	4,250	156	19	42	4	29	3
–1910	3,550	131	14	37	4	34	9
1910–1911	3,950	146	13	42	3	32	8

(Figures from *Anuario de la dirección de estadística de la República Argentina; Anuario estadístico de la provincia de Buenos Aires; . . . de Entre Ríos; . . . de Córdoba;* Ministry of Agriculture; Sociedad Rural Argentina; *Review of the River Plate;* and the United States Department of Agriculture.)

† Ministry of Agriculture statistics indicate 3,100,100 tons for 1902–1903 as opposed to the figure of the *Anuario de la dirección de estadística de la República Argentina.*

TABLE 7

Wheat, Agricultural, and Total Exports, Argentina, 1870–1910

Year	Total Exports (in thousands of gold pesos)	Agricultural (percentage of total)	Wheat (percentage of total)
1870	30,223		
1871	26,997		
1872	47,268		
1873	47,398		
1874	44,542		
1875	52,009	0.3	none
1876	48,091	0.9	infinitesimal
1877	44,770	1.4	0.02
1878	37,523	1.3	0.3
1879	49,358	4.5	2.6
1880	58,381	1.4	0.08
1881	57,938	2.5	0.02
1882	60,389	7.6	0.1
1883	60,208	7.8	4.0
1884	68,030	13.5	6.4
1885	83,879	unknown	3.8
1886	69,835	11.9	2.2
1887	84,422	25.2	11.3
1888	100,112	16.3	8.2
1889	90,145	15.8	1.8
1890	100,819	25.3	9.8
1891	103,219	25.7	15.4
1892	113,370	23.7	12.1
1893	94,090	32.8	24.9
1894	101,688	29.8	26.8
1895	120,068	34.5	17.7
1896	116,802	36.8	11.1
1897	101,169	23.1	3.4
1898	133,829	31.9	16.7
1899	184,918	35.2	20.6
1900	154,600	50.1	31.4
1901	167,716	42.7	15.6
1902	179,487	38.0	10.4
1903	220,985	47.6	18.6
1904	264,158	56.9	25.3
1905	322,844	52.7	26.6
1906	292,254	53.9	22.7
1907	296,204	55.4	27.9
1908	366,005	66.0	35.2
1909	397,351	58.0	26.8
1910	389,071	50.6	18.6

(Figures from Argentina, *Estadística general del comercio exterior,* and *Anuario de la Sociedad Rural Argentina, 1928.*)

TABLE 8

Imports of Agricultural Machinery, Argentina, 1890–1910

Year	Reapers	Threshers	Year	Reapers	Threshers
1890	1,045	43	1901	5,882	274
1891	1,382	47	1902	8,093	167
1892	4,908	328	1903	13,135	434
1893	9,034	338	1904	14,572	745
1894	9,633	1,569	1905	14,492	909
1895	2,723	299	1906	20,739	1,136
1896	3,054	93	1907	17,334	490
1897	1,985	31	1908	18,772	969
1898	5,872	22	1909	13,672	1,576
1899	11,058	152	1910	18,513	807
1900	6,094	228			

(Figures from *Boletín mensual de estadística del Ministerio de Agricultura* and *Anuario de la dirección de estadística de la República Argentina*.)

176

TABLE 9

Wheat Exports from the Three Leading Argentine Ports, 1879–1910
(in metric tons)

Year	Rosario	Buenos Aires	Santa Fe
1879	17,314	6,616	1,661
1880	582	578	-------
1881	-------	151	-------
1882	1,980	245	285
1883	5,148	4,690	12,013
1884	9,495	15,223	12,364
1885	25,390	28,033	10,863
1886	22,217	509	15,309
1887	140,660	33,133	25,825
1888	102,154	34,040	18,200
1889	10,603	4,112	2,888
1890	201,429	73,992	14,692
1891	152,100	172,333	28,127
			Bahía Blanca
1892	239,751	145,196	14,903
1893	390,209	303,630	37,899
1894†	790,007	305,231	51,981
1895	538,750	166,098	65,650
1896	352,689	48,396	36,941
1897	56,081	25,270	4,534
1898	384,061	77,124	38,408
1899	885,179	278,340	181,398
1900	797,214	405,221	271,158
1901	432,086	168,676	187,278
1902	85,672	194,694	277,872
1903	684,197	452,969	330,201
1904	963,368	349,405	542,744
1905	796,476	668,028	949,796
1906	616,763	565,764	101,875
1907	697,918	632,656	843,124
1908	1,075,945	783,160	1,032,046
1909	757,974	517,004	783,918
1910	516,843	601,755	641,308

(Figures from *Anuario de la dirección de estadística de la República Argentina.*)
† From 1894 on, the figure represents the amount shipped directly overseas.

A SELECTED BIBLIOGRAPHY

No attempt has been made to include in this selection all the items consulted or to list the many interviews with cereal merchants, grain brokers, and farmers. Consequently some items in the footnotes do not appear in the Bibliography.

I. BIBLIOGRAPHIES

Guides that have proved useful in the preparation of this monograph include:

Bagú, Sergio, *et al.*, *Bibliografía crítica sobre la historia de la estratificación social en la Argentina durante el período 1880–1959* (mimeo.; Buenos Aires, 1960). Compiled by the Department of Sociology of the University of Buenos Aires.

Estévez, Alfredo, *Colonización e inmigración. Bibliografía* (mimeo.; Buenos Aires, 1958). Prepared by the librarian of the Faculty of Economic Sciences of the University of Buenos Aires.

Millán, Roberto, *Bibliografía agrícola argentina hasta 1930* (Buenos Aires, 1935). Compiled by an agronomist of the Ministry of Agriculture.

———, *Catálogo de las publicaciones periódicas de la Argentina sobre agricultura* (Buenos Aires, 1932).

Museo Mitre, *Catálogo de la biblioteca* (Buenos Aires, 1907).

II. OFFICIAL PUBLICATIONS

A. *Censuses and Statistical Reports, Department [subsequently, Ministry] of Agriculture Reports, and Consular Reports* (Sessional Papers), *Great Britain, and Consular Reports, United States.*

Valuable commentaries as well as statistics are to be found in the national censuses:

Censo nacional de 1869 (Buenos Aires, 1872).

Censo nacional de 1895 (3 vols.; Buenos Aires, 1898).

Censo nacional de 1914 (10 vols.; Buenos Aires, 1916–1917).

Censo agropecuario nacional de la República Argentina en 1908 (3 vols.; Buenos Aires, 1909).

The provincial censuses add further detail:

Censo general de la provincia de Buenos Aires, 1881 (Buenos Aires, 1883).

Censo agrícola-pecuario de la provincia de Buenos Aires, 1888 (Buenos Aires, 1889).

Primer censo general de la provincia de Santa Fe, 1887 (Buenos Aires, 1888).

Argentine statistical publications for the period include:

Anuario del departamento nacional de estadística, since 1893 (published from 1870–1879 as *Estadística de la República Argentina; cuadro general del comercio exterior,* and from 1880–1892 as *Estadística del comercio exterior y de la navegación interior y exterior*).

Anuario estadístico de la provincia de Buenos Aires, since 1881 (published from 1854–1880 as *Registro estadístico de la provincia de Buenos Aires*).

Boletín mensual de estadística agrícola, published since 1900 by the Ministry of Agriculture with slight variations in title.

The Department of Agriculture, subsequently Ministry of Agriculture, published several important series of reports:

Anales de Agricultura de la República Argentina, 1873–1876.

Informe del departamento de agricultura, 1872–1876.

Boletín mensual del departamento de agricultura, 1878–1897.

Boletín del ministerio de agricultura, since 1904.

Memoria del ministerio de agricultura, since 1898.

Scattered references in the debates of the Cámara de Diputados, *Diario de sesiones* can be traced in two indexes—1854–1900 and 1901–1920. There is no such index for the Senate debates.

Occasional reference to Argentine agriculture is found in Great Britain, House of Commons, *Sessional Papers,* especially in Reports from Her Majesty's Consuls of the Manufactures, Commerce, etc., of their Consular Districts and in the Reports on Subjects of General and Commercial Interest, Miscellaneous Series. Similarly the United States, Department of State, *Consular Reports,* Nos. 1–357 (1880–1910), contain frequent comments on the Argentine rural scene. Also useful are United States, Department of Commerce, *Special Agent Series,* Nos. 8, 43, and 125.

B. *Special Studies by the Argentine Government and Foreign Governments.*

Amadeo, Tomás, *La enseñanza y la experimentación agrícolas en la República Argentina* (Buenos Aires, 1916). Ministry of Agriculture investigation.

André, Gustave, *Colonies agricoles de l'Entre-rios* (Louvain and Paris, 1890). Argentine government publication.

Beck-Bernard, Charles, *La République Argentine* (Lausanne, 1865). Official propaganda by an Argentine immigration agent in Europe.

Bialet Masse, Juan, *Informe sobre el estado de las clases obreras* (3 vols.; Buenos Aires, 1904). Study for the Ministry of Interior.

Bicknell, Frank W., *Alfalfa and Beef Production in Argentina* (Washington, D.C., 1904). One of four investigations by an agent of the U.S. Department of Agriculture.

——, *Animal Industry of Argentina* (Washington, D.C., 1903).

——, *Indian Corn in Argentina* (Washington, D.C., 1903).

——, *Wheat Production and Farm Life in Argentina* (Washington, D.C., 1904).

Cámara de Diputados, *Investigación parlamentaria sobre agricultura, ganadería, industrias derivadas y colonización* (Buenos Aires, 1898).

Campolieti, Roberto, *La chacra argentina* (Buenos Aires, 1914). Study by an outstanding agronomist of the Ministry of Agriculture.

Carrasco, Gabriel, *Descripción geográfica y estadística de la provincia de Santa Fe* (Buenos Aires, 1886). By the official publicist for the province of Santa Fe.

Cilley Vernet, José, *Los cereales y oleaginosos trillados en la provincia de Buenos Aires en la cosecha de 1895–1896* (La Plata, 1896). Study for the provincial government of Buenos Aires.

Dumas, A., *La crisis agrícola* (Santa Fe, 1902). An investigation by the provincial government of Santa Fe.

Fliess, Alois E., *La producción agrícola y ganadera de la República Argentina en el año 1891* (Buenos Aires, 1892). Study for the Argentine government.

Fuente, Diego G. de la, *Tierras, colonias y agricultura: recopilación de leyes, decretos y otras disposiciones nacionales, 1812–1897* (2 vols.; Buenos Aires, 1894–1897).

Girola, Carlos D., *Estudio sobre el cultivo del trigo en la provincia de Buenos Aires* (Buenos Aires, 1904). One of several studies by an agronomist of the Ministry of Agriculture.

——, *Estudio sobre el cultivo del trigo en la provincia de Entre Ríos* (Buenos Aires, 1901).

——, *Estudios sobre los trigos en la provincia de Santa Fe* (Buenos Aires, 1902).

——, *Investigación agrícola en la República Argentina. Preliminares* (Buenos Aires, 1904). Outline of an extensive province-by-province investigation made by the Ministry of Agriculture.

Gómez Langeheim, Antonio, *Colonización en la República Argentina* (Buenos Aires, 1906). Compilation of laws and decrees, 1810–1905.

Goyena, Juan, *Digesto rural y agrario* (3 vols.; Buenos Aires, 1892).

Huergo, Ricardo J., *Investigación agrícola en la región septentrional de la provincia de Buenos Aires* (Buenos Aires, 1904). Part of the Ministry of Agriculture's investigation under the direction of Carlos D. Girola.

Kaerger, Karl, *Landwirtschaft und Kolonisation im Spanischen Amerika* (2 vols.; Leipzig, 1901), Vol. I, *Die La Plata-Staaten,* especially pp. 1–220, 408–749. An exhaustive study by a German government agent.

Lahitte, Emilio, *Cosecha del año 1898–1899. Datos estadísticos* (Buenos

Aires, 1899). One of many studies by the director of Statistics and Rural Economics in the Ministry of Agriculture.

——, *Crédito agrícola. La cooperación rural* (Buenos Aires, 1912).

——, *La cuestión agraria. Informe* (Buenos Aires, 1912).

——, *Los impuestos en la provincia de Buenos Aires. Apuntes estadísticos* (Buenos Aires, 1900).

——, *Informes y estudios de la dirección de economía rural y estadística* (3 vols.; Buenos Aires, 1916).

——, *La producción agrícola y los impuestos en las provincias de Buenos Aires, Santa Fe, Córdoba y Entre Ríos* (Buenos Aires, 1899).

——, *La propiedad rural. Ventas, hipotecas, colonización, latifundios* (2 vols.; Buenos Aires, 1905–1906).

——, *La situación agrícola. Sociedades cooperativas* (Buenos Aires, 1907).

Larguía, Eduardo T., *La economía rural en la provincia. El trabajo* (La Plata, 1898). Study for the provincial government of Buenos Aires.

Larguía, Jonas, *Informe del inspector de colonias de la provincia de Santa Fe, 1872, 1876, 1879* (Santa Fe, 1872; Buenos Aires, 1876; Rosario, 1879).

López Mañan, Julio, *El actual problema agrario* (Buenos Aires, 1912).

Medina, Rodolfo, *Warrants. Datos sobre su legislación en la República Argentina y en el extranjero* (Buenos Aires, 1915).

Miatello, Hugo, *La chacra santafecina en 1905* (Buenos Aires, 1905). One of several studies by an agronomist, Ministry of Agriculture.

——, *El hogar argentino* (Buenos Aires, 1915). An investigation of rural dwellings and living conditions.

——, *Industrias agrícolas y ganaderas en la República Argentina. Datos para los inmigrantes agricultores* (Buenos Aires, 1901). Ministry of Agriculture's guide for immigrants.

——, *Investigación agrícola en la provincia de Santa Fe* (Buenos Aires, 1904). Part of the Ministry of Agriculture's investigation under the direction of Carlos D. Girola.

Molinas, Florencio T., *Santa Fe agrícola. Las cosechas de 1898–99 y 1899–1900* (Buenos Aires, 1901). Study for the Ministry of Agriculture.

Peyret, Alexis, *Une visite aux colonies de la République Argentine* (Paris, 1889). Argentine government publication.

Raña, Eduardo S., *Investigación agrícola en la provincia de Entre Ríos* (Buenos Aires, 1904). Part of the Ministry of Agriculture's investigation under the direction of Carlos D. Girola.

Salas, Carlos P., *La agricultura, ganadería, industria y comercio en la provincia de Buenos Aires en 1895* (La Plata, 1896). Study for the provincial government of Buenos Aires.

SVIMEZ, Associazione per lo sviluppo dell'industria nel Mezzogiorno, *Statistiche sul mezzogiorno d'Italia, 1861–1953* (Rome, 1954).

Wiener, Charles, *La République Argentine* (Paris, 1899), especially pp. 11–66, 303–408. Report by a French commercial agent.

Wilcken, Guillermo, *Las colonias. Informe sobre el estado actual de las colonias agrícolas de la República Argentina* (Buenos Aires, 1873). Study for the Argentine government.

III. NEWSPAPERS AND JOURNALS

Unless otherwise noted, the place of publication is Buenos Aires.

La Agricultura. Revista semanal ilustrada, 1893–1905.

Anales de la Sociedad Rural Argentina, consulted from 1867, the first year of publication, through 1915.

El Diario, consulted 1877–1878.

El Economista, consulted 1882–1892.

La Nación, consulted 1870–1885, 1895–1905.

El Plata Industrial y Agrícola, 1876–1878. Continuation as a private journal of the Department of Agriculture's *Anales de Agricultura*.

La Prensa, consulted 1905–1915.

La Producción Argentina. Revista semanal ilustrada de agricultura, ganadería, industria y comercio, 1894–1898.

Review of the River Plate, consulted from 1891, the first year of publication, through 1917.

Revista económica del Río de la Plata, 1st period, 1870–1871; 2d period, 1892–1893; 3d period, 1899–1900.

La Semana Rural. Revista industrial mensual, de agricultura y ganadería nacional, 1894–1907.

The Standard, consulted 1880–1895, 1900–1910.

La Unión (Esperanza), consulted 1891–1894.

IV. GENERAL STUDIES, MONOGRAPHS, AND TRAVELERS' ACCOUNTS

Akers, Charles E., *Argentine, Patagonian and Chilian Sketches with a few notes on Uruguay* (London, 1893), especially pp. 56–97.

Alsina, Juan A., *La inmigración en el primer siglo de la independencia* (Buenos Aires, 1910). By the director of the Argentine Immigration Office.

———, *La inmigración europea en la República Argentina* (Buenos Aires, 1898).

———, *El obrero en la República Argentina* (2 vols.; Buenos Aires, 1905).

———, *Población, tierras y producción* (Buenos Aires, 1903).

Aparicio, Francisco de, and Horacio A. Difrieri (eds.), *La Argentina. Suma de geografía* (9 vols.; Buenos Aires, 1958–1963).

Armaignac, Henry, *Voyages dans les pampas de la république Argentine* (Tours, 1883). A description of frontier conditions in the 1870's.

Arnold, Samuel G., *Viaje por América del Sur, 1847–1848* (Buenos Aires, 1951).

Avellaneda, Nicolás, *Estudios sobre las leyes de tierras públicas* (Buenos Aires, 1865). Law thesis by the president responsible for formulating the 1876 law on public lands.

Barba, Enrique, *Rastrilladas, huellas y caminos* (Buenos Aires, 1956).

Barra, Francisco de la, *La inmigración en la República Argentina* (Buenos Aires, 1904).

Beck-Bernard, Lina, *Le Rio Parana; cinq années de séjour dans la République Argentine* (Paris, 1864). By the wife of the colonizer and immigration agent Charles Beck-Bernard.

Becker, Max, *Der argentinische Weizen im Weltmarkte* (Jena, 1903). A detailed investigation of the aspects of international commerce.

Beco, Pedro, "El trigo en la República Argentina," *Revista zootécnica* (Buenos Aires), V (1914), 509–520, 562–582. An agronomy dissertation.

Bernárdez, Manuel, *La nación en marcha; viajes por la República Argentina* (Buenos Aires, 1904), especially pp. 135–188 for descriptions of river ports.

Bidabehere, Fernando A., *Bolsas y mercados de comercio en la República Argentina* (Buenos Aires, 1930).

Bishop, Nathaniel H., *A Thousand Miles' Walk across South America* (11th ed.; Boston, 1883).

Bonino, Alfredo, and Pedro del Carril, *La subdivisión de nuestras tierras y la evolución agraria del país* (Buenos Aires, 1926).

Borda, Julio C., *Breve estudio sobre legislación agraria* (Buenos Aires, 1898).

Bóveda, Ramón M., *Legislación rural argentina* (Buenos Aires, 1903).

Bunge, Alejandro, *Ferrocarriles argentinos. Contribución al estudio del patrimonio nacional* (Buenos Aires, 1918).

———, *Una nueva Argentina* (Buenos Aires, 1940).

———, *Riqueza y renta de la Argentina* (Buenos Aires, 1917).

Burgin, Miron, *Economic Aspects of Argentine Federalism* (Cambridge, Mass., 1946). A masterly study of the economic scene during the first half of the nineteenth century.

Burmeister, Hermann, *Reise durch die La Plata-staaten, mit besonderer Rücksicht auf die physische Beschaffenheit und den Culturzustand der Argentinischen Republik* (2 vols.; Halle, 1861), especially I, 86–150, 386–495. By a German naturalist who subsequently compiled a second-rate study of Argentina's natural resources for the national government.

Campolieti, Roberto, *La organización de la agricultura argentina. Ensayo de política agraria* (Buenos Aires, 1927). By an important agronomist in the Ministry of Agriculture.

Canepa, Luis R., *Economía agraria argentina* (Buenos Aires, 1942).

Cárcano, Miguel A., *Evolución histórica del régimen de la tierra pública, 1810–1916* (2d ed.; Buenos Aires, 1925). A classical study of the legal aspects of public lands.

Ceppi, José, *Cuadros sudamericanos* (Buenos Aires, 1888), especially pp. 10–95.

Cervera, Manuel M., *Boceto histórico sobre colonización argentina y fundación de Esperanza, 1856–1906* (Esperanza, 1906).

Child, Theodore, *The Spanish American Republics* (New York, 1891), especially pp. 1–19, 261–350.

Clemens, Eliza J. M., *La Plata Countries of South America* (Philadelphia, 1886), especially pp. 95–237. An account of a trip in 1880 with a description of Rosario and environs.

Coni, Emilio A., *El mercado ordenado de trigo argentino* (Buenos Aires, 1932).

Crommelin, Mary, *Over the Andes from the Argentine to Chile and Peru* (London, 1896), especially pp. 9–106.

Cuneo, Nicollò, *Storia dell emigrazione italiana in Argentina, 1810–1870* (Milan, 1940).

Daireaux, Emile, *La vie et les moeurs à la Plata* (2 vols.; Paris, 1888), especially II, 135–372. A complete and acute survey.

Darbyshire, Charles, *My Life in the Argentine Republic* (London, 1917).

Daus, Federico A., *Geografía de la República Argentina* (2 vols.; Buenos Aires, 1954–1958). A standard guide to Argentine geography.

Denis, Pierre, *The Argentine Republic, its Development and Progress* (New York, 1922). An excellent geographical study originally published in French.

Drago, José M., *Excursiones rurales. Breves apuntes sobre ganadería en la provincia de Buenos Aires* (Buenos Aires, 1900).

Ducos, Octavio F., *Cincuentenario de la colonia francesa de Pigüé, 1884–1934* (2 vols.; Buenos Aires, 1934).

Etcheverry, Victor D., *Las cooperativas agrícolas en Entre Ríos* (Concepción del Uruguay, 1914).

Foerster, Robert F., *The Italian Emigrant of Our Times* (Cambridge, Mass., 1924).

Fraser, John F., *The Amazing Argentina; a New Land of Enterprise* (London, 1914), especially pp. 21–198.

Frers, Emilio, *Cuestiones agrarias* (2 vols.; Buenos Aires, 1918). Observations by Argentina's first Minister of Agriculture and a leader of the Sociedad Rural.

———, *El prohibicionismo y la política comercial argentina. Cartas de un hombre de estado* (Buenos Aires, 1902).

Giberti, Horacio C. E., *Historia económica de la ganadería argentina* (2d ed.; Buenos Aires, 1961). An outstanding monograph on the pastoral industries.

Gibson, Herbert, *The History and the Present State of the Sheepbreeding Industry in the Argentine Republic* (Buenos Aires, 1893). By a British merchant and *estanciero* of long residence in Argentina.

———, *The Land We Live On* (Buenos Aires, 1914).

Giménez, Ovidio, *Del trigo y su molienda* (Buenos Aires, 1962). By a director of one of Buenos Aires' largest flour mills, with emphasis on commercial and milling aspects of wheat.

Goodwin, William, *Wheat Growing in the Argentine Republic* (Liverpool, 1895). Commercial information compiled by a British merchant of long residence in Argentina.

Gori, Gastón, *Colonización. Estudio histórico y social de la colonia Humboldt* (Colmegna, Santa Fe, 1948). One of several works by the outstanding novelist and historian of the Santa Fe colonies.

———, *Familias colonizadores* (Santa Fe, 1952).

———, *Ha pasado la nostalgia* (Colmegna, Santa Fe, 1950).

———, *La pampa sin gaucho; influencia del inmigrante en la transformación de los usos y costumbres en el campo argentino en el siglo XIX* (Buenos Aires, 1952).

———, *El pan nuestro* (Buenos Aires, 1958).

Gouchon, Emilio, *Apuntes sobre inmigración y colonización* (Buenos Aires, 1889).

Grela, Plácido, *El grito de Alcorta. Historia de la rebelión campesina de 1912* (Buenos Aires, 1958).

Gschwind, Juan J., *Historia de San Carlos* (Rosario, 1958).

Guglieri, Pablo, *Las memorias de un hombre del campo. Treinta años de permanencia en la República Argentina* (Buenos Aires, 1913).

Hadfield, William, *Brazil and the River Plate in 1868 showing the progress of those countries since his former visit in 1853* (London, 1869).

———, *Brazil and the River Plate, 1870–1876* (London, 1877).

Hammerton, John A., *The Real Argentine. Notes and Impressions of a Year in the Argentine and Uruguay* (New York, 1915), especially pp. 289–339.

Heusser, J. Chr., *Drei Aufsaetze betreffend die europaische Auswanderung nach den Argentinischen Provinzen, Buenos Aires, Sta Fe und Entrerios* (Zurich, 1885).

Hinchliff, Thomas, *South American Sketches* (London, 1863).

Holland, William J., *To the River Plate and Back* (New York, 1913). Perceptive observations by a visiting natural scientist.

Horne, Bernardino C., *Un ensayo social agrario. La colonia San José, Entre Ríos, 1857–1957* (Buenos Aires, 1957).

Hotschewer, Curto E., *Evolución de la agricultura en la provincia de Santa Fe* (Santa Fe, 1953).

Huret, Jules, *En Argentine. De Buenos Aires au Gran Chaco* (Paris, 1911), especially pp. 20–192, 407–516. By an acute observer of social and economic development.

———, *En Argentine. De La Plata à la Cordillière des Andes* (Paris, 1913), especially pp. 1–175, 301–491.

Hutchinson, Thomas J., *Buenos Ayres and Argentine Gleanings* (London, 1865), especially pp. 10–108, 237–265. By the British consul at Rosario.

———, *The Paraná; with Incidents of the Paraguayan War, and South American Recollections, from 1861 to 1868* (London, 1868), especially pp. 166–204.

Irigoyen, Bernardo de, *Colonización e inmigración en la Argentina; datos y antecedentes* (La Plata, 1901).

James, Preston, *Latin America* (3d ed.; New York, 1959). The standard reference in English on Latin-American geography.

Jefferson, Mark, *Peopling the Argentine Pampa* (New York, 1926).

Jewish Colonization Association, *Su obra en la República Argentina, 1891–1941* (Buenos Aires, 1942).

Koebel, William H., *Argentina, Past and Present* (2d ed.; London, 1914), especially pp. 132–291, 377–459.

Koenig, Abraham, *A través de la República Argentina; diario de viaje* (Santiago de Chile, 1890), especially pp. 227–390.

Kuczynski, Robert R., "Freight Rates on Argentine and North American Wheat," *Journal of Political Economy* (Chicago), Vol. X, No. 3 (June 1902), pp. 333–360.

Kuehn, Franz, *Grundriss der Kulturgeographie von Argentinien* (Hamburg, 1933). An outstanding geographical study.

Lagos, Hector, *Carlos Casado de Alisal* (Buenos Aires, 1949). Biography of an early colonizer and exporter of wheat.

Lamas, Andrés L., *Tierras públicas y colonización* (2 vols.; Buenos Aires, 1899).

Larden, Walter, *Argentine Plains and Andine Glaciers* (London, 1911). Based on considerable experience and residence in Argentina.

Lastra, Raúl A., *El cultivo del trigo y del maíz* (2d ed.; Buenos Aires, 1908).

Latham, Wilfrid, *The States of the River Plate* (2d ed.; London, 1868). An excellent work on sheep raising by a British *estanciero* of long residence in Argentina.

Latzina, Francisco, *La Argentina considerada en sus aspectos físicos, so-*

ciales y económicos (2 vols.; Buenos Aires, 1902). A semiofficial work by the director of the National Department of Statistics.

Lemée, Carlos, *La agricultura y la ganadería en la República Argentina* (La Plata, 1894).

——, I. *El chacarero.* II. *El estanciero* (2 vols.; La Plata, 1902).

Liebermann, José, *Tierra soñada. Episodios de la colonización agraria judía en la Argentina, 1889–1959* (Buenos Aires, 1959).

Lix Klett, Carlos, *Estudios sobre producción, comercio, finanzas e intereses generales de la República Argentina* (2 vols.; Buenos Aires, 1900).

Lonfat, Germain, *Les colonies agricoles de la République Argentine décrites après cinq années de séjour* (Lausanne, 1879).

MacCann, William, *Two Thousand Miles' Ride Through the Argentine Provinces* (2 vols.; London, 1853).

McGann, Thomas F., *Argentina, the United States and the Inter-American System, 1880–1914* (Cambridge, Mass., 1957). An outstanding study of the "Generation of Eighty" in Argentina as well as an examination of Argentine–United States relations.

Malaurie, Clement, *L'émigrant à la Plata* (Paris, 1883). A shockingly honest guide for prospective immigrants.

Malenbaum, Wilfred, *The World Wheat Economy, 1885–1939* (Cambridge, Mass., 1953). Monograph on international aspects of production and trade.

Martin de Moussy, J. A. Victor, *Description géographique et statistique de la Confédération Argentine* (3 vols. and atlas; Paris, 1860–1873). By a French geographer commissioned by the Argentine government.

Martínez, Alberto R., and Maurice Lewandowski, *The Argentine in the Twentieth Century* (London, 1911). A semiofficial handbook of general economic data.

Mendoza, Prudencio de la C., *Historia de la ganadería argentina* (Buenos Aires, 1928).

Miatello, Hugo, *La agricultura y la ganadería en la República Argentina. Su evolución y progresos* (Buenos Aires, 1916). By an agronomist with the Ministry of Agriculture.

Molinas, Florencio T., *La colonización argentina y las industrias agropecuarias* (Buenos Aires, 1910).

Molins, Wenceslao J., *La pampa* (Buenos Aires, 1918).

Montoya, Alfredo J., *Historia de los saladeros argentinos* (Buenos Aires, 1956). An excellent brief monograph.

Mulhall, Edward T., and Michael G. Mulhall, *Handbook of the River Plate* (6th ed.; Buenos Aires, 1892). First published in 1863 by the editors of *The Standard,* Buenos Aires' most important English newspaper.

Oddone, Jacinto, *La burguesía terrateniente argentina* (3d ed.; Buenos

Aires, 1956). A study of the concentration of landownership in a few hands.

Olivera, Eduardo, *Historia de la ganadería, agricultura e industrias afines de la República Argentina, 1515–1927* (Buenos Aires, 1928). A ninety-page prospectus of a promising work which never appeared.

Ortiz, Ricardo M., *Historia económica de la Argentina, 1850–1930* (2 vols.; Buenos Aires, 1955).

Patroni, Andriani, *Los trabajadores en la Argentina: datos acerca de salarios, horarios, habitaciones obreras, costo de vida, etc.* (Buenos Aires, 1898).

Pennington, A. Stuart, *The Argentine Republic* (New York, 1910).

Perkins, William, *The Colonies of Santa Fe. Their origin, progress and present condition with general observations on emigration to the Argentine Republic* (Rosario, 1864).

Podestá, José P., "La pequeña propiedad rural en la República Argentina," *Investigaciones de seminario de la facultad de ciencias económicas de la Universidad de Buenos Aires,* III (1923), 3–144.

Posada, Adolfo, *La República Argentina* (Madrid, 1912).

Pozzo Ardizzi, Luis, *Hombres del surco, semblanzas de agricultores* (Buenos Aires, 1955).

Rumbold, Horace, *The Great Silver River; notes of a residence in Buenos Ayres in 1880 and 1881* (London, 1887), especially pp. 68–167. By a former British minister to Argentina.

Rutter, William P., *Wheat Growing in Canada, United States and Argentina* (London, 1911).

Sbarra, Noel H., *Historia del alambrado en la Argentina* (Buenos Aires, 1955).

——, *Historia de las aguadas y el molino* (La Plata, 1961).

Scardin, Francisco, *La Argentina y el trabajo* (Buenos Aires, 1906).

Schmidt, Ernst W., *Argentinien in geographischer geschichtlicher und wirtschaftlicher Beziehung* (Hannover, 1912), especially pp. 196–221.

Schmieder, Oscar, "The Pampa—A Natural or Culturally Induced Grass-Land?" *University of California Publications in Geography,* Vol. II, No. 8 (1927), pp. 255–270.

——, "Alteration of the Argentine Pampa in the Colonial Period," *ibid.,* Vol. II, No. 10 (1927), pp. 303–321.

Schobinger, Juan, *Inmigración y colonización suizas en la República Argentina en el siglo XIX* (Buenos Aires, 1957).

Schopflocher, Roberto, *Historia de la colonización agrícola en Argentina* (Buenos Aires, 1955).

Schuster, Adolf N., *Argentinien: Land, Volks, Wirtschaftsleben, und Kolonisation* (2 vols.; Munich, 1913), especially I, 105–120, 404–450.

Seymour, Richard A., *Pioneering in the Pampas; or, the first four years of a settler's experience in the La Plata camps* (2d ed.; London, 1870).

Smith, Rollin E., *Wheat Fields and Markets of the World* (St. Louis, Mo., 1908).

Taylor, Carl C., *Rural Life in Argentina* (Baton Rouge, La., 1948). An outstanding sociological study of rural problems.

Tenembaum, Juan L., *Orientación económica de la agricultura argentina* (Buenos Aires, 1946).

Torino, Damian M., *El problema del inmigrante y el problema agrario en la Argentina* (Buenos Aires, 1912).

Tornquist & Co., Ernesto, *The Economic Development of the Argentine Republic in the Last Fifty Years* (Buenos Aires, 1919). A collection of statistical tables published in several languages.

Turner, Thomas A., *Argentina and the Argentines; Notes and Impressions of a Five Years' Sojourn in the Argentine Republic, 1885–90* (London, 1892).

Vázquez de la Morena, Ignacio, *Contribución al estudio de los problemas agrarios* (Buenos Aires, 1898).

Velasco, Leopoldo, "El éxodo hacia Buenos Aires," *Revista Argentina de Ciencias Políticas* (Buenos Aires), XVI (1918), 346–355.

Vicuña Mackenna, Benjamín, *La Argentina en el año 1855* (Buenos Aires, 1936).

Villanueva, Carlos E., *El litoral y el interior. Observaciones sobre ganadería y agricultura* (Buenos Aires, 1887).

Vollenweider, Heinrich, *Diario del colonizador Enrique Vollenweider* (Santa Fe, 1958).

Weill, Simon, *La contribution française au développement de l'agriculture et de l'élevage en Argentine* (Buenos Aires, 1957).

Zeballos, Estanislao S., *Descripción amena de la República Argentina* (3 vols.; Buenos Aires, 1881–1888).

———, "Problemas conexos con la inmigración," *Revista de Derecho, Historia y Letras* (Buenos Aires), XV (1903), 544–552.

Cuba: as market for salted meat, 42

Cullen, Patricio: and land policy, 115

Dársena Norte: effect of, 107, 108

Darwin, Charles: on formation of pampa dunes, 22

d'Herculais, Jules: and locust problem, 146

Diamante, Entre Ríos: wheat of region of, 109–110; mentioned, 20

Dreyfus: as export firm, 93, 101; effect of establishment of, 100; as source of credit, 102; and Comisión de la Defensa Agrícola, 147. See also "Big Four"

Dulce River: 10

education, agricultural: attempts at, 148–151; reasons for failure of, 148, 149, 150; mentioned, 138

Education, Ministry of: and immigrants' schools, 127

El Plata Industrial y Agrícola: agricultural bulletins of, 134; mentioned, 145

Emilia, Italy: immigrants from, 56

England: Argentine exports to, 5, 38, 52, 110; and investment in Argentine railroads, 36, 96, 121; and packing plants, 44; equipment imports from, 82, 83; trade balance with, 99, 110

—, immigrants from: as colonists, 31–32, 56; as undesirables, 122; to United States, 124; mentioned, 29, 30, 127

Entre Ríos (province): soil of, 18, 22, 72–73, 78; relief and drainage of, 20; weather conditions in, 20, 23, 74, 139; wildlife in, 25; wheat of, 42, 48, 50, 109–110; agricultural practices in, 78–79; flour production of, 112; landowners in, 115; seed-funds committee in, 139; statistics of, 142, 144; locust plague in, 145; agricultural station in, 149; tax on cereals in, 156; mentioned, 15, 43, 50, 87

—, colonies of: government contracting of, 32; number of, 35, 46; of Russian Jews, 62–63, 124–125; cooperatives in, 141; mentioned, 120, 140

equipment, agricultural: threshers as, 80, 83, 109; early, 82; and factors encouraging mechanization, 82–83; cost of, 82, 83, 84; import of, 82, 83, 85; reapers as, 83; effect of, on tenant farming, 83–84; mentioned, 77

Escalante, Wenceslao: as agriculture minister, 136; on agricultural budget, 137

Escuela de Agricultura y Ganadería: as agricultural school, 150

Escuela de Arboricultura y Sacaritécnica: as agricultural school, 150

Escuela de Vinicultura: as agricultural school, 150

Esperanza, Santa Fe: soil of, 72; agricultural congress in, 154; governor at ceremony at, 154; mentioned, 82

—, colony of: preparations for, 33; outcome of, 33; relocation of, 34; experiences of, 34; growth of, 34–35; plowing in, 79; flour mills of, 111; mentioned, 35, 58, 63

estancia: description of, 12; mentioned, 6, 25

estancieros: attitude of, toward resources, 13; use of land by, 31; and land values, 45; need of, for tenant farmers, 46; and Sociedad Rural, 138; and locust elimination, 146; and rural settlement, 162. See also cattlemen

Europe: Argentine immigrants from, 29; wheat export to, 38; farming in, 76–77; commercial houses and cereal firms of, 81–82; agricultural labor force of, 87; as wheat market, 87; milling facilities of, 113; immigration agents in, 122; mentioned, 36, 55, 105, 141, 162

export: of wool, 5, 42; of cotton, 12; of meat, 42–43, 52–53; increase in,